The Irela Championship 2005

The All-Ireland Hurling and Gaelic Football Championships

Damian Cullen

CW01472037

PENGUIN BOOKS

PENGUIN IRELAND

Published by the Penguin Group

Penguin Ireland,
25 St Stephen's Green, Dublin 2, Ireland
(a division of Penguin Books Ltd)

Penguin Books Ltd,
80 Strand, London WC2R 0RL, England

Penguin Group (USA) Inc.,
375 Hudson Street, New York, New York 10014, USA

Penguin Group (Australia),
250 Camberwell Road,Camberwell, Victoria 3124, Australia
(a division of Pearson Australia Group Pty Ltd)

Penguin Group (Canada),
10 Alcorn Avenue, Toronto, Ontario, Canada M4V 3B2
(a division of Pearson Penguin Canada Inc.)

Penguin Books India Pvt Ltd,
11 Community Centre, Panchsheel Park, New Delhi – 110 017, India

Penguin Group (NZ),
cnr Airborne and Rosedale Roads, Albany, Auckland 1310, New Zealand
(a division of Pearson New Zealand Ltd)

Penguin Books (South Africa) (Pty) Ltd,
24 Sturdee Avenue, Rosebank 2196, South Africa

Penguin Books Ltd. Registered Offices: 80 Strand, London WC2R 0RL, England

www.penguin.com

First published 2005

Photo credits:
p. 1: Damien Eagers / SPORTSFILE
p. 31: Ray McManus / SPORTSFILE
p. 49: Brendan Moran / SPORTSFILE
p. 103: Brendan Moran / SPORTSFILE
p. 179: Bryan O'Brien, IRISH TIMES
p. 191: Brian Lawless / SPORTSFILE

Designed by Richard Marston
Printed in Italy by LegoPrint S.p.A

ISBN 1-844-88067-2

Contents

4

Football Championship 2005   103

5

Women's Senior Camogie and Football Championships   179

6

Results 2004   191

Introduction

In 1997, Cavan reached the All-Ireland Under-21 football final – bringing about a magnificent upsurge in interest in a part of Ireland that had fallen on hard times in footballing terms. And on a beautiful summer's day, a large and enthusiastic crowd followed the players down to Tipperary for a meeting with Kerry.

For many travellers from Cavan, it would be their first visit to the Gaelic Athletic Association's second-largest stadium. When traffic arriving from the north side of Thurles was held up briefly (apparently due to a lorry breaking down), some decided to park their cars and walk to the stadium, believing they were on the outskirts of the town.

Of course, as every GAA fan has witnessed, parking on match day often involves a domino effect: seeing the parked cars and the walking supporters, others followed suit, and soon a long line of blue-and-white-clad fans were walking along a county road – over four miles from the edge of Thurles. Clued-in supporters and locals began stopping and loading up their cars with grateful fans; two Tyrone men even sat in the open boot of a car (the driver of which will remain nameless).

It was an episode that showed how used to being kept in the dark GAA fans have become – and as such it formed part of the inspiration for this book. On the pages that follow we attempt to shed a little more light on the greatest show on Earth – providing supporters with all the little bits of vital information that help in supporting a team through the championship season.

Chapter One provides guides to some of the most important stadiums on the island, and the towns in which they are located – in all four provinces.

Chapter Two provides background on the GAA's history and rather complicated structure. It also suggests the most helpful web links; chronicles the scores of past All-Ireland finals; lists the reigning champions at all levels; and sheds light on some of the trickier rules of Gaelic games.

Chapter Three previews this year's All-Ireland hurling championship. It explains the format of the competition, lists the fixtures, provides a chart for supporters to fill in the results as they happen, and offers detailed information and analysis on each county side. Chapter Four does the same for football.

Chapter Five notes the rise and rise of the women's codes, previews the All-Ireland championships in Gaelic football and camogie, and lists all the results from 2004. And Chapter Six gives full results from the men's championships of 2004.

Enjoy.

Watching the Championship

Watching the
Championship

Towns and Stadiums

Thanks to new championship formats and (in some places) better roads and public transport facilities, provincial borders are simply no longer a barrier for hurling and football teams and supporters. In just the past couple of years, first-team supporters from Armagh, Limerick and Cork have been to Roscommon; Laois fans have travelled to Limerick; Carlow and Offaly spectators have visited Tipperary and supporters of Westmeath, Dublin, Meath and Longford have all found themselves in Monaghan. Road maps can only point you in the right direction; here we attempt to take you the rest of the way, with advice on traffic, parking, pubs, hotels and other supporters' landmarks.

Clones

St Tiernach's Park

Clones, Co. Monaghan
Stadium capacity: 36,000

The stadium

There are many reasons why Clones was chosen and developed over the years as the main GAA stadium in Ulster. The area has been associated with Gaelic games from the early days of the organization: Clones contested the first-ever Monaghan club championship in the late 1880s. Last season, however, was something of a wake-up call, with the Ulster football final being moved from its traditional home to Croke Park. Still, there's no need for locals to panic: the Qualifier system has resulted in the stadium hosting more and more matches each season. And the £1 million development of the west stand has ensured the importance of St Tiernach's Park in the province for many years to come.

Getting there

Situated near the Fermanagh border in west Monaghan, Clones is the ideal location for a major GAA stadium in Ulster – at least when you look at where it is on a map. But it's a long, long time since the town was a major railway hub, and driving to Clones on big match days can be a gruelling experience, especially when the supporters of the competing counties are approaching from the same direction, which is often the case. However, if you can

Clones

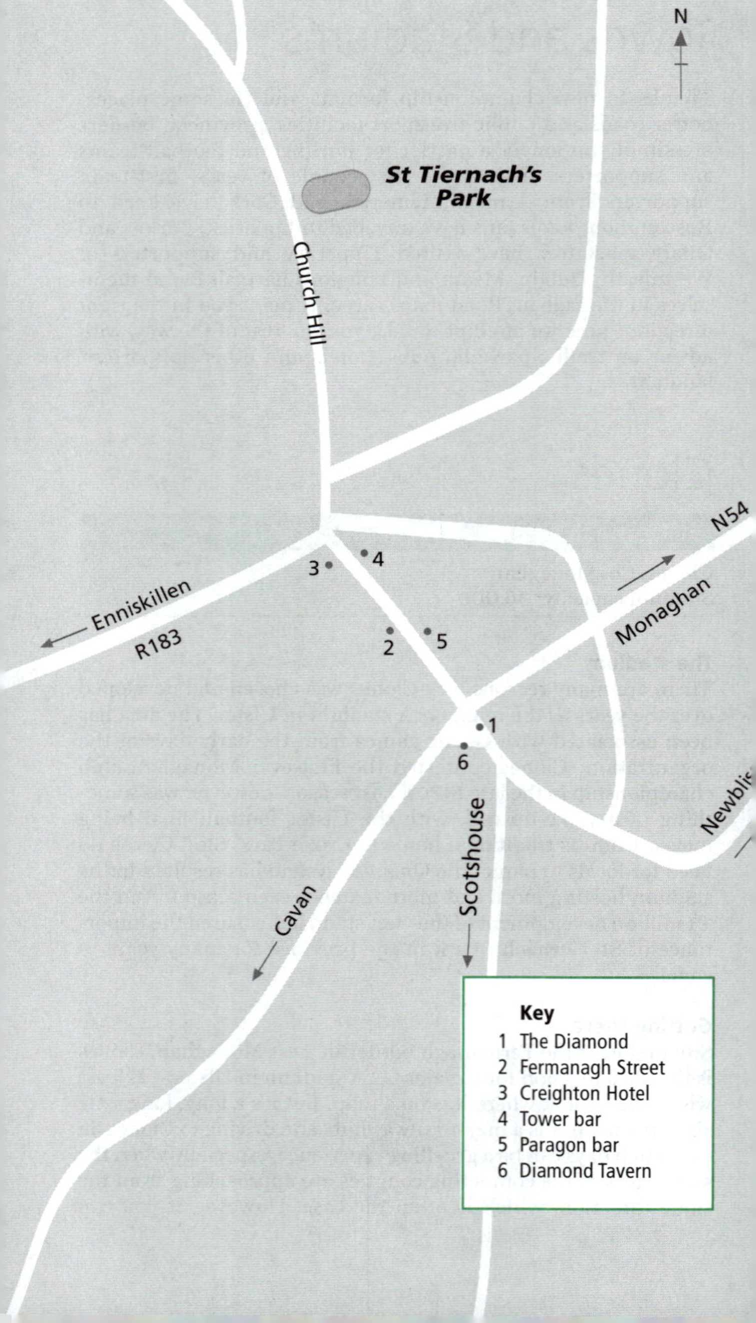

St Tiernach's Park

Church Hill

N54

Enniskillen

R183

Monaghan

Newblis

3

4

2

5

1

6

Cavan

Scotshouse

N

Key
1 The Diamond
2 Fermanagh Street
3 Creighton Hotel
4 Tower bar
5 Paragon bar
6 Diamond Tavern

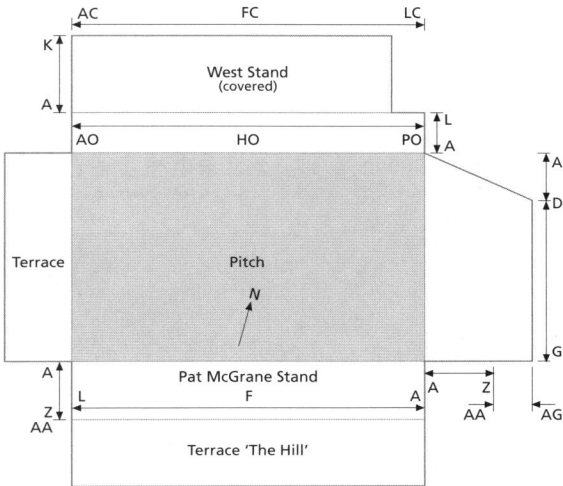

approach the town from a direction that does not link directly to a participating county, you'll have no difficulty parking within a brief walk of the town centre.

The town

For travelling supporters, there are two main areas of interest in the town: the Diamond (1) and Fermanagh Street (2) – both of which have received face-lifts in the past few years. Supporters congregate on Fermanagh Street on match days and it is the main route taken by most to the stadium on Church Hill. At the north end of Fermanagh Street is the Creighton Hotel (3), which has a large outdoor area for supporters on match days. At the other side of the road is the Tower Bar (4), and closer to the centre of town is the Paragon Bar (5), a great spot for GAA fans to meet before and after the game. If there's such a thing as a Gaelic football bar, this is it – the walls of the Paragon (and the adjoining pub, called Under the Bar) are decorated with pictures of famous Ulster footballers. The Diamond area of the town also has a number of restaurants and bars that are well worth a visit, including the Diamond Tavern (6) and the Cuildarach Bar and Restaurant.

Travel distances

Belfast	111 km (69 miles)	Dublin	128 km (80 miles)
Derry	107 km (66 miles)	Newry	70.5 km (44 miles)
Donegal	93 km (58 miles)	Omagh	54 km (33 miles)

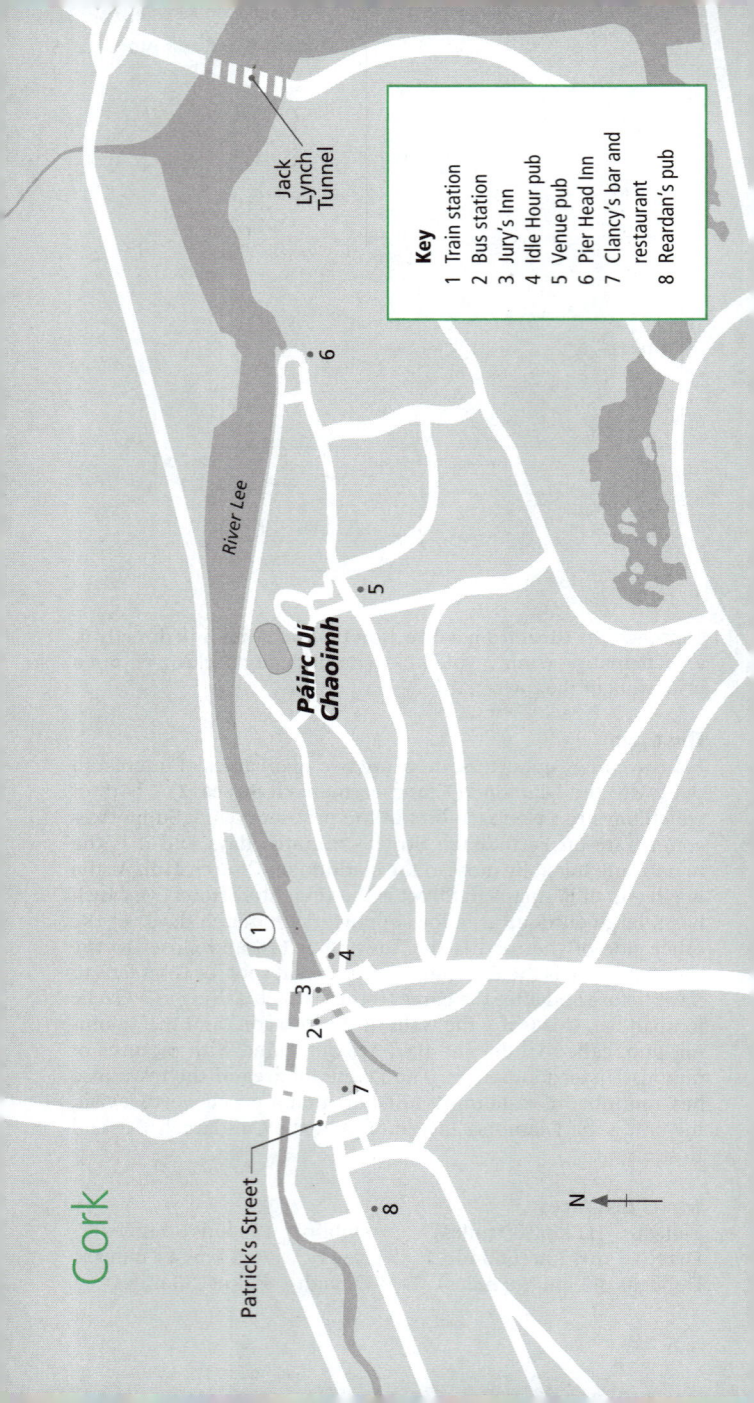

Cork

Key

1 Train station
2 Bus station
3 Jury's Inn
4 Idle Hour pub
5 Venue pub
6 Pier Head Inn
7 Clancy's bar and restaurant
8 Reardan's pub

Jack Lynch Tunnel

River Lee

Páirc Uí Chaoimh

Patrick's Street

N

Cork

Cork city
Stadium capacity: 43,000

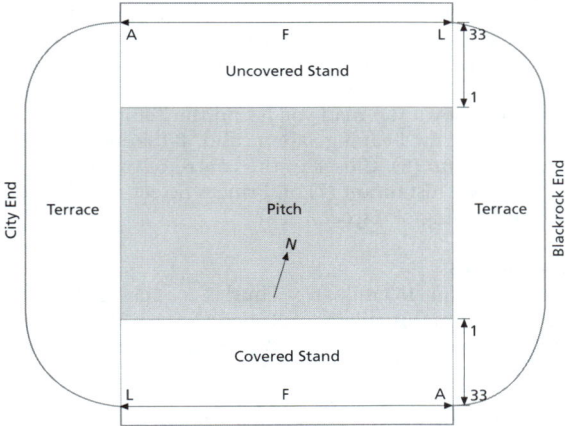

The stadium

Known for decades as the Cork Athletic Grounds, Páirc Uí Chaoimh was re-christened in 1976, the same year that the Rebels defeated Limerick in the Munster senior hurling final at the venue. For locals, especially, there is nothing to compare with a full ground on a championship afternoon in the summer, with most of the home supporters occupying the City End. Rumours of future major improvements and expansions are frequent; but probably the most significant change of recent years was made in 1999, when the playing surface was upgraded. Accepting that they couldn't stop the rain from falling, Cork officials did the next best thing, improving the drainage system and reseeding the entire field.

Getting there

Many travelling supporters use the city's train station (1) and main bus station (2). The train station, especially, is always full of fans on the morning of a big game. The opening of the Jack Lynch Tunnel in 1999 was a godsend, allowing travelling supporters to bypass the city centre on their way to the stadium. There is very little available parking near the stadium, and the roads around the ground are usually blocked off to everyone except pedestrians and local residents on the big summer Sundays.

The town

Because of the route GAA fans must take to get from the train station and the city centre to the Cork ground, some of the most popular meeting places and watering holes are along by the docks – with Jury's Inn (3) always busy on match day. Around the corner, public houses such as Idle Hour (4) and the nearby Port Bar and Marina Bar are usually kept very busy. One of the closest pubs to Páirc Uí Chaoimh is the Venue (5) in Ballintemple, while a little further down the road you'll find the Temple Inn (which also serves food), the Leaping Salmon and, at the end of the road, the Pier Head Inn (6). Closer to the centre of town you'll find Clancy's bar and restaurant (7) on Princes Street, and Reardan's pub (8) on Washington Street.

Travel distances

Dublin	252 km (157 miles)	Thurles	115 km (71 miles)
Kilkenny	143 km (89 miles)	Tralee	112 km (70 miles)
Limerick	97 km (60 miles)	Waterford	122 km (76 miles)

Dublin

Croke Park

Jones Road, Dublin 3
Stadium capacity: 82,300

The stadium

Croke Park stands on the site formerly occupied by the City and Suburban Racecourse, a ground used regularly by the GAA before the organization purchased the 14-acre site for £3,500 in 1913 and renamed it after the association's first patron, Archbishop Croke.

The Hill 16 terrace was constructed in 1917, using rubble from the Easter 1916 rebellion. On 21 November 1920 the ground was stormed by Black and Tans, who shot dead 11 supporters and one player during a football match between Tipperary and Dublin. Four years later, the Hogan Stand was built and dedicated to the fallen player, Tipperary captain Michael Hogan. An upper deck was added to the Cusack Stand in 1936. The Canal End terrace was constructed in 1948 and the Nally Stand in 1952.

Over the past decade the GAA has replaced the old stands and terraces with a more fitting monument to the national games.

Phase One of the reconstruction involved the razing of the Cusack Stand and its replacement with a modern three-tiered stand, completed in 1997 with a seating capacity of 25,000. Phase Two extended the new stand around the canal side of the stadium and Phase Three involved the replacement of the Hogan Stand, completing the horseshoe. In 2003 the final phase began, with the replacement of the Nally Stand and the Hill 16 terrace with a new terrace at the railway end. The completion of this phase has brought the capacity of Croke Park up to a remarkable 82,300.

Getting there

This season, GAA supporters travelling by train to Dublin from the south and west will be able to use the Luas tram line to take them from Heuston Station to O'Connell Street (1) or to Connolly Station (2). Fans arriving from the north and north-west of the island to Connolly will have no need for the new tram service, of course, as the station is only a short walk from Croke Park, as is Busáras (3) – Dublin's central bus station.

There is one word to keep in mind above all others if you are travelling to Croke Park by car: clampers. Apart from GAA fans, no one loves a big game at Croker better than your friendly neighbourhood clamper. There is nothing worse than paying €30 or €40 for a ticket, watching your team lose easily at head-

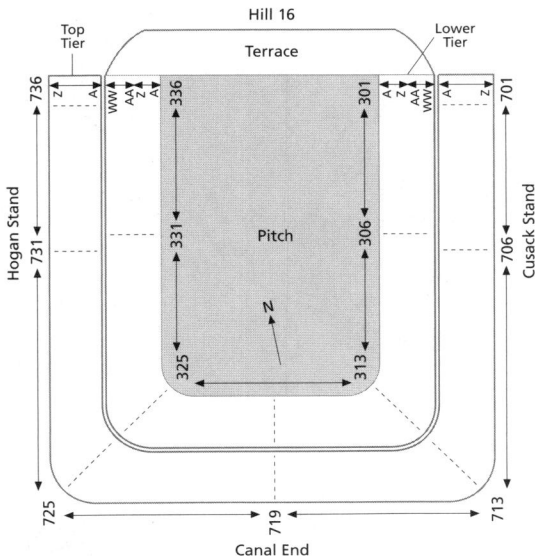

Hill 16

Top Tier — Terrace — Lower Tier

Hogan Stand

Cusack Stand

736 Z A WW AA Z A 336 331 Pitch 306 301 A Z AA WW A Z 701 706 725 331 325 Z 313 306 719 713

Canal End

Dublin

Key
1. O'Connell Street
2. Connolly Station
3. Busáras
4. Quinn's pub
5. McGrath's pub
6. The Big Tree pub
7. Barry's Hotel
8. Hill 16 pub
9. The Hogan Stand pub
10. Cusack's pub
11. Chaplin's pub
12. Doyle's pub
13. Palace Bar
14. Gresham Hotel

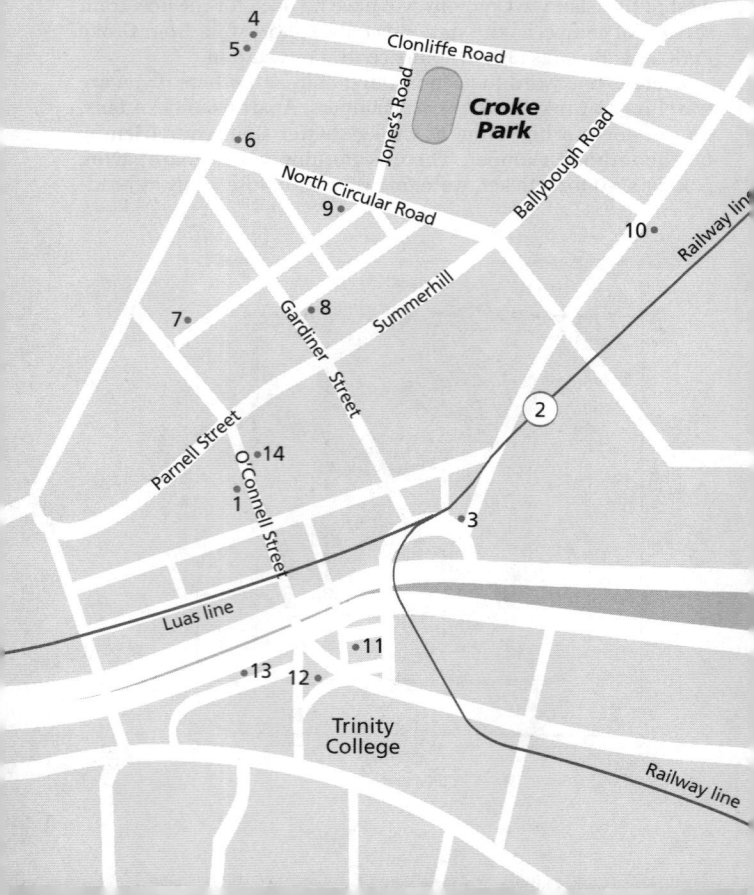

N

Clonliffe Road

Jones's Road

Croke Park

Ballybough Road

North Circular Road

Railway line

Summerhill

Gardiner Street

Parnell Street

O'Connell Street

Luas line

Trinity College

Railway line

quarters, and then trudging out of the stadium to find that your car is going nowhere. There's plenty of legal and safe parking around the city, and one suspects that some supporters may begin this year to leave their cars in the 'park & ride' areas outside town, such as the one at the Red Cow stop, and then use the Luas to ferry them in and out.

The city
There are a number of public houses in Dublin that are associated with particular counties, and others that attract GAA supporters on big match weekends, no matter who is playing. The Drumcondra Road is probably the most popular stop for supporters en route to Croke Park, with Quinn's (4) a particular pre- and post-match favourite (there is a restaurant upstairs). A few doors down is McGrath's (5), and on the opposite side of the road, at the corner of North Circular Road, is the recently refurbished Big Tree (6), which is usually full of GAA fans on summer Sundays.

Barry's Hotel (7) on Denmark Street has a long and proud tradition as a meeting place for Gaelic games enthusiasts, especially fans who don't want to watch the match on an empty stomach. Nearer the city centre, the Gresham Hotel (14) on O'Connell Street and the new Jury's Inn on Parnell Street are equally happy to accommodate fans and send them up to Croke Park with a full stomach on match day. Hill 16 (8), a public house in Middle Gardiner Street, has strong Mayo connections but has proven a popular location for GAA supporters from all corners of the island. Dublin supporters especially seem to enjoy the pub's pre-match atmosphere, usually leaving it until the last minute before making the dash to the other Hill 16.

A little closer to Croke Park is the Hogan Stand pub (9). And on North Strand Road, Cusack's (10) is popular with supporters who are breaking the journey between Connolly Station and the stadium, or who are using the on-street parking in the area.

Just across the Liffey, Chaplin's (11) on Hawkins Street is a well-known GAA bar, as is Doyle's (12) around the corner. Temple Bar hosts several GAA haunts, most notably the Palace Bar (13), which displays tributes to legendary journalist Con Houlihan on its walls.

Tips
If the weather isn't good, a double-letter Croke Park stand ticket (e.g. KK) is much more valuable than a single-letter ticket. Depending on the direction of the wind and rain, the first 30 rows are open to the elements.

If you are approaching the stadium from a side that your ticket is not for, please note it can take a long time to push through the crowds to the correct side of the stadium.

The Lower Cusack Stand starts at Section 301 and ends at 312, the Lower Canal End goes from Section 313 to 324 and the Lower Hogan from 325 to 336. The Upper decks are 701 to 712 (Cusack), 713 to 724 (Canal) and 725 to 736 (Hogan).

While many assume that lower-tier tickets are better than upper-tier ones, there is a considerably better view from the front row of the middle section of the Upper Cusack Stand, for example, than from the back row of the corner section of the Lower Cusack – so be careful when buying or swapping tickets.

Travel distances

Belfast	164 km (102 miles)	Kilkenny	115 km (72 miles)
Cork	252 km (157 miles)	Limerick	191 km (119 miles)
Derry	228 km (142 miles)	Sligo	207 km (129 miles)
Galway	213 km (132 miles)	Waterford	166 km (103 miles)

Kilkenny

Nowlan Park

Kilkenny city
Stadium capacity: 30,000

The stadium

Considering its location and standard, Nowlan Park is under-exploited – for inter-county games in particular. The ground doesn't attract as many of the bigger provincial, Qualifier and All-Ireland championship clashes as it should, in spite of regular improvements over the past few decades. The construction of the covered New Stand, replacing the old bank, has elevated the stadium to a much higher status. And when the stadium is full, for games such as the Kilkenny–Waterford senior hurling championship tie in 2003, the atmosphere in the stands and terraces is simply second to none.

Getting there

Kilkenny is situated on the Dublin–Waterford railway line, and McDonagh Station (1) is within a 10-minute walk of Nowlan Park. More or less equidistant from Cork and Dublin, the city is adequately served by national primary roads, and the ring road – which runs across the south side of the city – has made the stadium much more easily accessible for supporters travelling from the south. No matter from which direction you approach

Kilkenny

Key
1 McDonagh Station
2 M.J. McGuinness's pub
3 Langton's pub
4 Newpark Hotel
5 Hotel Kilkenny

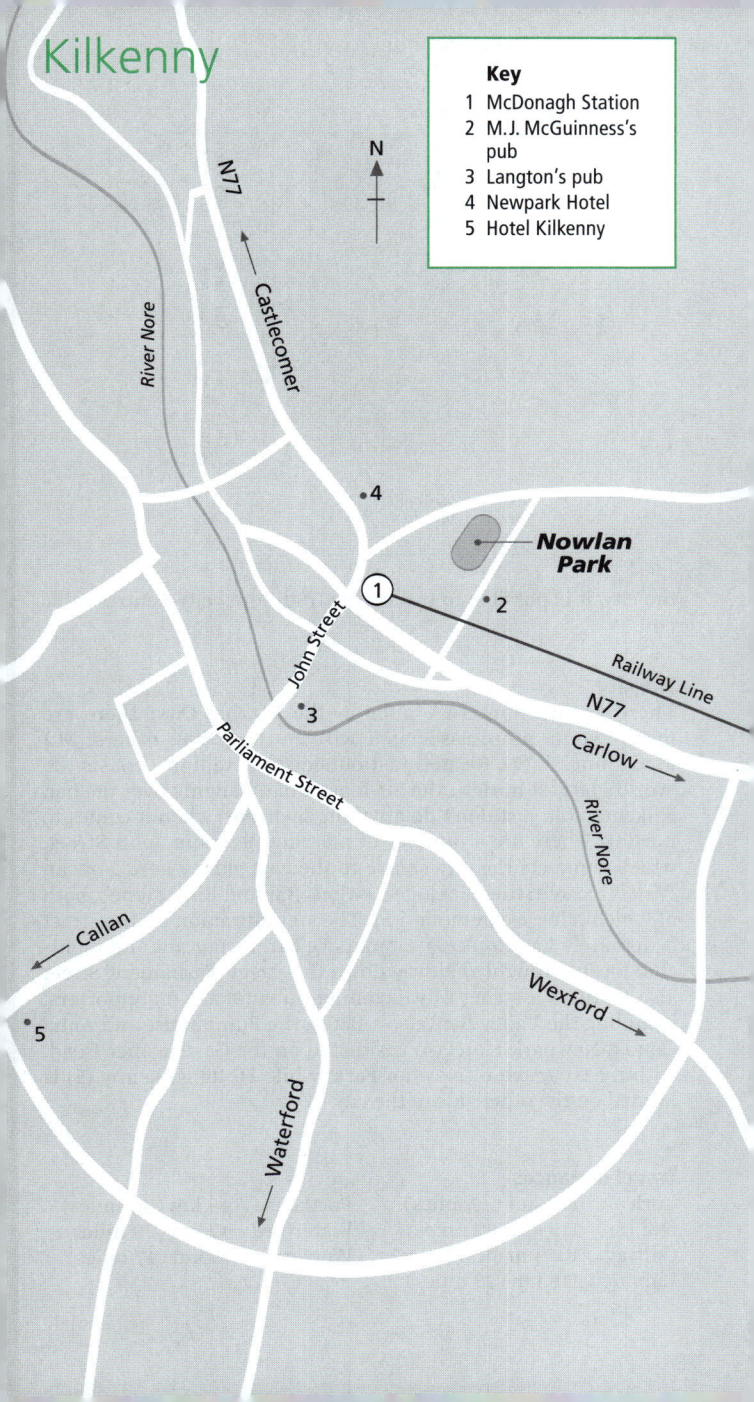

N

N77

River Nore

Castlecomer

4

Nowlan Park

1

2

John Street

Railway Line

N77

Carlow →

3

Parliament Street

River Nore

← Callan

Wexford →

5

Waterford

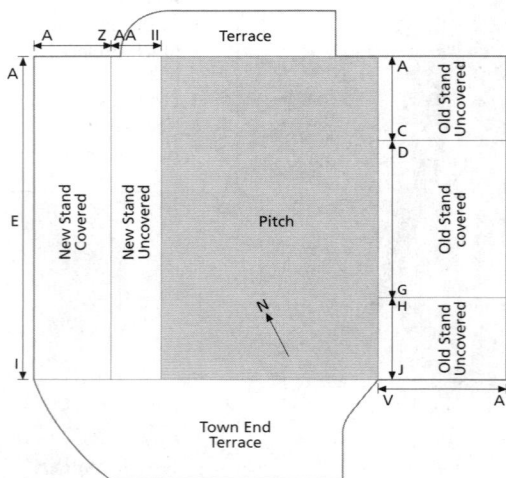

the city, it is possible to bypass the traditional city-centre traffic jam.

The city

There are no non-GAA pubs in the Marble City; there are merely some more associated with hurling than others. MJ McGuinness's (2), located just outside the stadium, boasts the 'world's largest hurley': the 20-foot camán hanging over the bar. Kilkenny folk just don't do anything by halves when it comes to hurling. There are a number of meeting-places in John Street, which connects the city centre to the east side, where Nowlan Park is located; these include Lawlor's Bar and Billy Byrne's, both of which offer accommodation. The star attraction on the street is definitely Langton's (3) – a massive bar, restaurant and nightclub located roughly halfway down the street. Parliament Street also features a string of welcoming pubs for GAA supporters, including the Bailey Bar (also a B&B), the Pumphouse and Anna Conda. Newpark Hotel (4) is situated on the Castlecomer Road, within easy reach of Nowlan Park, while Hotel Kilkenny (5) is located on the other side of the city.

Travel distances

Cork	143 km (87 miles)	Portlaoise	49 km (30 miles)
Dublin	115 km (72 miles)	Waterford	47 km (29 miles)
Galway	165 km (103 miles)	Wexford	75 km (47 miles)
Limerick	118 km (73 miles)		

Limerick

Gaelic Grounds

Limerick city
Stadium capacity: 49,500

The stadium

The recent €12 million development – which added 19,000 to the stadium's capacity – has transformed the Gaelic Grounds in Limerick. Suggestions before last season's Waterford–Cork Munster hurling final that the game could be staged at the venue may have been offered more in hope than confidence, but they were a signal of intent: Semple Stadium's capacity now exceeds that of the Limerick ground by only a few thousand.

The main stand is named in memory of legendary Limerick forward Mick Mackey, who played at the official opening of the ground in 1928. When Croke Park replaced its Hogan Stand in the late 1950s, Limerick gratefully accepted the old stand – a boost that allowed over 60,000 spectators to watch the Munster hurling final between Cork and Tipperary in 1961. The Mackey Stand was completed in 1988, with another Munster final between Cork and Tipperary marking its official opening. With a new 12,000-seat uncovered stand now facing the Mackey – and modern terraces on both sides – the Gaelic Grounds will be a serious contender for major games in the Munster and All-Ireland Qualifier competitions for the foreseeable future.

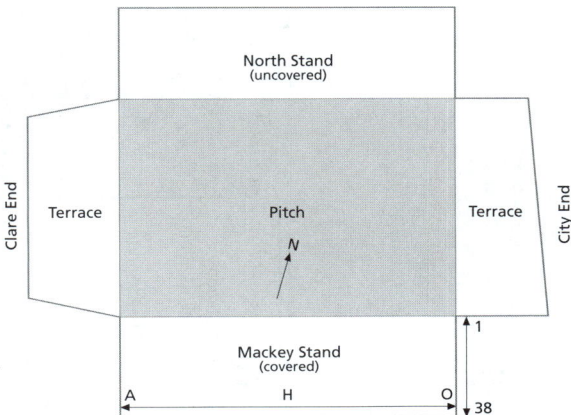

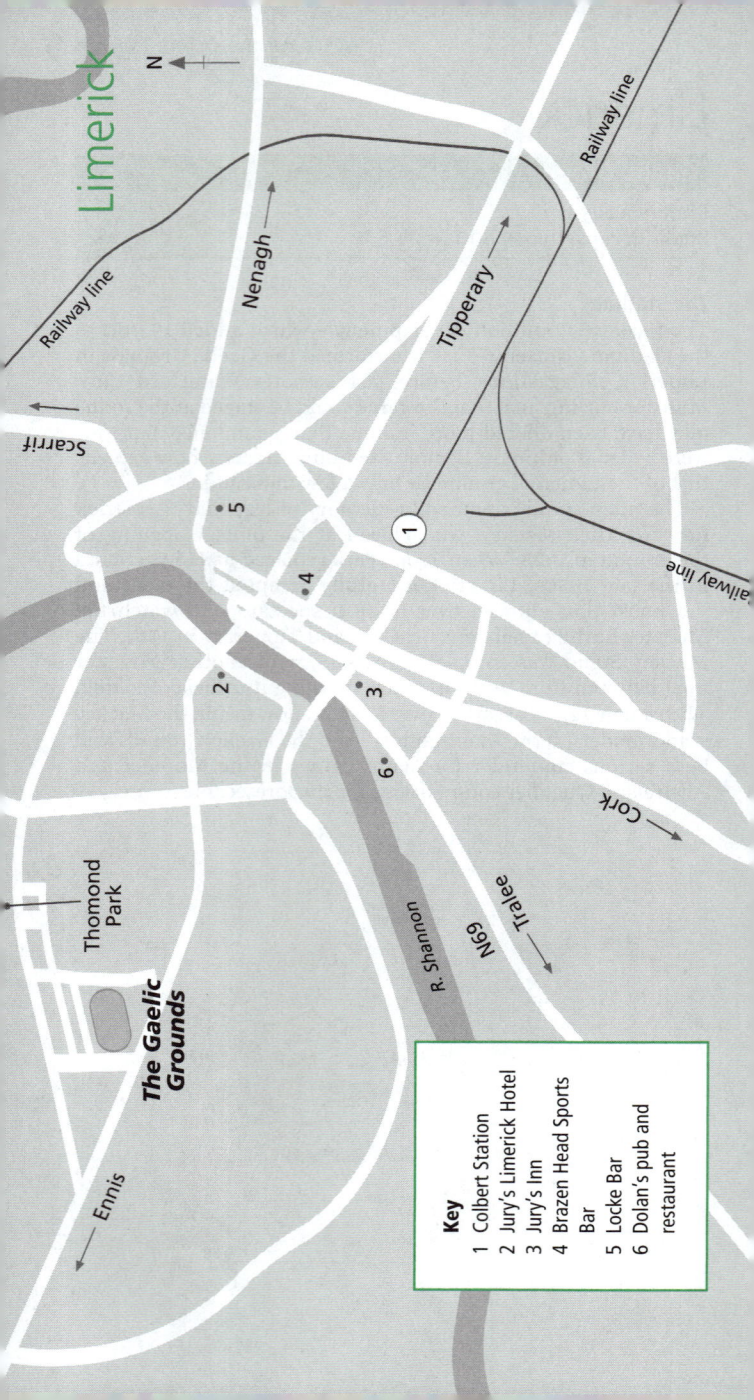

Limerick

N

Railway line

Railway line

Nenagh

Tipperary

Scarrif

(1)

Railway line

5

4

2

3

6

Cork

Tralee

N69

R. Shannon

Thomond Park

The Gaelic Grounds

Ennis

Key

1 Colbert Station
2 Jury's Limerick Hotel
3 Jury's Inn
4 Brazen Head Sports Bar
5 Locke Bar
6 Dolan's pub and restaurant

Getting there

It is simply impossible to estimate the time it will take to drive from the outskirts of the city to the Gaelic Grounds, or vice versa, on match day. Suffice it to say that leaving home in plenty of time is probably more important for this destination than for any other GAA stadium. And if there is a rugby game at Thomond around the same time, well, don't make any other plans for the day. Congestion on the roads is possibly the reason many supporters prefer public transport, arriving into the city by train or bus to Colbert Station (1).

The city

Limerick is a compact city, with most of the restaurants, bars and hotels within walking distance of each other. Close to the Gaelic Grounds on the Ennis Road is the Davin Arms, a popular spot for GAA supporters on the morning and evening of a game, while Bard Hogan's – despite being situated close to Thomond Park – is also a favourite with hurling and football fans. There are two Jury's – Jury's Limerick Hotel (2) and Jury's Inn (3) – both within easy reach of the ground and the city centre. The spacious Brazen Head Sports Bar (4) – which also serves food daily – is popular with fans, while the Locke Bar (5) is located on George's Quay. On the Dock Road fans will find Dolan's pub and restaurant (6).

Travel distances

Athlone	118 km (74 miles)	Galway	89 km (55 miles)
Cork	97 km (60 miles)	Kilkenny	118 km (74 miles)
Dublin	191 km (118 miles)	Tralee	101 km (62 miles)
Ennis	36 km (23 miles)		

Roscommon

Dr Hyde Park

Roscommon town
Stadium capacity: 30,000

The stadium

Raftery's Field was long used by the GAA for various grades of competition before 1969, when the organization purchased the site and renamed it Dr Hyde Park. Additions to the stadium since then include the Hyde Centre and Bar Complex, which was constructed in the 1970s. The grass banks around the three sides of the ground were replaced by modern terracing in the early

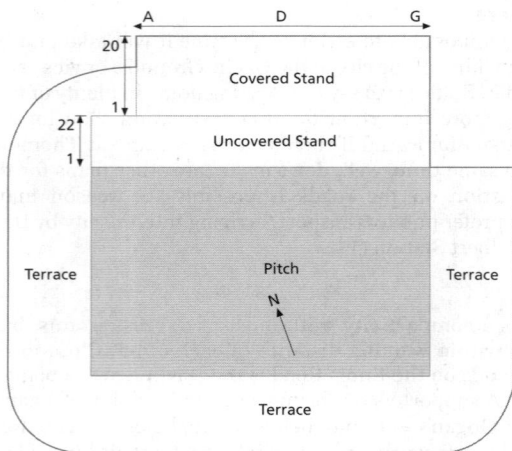

1990s. More recently, a covered stand was built behind open seating – which added significantly to the stadium's attractiveness, not just for Connacht championship games, but also for Qualifier ties, such as last season's encounter in the football championship between Limerick and Derry.

Getting there

The railway line that runs through Roscommon town serves Ballina and Westport to the north and joins the Dublin–Galway line to the south. With Dr Hyde Park well within the town boundaries, it is a short walk for supporters from the train station (1). The town is relatively well served by national roads, though Lough Ree has to be circumvented if you are travelling from the east or south-east. Parking is not usually a significant problem, though there has been a tendency by some fans, usually late for the big match, to abandon their cars in the first available 12-foot by 6-foot space. Of course, this occurs in the vicinity of nearly every GAA pitch on the island, but it tends to cause even more disruption than normal on the road to Athlone.

The town

The centre of Roscommon is Market Square (2), where GAA fans frequent Gleeson's Townhouse and Restaurant, and Regan's Guesthouse. Just off Main Street is Church Street (3), where you will find Church Street Station, a public house that has walls decorated with former Roscommon footballing heroes, and Down the Hatch, another bar with strong local GAA connections. A hospital (4) is situated beside the GAA

Roscommon

N

Four Mile House

N60
Ballymoe

Longford
N63

2

3

Dr Hyde Park

N61
4
5
Athlone

Main Street

1

N63

Athlegue

Railway Line

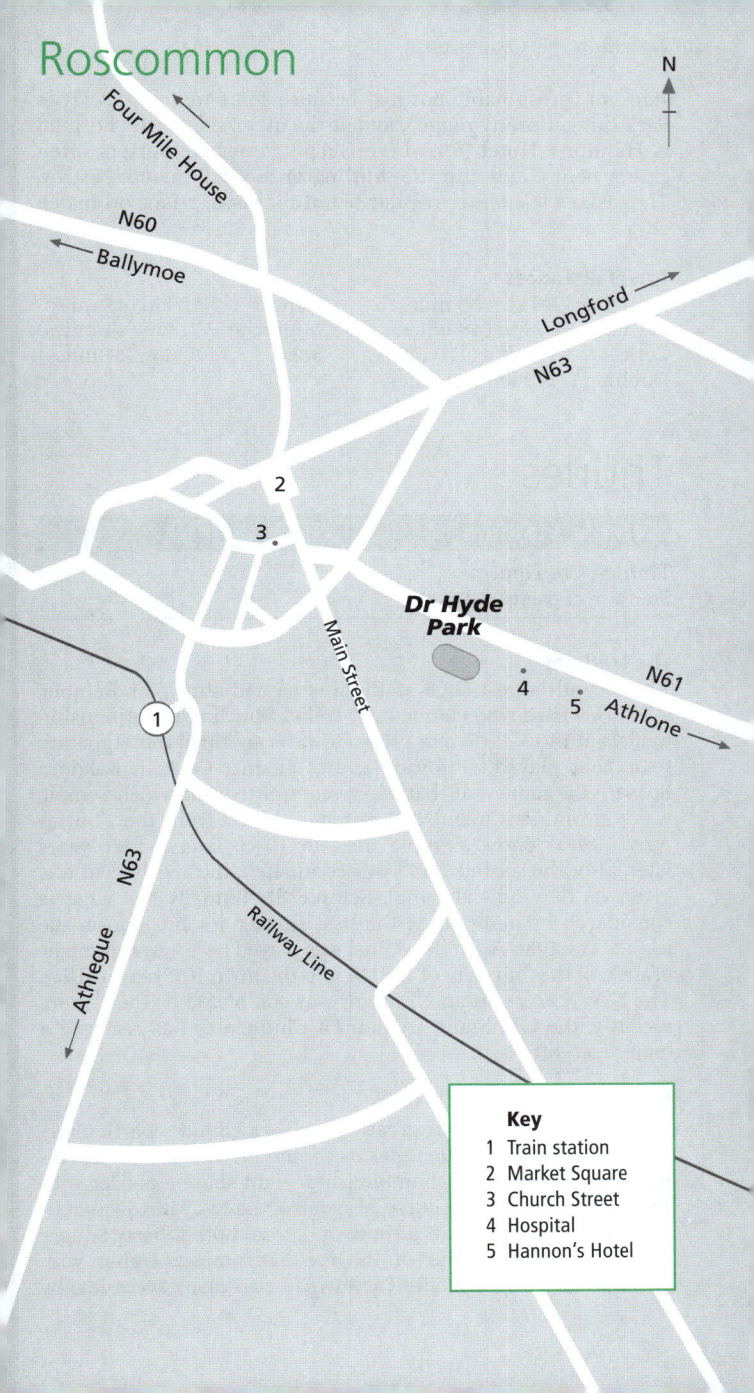

Key
1 Train station
2 Market Square
3 Church Street
4 Hospital
5 Hannon's Hotel

stadium (presumably not just because some matches at Hyde Park can get pretty rough), and at the other side of the hospital is Hannon's Hotel (5), where Gaelic games supporters often gather before and after the hurling or football match. Nearby, Thos Foxe's is another regular haunt for visiting fans on match days.

Travel distances

Castlebar	86 km (53 miles)	Galway	78 km (48 miles)
Cavan	77 km (48 miles)	Mullingar	71 km (44 miles)
Cork	239 km (149 miles)	Sligo	83 km (51 miles)
Dublin	148 km (92 miles)		

Thurles

Semple Stadium

Thurles, Co. Tipperary
Stadium capacity: 53,000

The stadium

The second-largest GAA stadium is named after Tom Semple, a Thurles man who claimed All-Ireland hurling championship medals in 1900, 1906 and 1908. He also captained the Tipperary team that played exhibition games against Cork in Belgium in 1910, the same year that a local committee – of which Semple was a prominent member – purchased land from the Thurles Agricultural Show. Semple died in 1943. Twenty-four years later, after the second stand was completed, the sports field was given its new official name, Semple Stadium. It has what is considered by many to be the best surface for hurling on the island. The 1984 All-Ireland final was played here – in commemoration of the founding of the GAA in the town 100 years earlier. The New Stand (Ardan Uí Riain) was completed by then; more recently, the Old Stand (Ardan Uí Chuineain) has received a major face-lift.

Getting there

Semple Stadium benefits greatly from its location – particularly for hurling games. Of the 12 teams competing in this season's All-Ireland senior hurling championship, eight share a border with Tipperary (which is, of course, also one of the 12). The town's railway station (1) – which is a short walk from both Liberty Square (2) and the stadium – lies on the line that connects Dublin with Cork, Tralee and Limerick. The town is also easily accessible by

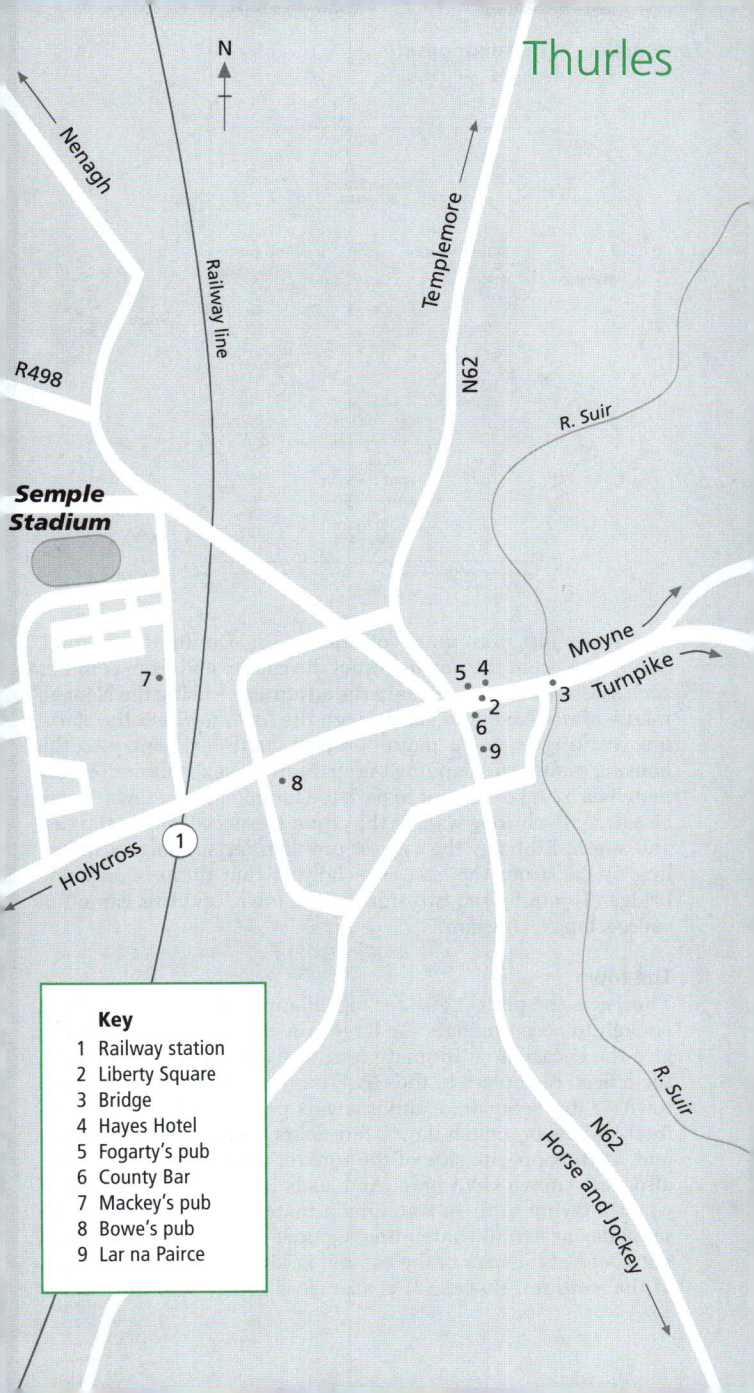

Thurles

Key
1 Railway station
2 Liberty Square
3 Bridge
4 Hayes Hotel
5 Fogarty's pub
6 County Bar
7 Mackey's pub
8 Bowe's pub
9 Lar na Pairce

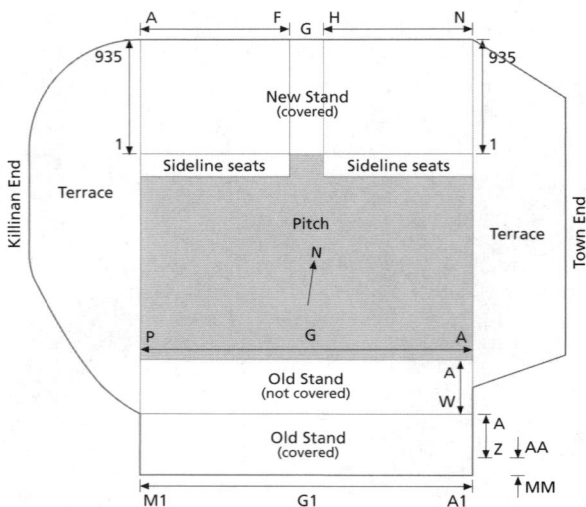

car, lying just ten miles off the main Dublin–Cork road. Supporters from the north-west of the county and from counties such as Clare and Galway have the advantage – using the Nenagh road – of not having to get through the town to reach the stadium. Parking is not a major problem, although entry to the housing estates surrounding the stadium is usually limited on big match days. Take care not to park too far outside the town: it can be a deceptively long walk to the ground, especially from the east and south. Probably the biggest problem for supporters travelling by car, from the east especially, is that there is only one bridge (3) joining the two sides of the town, and this can often cause a long traffic jam.

The town

Thurles is the perfect size for big championship weekends: big enough to accommodate the large crowds, but small enough to give the occasion an intimate festival flavour. Hayes' Hotel (4), the official birthplace of the GAA, is situated in the heart of the town – Liberty Square – and is always popular with hurling and football fans on match day. A few doors away, Fogarty's pub (5) and, at the opposite side of the square, the County Bar (6), are also well-known GAA bars. And, as is increasingly the case, if you are trying to fit in watching a match on television on the same day as actually attending a game, Mackey's pub (7) has a big screen at the back of the bar and is within a two-minute dash of the stadium. Bowe's (8) is also close to the stadium, and is especially popular with supporters using the train station. Apart from Hayes', the Anner Hotel on the edge of town is also usually kept very busy accommodating fans – and often players – on summer weekends.

Also in the town is Lar na Pairce (9), a GAA museum just off Liberty Square, that houses – among its impressive collection of jerseys, trophies, books, videos and photographs – the world's oldest hurley.

Travel distances

Cork	75km (46 miles)	Limerick	128km (80 miles)
Dublin	142km (88 miles)	Waterford	46km (29 miles)
Galway	114km (71 miles)	Wexford	76.5km (47.5 miles)
Kilkenny	114km (71 miles)		

How to get tickets

When it comes to securing tickets for big GAA matches, 'what you know' has, for a long time, been lagging well behind 'who you know'. Attitudes and procedures, however, have been changing, and the Association has finally woken up to the reality that there is a huge under-exploited market for tickets.

Of course, securing a golden ticket for an All-Ireland hurling or football final remains an exhausting sport in itself – with clubs from participating counties regularly being asked to perform 'loaves and fishes' tricks with their meagre allocations. But on other days, when attendance figures might not necessarily test the capacity limits, the GAA has been actively encouraging non-members, as well as members, to go along to the games.

Surely the biggest step forward in ticket sales in recent years – especially for non-members of the association – has been the availability of inter-county GAA tickets online. The official website www.gaa.ie offers supporters the opportunity to purchase tickets for many championship games – and nearly all games held at Croke Park. Tickets are generally offered about a week in advance of the game; if you have left it too late to receive your tickets by post, you can pick them up at the GAA's offices on Prince's Street in Dublin's city centre (from the south end of O'Connell bridge, facing south, turn left down City Quay; Prince's Street is the first right). Wheelchair-access tickets, family tickets and reduced-price tickets for students or pensioners are not available from the website, unfortunately, so it's back to your club or county board for those. Ticketmaster has also been getting in on the act, selling tickets for most important GAA ties.

On big match days in Croke Park, any tickets remaining unsold will be available from several outlets surrounding the stadium – the GAA's traditional outlets include Matt Talbot Credit Union on Fitzgibbon Street, the Drumcondra Laundrette on Drumcondra Road and a ticket booth opposite Quinn's Pub, at the junction of Drumcondra Road and Clonliffe Road. And do try to secure a ticket from an official source, before you resort to engaging the services of a ticket tout – they are no friend of GAA supporters.

If you are collecting tickets, so are hundreds of other supporters – usually all around the same time – so be sure to leave plenty of time. Do not imagine that you can just stroll up to the counter, collect your tickets and wander into the stadium minutes before the match begins.

Due to ever-increasing demand, tickets for the senior hurling and football finals are available only via club or county-board channels: they never go on general sale and are not available on-line – not on the official website, anyway.

Prices and concessions

Ticket prices for this September's All-Ireland hurling and football finals will be €60 for the stands and €30 for the terrace. To attend a semi-final you will have to part with €40 for a seat, or €25 for a place on the terrace. Quarter-final tickets will cost €35 and €20, but if a quarter-final tie is played outside Croke Park the stand ticket will be €30.

A new ticket scheme has been introduced for all games in Croke Park, and your colour-coded ticket will direct you to the correct side of the stadium, as well as to the right turnstile and seating block. And please note that all patrons, no matter what age, require a ticket to enter Croke Park – the days of lifting half the family over the stiles are gone.

Student tickets have long been the bane of many sporting organizations, but their importance and appeal are obvious. Card-carrying students have been known to buy several student tickets and hand them out to non-student friends, and stile operators often don't feel they have time to demand or check a student card when there is a long queue to enter the stadium. One of the more recent and confusing schemes has involved selling tickets to students at full price, but allowing them to claim back part (usually half) of the cost at the turnstile on the way into the stadium – a system that makes it impossible for student tickets to be sold on to non-students. This has resulted in the rather amusing sight of stile operators handing cash to spectators as they enter the stadium.

Remember, you must have a valid student card to avail of the scheme – strange as it may seem, many people believe just claiming to be a student should be enough. And be aware of what stiles will be operating the refund system: there's nothing worse than being told you are at the wrong side of the stadium a minute before the throw-in.

Championship diary

May

May 1
Connacht Football Championship, quarter-final
New York v Galway (Gaelic Park, New York)

May 8
Leinster Football Championship, first round
Offaly v Louth (Navan)

May 15
Ulster Football Championship, first round
Armagh v Fermanagh
Leinster Football Championship, first round
Wicklow v Kildare (Croke Park)
Dublin v Longford (Croke Park)
Ulster Hurling Championship, quarter-final
Down v London
Munster Hurling Championship, quarter-final
Tipperary v Limerick (Thurles)

May 22
Leinster Hurling Championship, first round
Dublin v Laois (Kilkenny)
Ulster Hurling Championship, semi-finals
Derry v Down/London
New York v Antrim (New York)
Munster Hurling Championship, semi-final
Cork v Waterford (Thurles)
Connacht Football Championship, quarter-final
Sligo v Leitrim (Carrick-on-Shannon)
Ulster Football Championship, quarter-final
Tyrone v Down

May 29
Munster Football Championship, quarter-finals
Tipperary v Kerry
Waterford v Clare (Ennis)
Connacht Football Championship, quarter-final
London v Roscommon (London)
Leinster Football Championship, quarter-finals
Offaly/Louth v Laois (Croke Park)
Wicklow/Kildare v Westmeath (Croke Park)

Ulster Football Championship, quarter-final
Cavan v Antrim

June

June 4
Hurling Tier 2, Group B, round 1

June 5
Ulster Hurling Championship Final
Leinster Football Championship, quarter-finals
Dublin/Longford v Meath (Croke Park)
Carlow v Wexford (Croke Park)
Ulster Football Championship, quarter-final
Monaghan v Derry
Munster Hurling Championship, semi-final
Clare v Limerick/Tipperary (Thurles or Limerick)

June 11
Hurling Tier 2, Group A, round 1
Hurling Tier 2, Group B, round 2

June 12
Leinster Hurling Championship, semi-finals
Wexford v Laois/Dublin (Croke Park)
Kilkenny v Offaly (Croke Park)
Connnacht Football Championship, semi-final
Sligo/Leitrim v New York/Galway
Munster Football Championship, semi-final
Cork v Clare/Waterford (Ennis/Dungarvan)
Ulster Football Championship, quarter-final
Donegal v Armagh/Fermanagh (Enniskillen or Ballybofey)

June 18
All-Ireland Football Championship Qualifiers, round 1
All-Ireland Hurling Championship Round 1
Hurling Tier Two, Group A, round 2
Hurling Tier Three, round 1

June 19
Connnacht Football Championship, semi-final
Mayo v Roscommon/London (Roscommon)
Leinster Football Championship, semi-finals
Offaly/Louth/Laois v Wicklow/Kildare/Westmeath (Croke Park)
Dublin/Longford/Meath v Carlow v Wexford (Croke Park)
Munster Football Championship, semi-final
Kerry/Tipperary v Limerick (Limerick or Cork)
Ulster Football Championship, semi-final
Tyrone/Down v Cavan/Antrim (Clones)

June 25
> Hurling Tier Two, round 3
> Hurling Tier Three, round 2

June 26
> Munster Hurling Championship Final
> Ulster Football Championship, semi-final
> Armagh/Fermanagh/Donegal v Monaghan/Derry (Clones)

July

July 2
> All-Ireland Football Championship Qualifiers, round 2
> All-Ireland Hurling Championship, round 2
> Hurling Tier 2, round 4

July 3
> Leinster Hurling Championship Final

July 9
> Hurling Championship Round 3
> Hurling Tier Three, round 3
> Preliminary Hurling Championship Quarter Final
> (if necessary – if Down or Derry)

July 10
> Connacht Football Final
> Munster Football Final

July 16
> All-Ireland Football Championship Qualifiers, round 3
> Hurling Tier Two, round 5

July 17
> Leinster Football Final (Croke Park)
> Ulster Football Final

July 24
> All-Ireland Hurling Championship, quarter-finals
> Munster champions v Group qualifiers
> Leinster runners-up v Group Qualifiers
> Hurling Tier Three, quarter-final

July 30
> All-Ireland Football Championship Qualifiers, round 4
> Connacht runners-up v round 3 winner
> Munster runners-up v round 3 winner

July 31
> All-Ireland Hurling Championship quarter-finals

Leinster champions v Group qualifiers
Munster runners-up v Group qualifiers
Hurling Tier Two, semi-finals
Hurling Tier 2, relegation semi-finals

August

August 6
All-Ireland Football Championship Qualifiers, round 4
Leinster runners-up v round 3 winner
Ulster runners-up v round 3 winner
Hurling Tier three, semi-finals

August 7
All-Ireland Football Championship, quarter-finals
Munster champions v Qualifier round 4 winner
Connacht champions v Qualifier round 4 winner

August 13
All-Ireland Football Championship, quarter-finals
Leinster champions v Qualifier round 4 winner
Ulster champions v Qualifier round 4 winner
Hurling Tier Two, relegation final

August 14
All-Ireland Hurling Championship, first semi-final (Croke Park)
Hurling Tier Two championship final (Croke Park)

August 21
All-Ireland Hurling Championship, second semi-final (Croke Park)
Hurling Tier Three championship final (Croke Park)

August 28
All-Ireland Football Championship, first semi-final
Connacht champions/QF Winners v Munster champions/QF winners (Croke Park)

September

September 4
All-Ireland Football Championship, second semi-final
Leinster champions/QF Winners v Ulster champions/QF winners (Croke Park)

September 11
All-Ireland Hurling Championship Finals (Croke Park)

September 18
All-Ireland Camogie Final (Croke Park)

September 25
All-Ireland Football Championship Finals (Croke Park)

October

October 2
All-Ireland Women's Football Final (Croke Park)

October 21
International Rules: Australia v Ireland (provisional)

October 28
International Rules: Australia v Ireland (provisional)

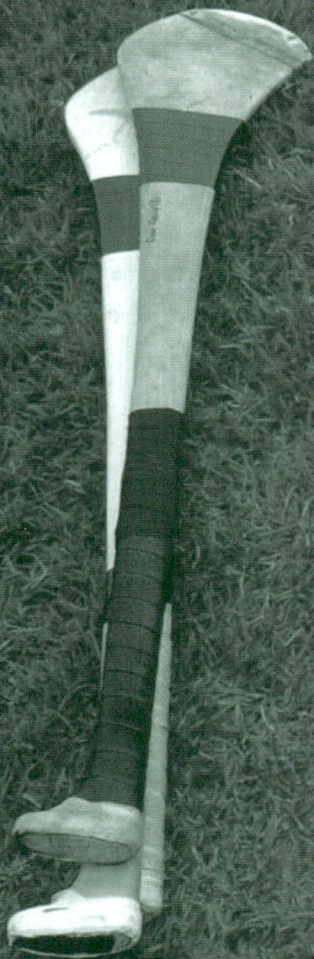

The GAA

2
The GAA

Structure of the GAA

The primary function of the GAA (Gaelic Athletic Association) is the promotion of the national games: Gaelic football, hurling, handball and rounders. The organizations that administer women's football and camogie are officially separate from the GAA, but the women's codes receive most of the benefits of GAA membership. Membership of the association can only be obtained through GAA clubs, and full membership is open to all over the age of 18. The association's structure has five primary layers, which have not changed fundamentally since they were devised over 100 years ago.

The Club
The club is the basic unit of the GAA. At least 15 playing members are needed before a club can be accepted into the organization. The members of the club elect a chairperson, secretary and other members annually to organize and control the assets and affairs of the club. There are over 2,500 GAA clubs.

Did you know? While many clubs are named after former local heroes, a GAA club cannot be named after a living person.

The County
The 32 county boards usually have a number of divisional or juvenile boards to organize competitions at district and youth levels. The boards are, of course, also responsible for the organization and facilitation of teams at inter-county level – at all age groups from Under-10 to Senior. Some boards have a particular interest in one of the codes, which usually leads to the neglect of the other (or even to its non-existence). An annual county convention is held before the end of each calendar year – with two delegates representing each adult club in the county – at which the chairperson, secretary and other officials are elected or re-elected for the following year. Being a member of a county board is a rather thankless job in the GAA, with fans only really getting interested when the board has to make difficult decisions.

Did you know? Missing three consecutive county board meetings automatically disqualifies a representative from attending meetings for the rest of the year, unless he or she can come up with a good excuse.

The Province
The four provincial councils organize the provincial championships for clubs and counties in both hurling and football, and

the inter-provincial teams in hurling and football; they also control many of the financial matters of the association within the province.

By secret ballot a chairperson and other officials are elected to serve on the provincial committee. All candidates for election as a provincial officer have to be nominated from county level. (A maximum of six representatives are allowed from each county at the provincial convention.) The provincial council consists of a chairperson, vice-chairperson, treasurer, PRO, secretary and two representatives from each county.

Did you know? At the start of each year, the provincial council has to give Central Council a fee of €1 for each club in its area.

National

The GAA is run by Central Council (Árd Comhairle), with the management committee controlling day-to-day affairs. The council runs the All-Ireland series of the club and county championships. Ever since Maurice Davin became the first president of the GAA in 1884, rule changes and amendments to GAA structures have been implemented at national level. Major changes to GAA affairs have to be ratified by these bodies.

The Central Council usually consists of the president, director-general, vice-presidents, two trustees, and a representative from each county in Ireland, as well as delegates from Britain, London, New York, handball, the players' committee and each of the first-, second- and third-level schools' committees.

Between the annual congresses, the Central Council is the supreme governing body of the Gaelic Athletic Association. Its decisions are binding and final.

Did you know? The Central Council vice-presidents are always the presidents of the provincial councils.

Annual Congress

The annual congress takes place before May each year, at a venue of the Central Council's choosing. It comprises the outgoing council, past presidents, and up to ten delegates from each county. Each county or provincial committee is allowed to submit one motion.

The main functions of the annual congress are to debate and (sometimes) vote on motions – various motions relating to Rule 42, which forbids the use of GAA stadiums for 'foreign' games, being the most talked-about in recent years – and to elect a president by secret ballot (a GAA president cannot hold office for more than three consecutive years).

Did you know? The GAA is committed to holding a Youth Congress, comprising delegates under 18 years of age, every second year.

Timeline

1884 The GAA is founded in Miss Hayes's Commercial Hotel in Thurles.

1885 Rules for hurling and football are agreed.

1886 County committees introduced, with Wexford being the first formed.

Artane Boys' Band gives its first GAA public performance.

1887 First All-Ireland Championship in hurling and football, involving club champions.

1888 First All-Ireland Championship finals (of 1887 competition) played.

Members of Royal Irish Constabulary banned from playing GAA sports.

1892 Teams reduced from 21 to 17 players a side.

1894 Over 10,000 attend All-Ireland football final replay.

1895 Cork fields a county side for inter-county competition (instead of using club champions).

1896 Goal reduced from five to three points.

1900 Provincial structure introduced.

1904 First public camogie game held in Navan, Co. Meath.

1905 Foundation of Cumann Camogaiochata, with Máire Ní Chinneide as President.

1912 Junior All-Ireland Championships introduced.

1913 GAA purchases Croke Park for £3,500.

Teams reduced to 15 players a side.

1918 Dublin Castle proscribes GAA as a dangerous organization.

1920 Twelve people killed in Croke Park by Black and Tans during Tipperary–Dublin football match.

1921 Liam McCarthy Cup established as the prize for the All-Ireland hurling champions; Limerick are the first winners.

1922 GAA relinquishes control of athletics to a new national athletics body.

1926 Galway v Kilkenny hurling game broadcast on radio.

National Leagues introduced.

Tipperary hurlers tour America.

1927 Sam Maguire dies of tuberculosis in west Cork at the age of 48.
Railway Cups introduced.
Birth of minor championships.

1928 Sam Maguire Cup established as prize for the All-Ireland football champions; Kildare are the first winners.

1931 GAA adopt the name Cumann Luthcleas Gael.

1932 First All-Ireland camogie championship.

1933 Ulster finally produces an All-Ireland champion, with Cavan claiming the football title.

1937 Cusack Stand opened at Croke Park.

1938 Mícheál O'Hehir commentates on his first GAA match.

1939 'Thunder & Lightning' hurling final between Cork and Kilkenny.

1947 In an attempt to boost the profile of the game abroad, the All-Ireland football final between Cavan and Kerry is played in the Polo Grounds, New York.

1954 84,856 attend Cork–Wexford All-Ireland hurling final at Croke Park.

1956 Cork's Christy Ring appears in his tenth All-Ireland senior hurling final.

1959 New cantilevered Hogan Stand opened at Croke Park.

1961 90,556 attend Down–Offaly All-Ireland football final at Croke Park.
Intermediate hurling competition introduced.

1962 RTE broadcasts GAA match live on television for first time.

1964 Under-21 competition introduced.
All-Ireland camogie club championship introduced.
Five countries compete in first world handball championships in New York.

1967 Tipperary's John Doyle equals Christy Ring's record, appearing in his tenth All-Ireland senior hurling final.

1970 World handball championship staged in Croke Park.

1971 First All-Star awards scheme.
Ban on playing 'foreign' games is lifted.
Tipperary beat Waterford in what is believed to be the first inter-county women's football match.

1973 Junior championships discontinued.

1974 Ladies Gaelic Football Association officially founded.
First All-Ireland B Championship.

1976 Páirc Uí Chaoimh in Cork is offcially opened.

1980 National League structure revamped, with promotion and relegation between divisions.

1983 Junior championships re-introduced.

Kilkenny's Noel Skehan wins record ninth All-Ireland hurling winner's medal.

1984 All-Ireland hurling final staged at Semple Stadium in GAA's centenary year.

1989 Nicky English of Tipperary claims highest-ever individual score in senior hurling final – 2-12 against Antrim.

1997 First phase of new Croke Park development completed (Cusack Stand side).

'Back door' system introduced in senior hurling championship.

2001 Qualifier format introduced in senior football championship.

2003 Last phase of Croke Park development begins (replacement of Hill 16 and Nally Stand).

2004 Westmeath win Leinster senior football crown, leaving only two teams – Fermanagh and Wicklow – still without a senior hurling or football championship title.

Camogie celebrates 100th anniversary, with 24,500 attending All-Ireland senior and junior camogie final.

2005 Three-tier senior hurling championship introduced.

The Pitch

GAA supporters have long maintained a tradition of dual measurement – yards and metres. Simultaneous calls can be heard at hurling and football matches for a '21' (yards) or a '20' (metres). Demanding a '50' or a '45' also means exactly the same thing (in sporting if not mathematical terms), and, similarly, you can claim either a '70' or a '65' and the referee will know what you mean.

Playing pitches are officially measured in metres, and, as the government is encouraging everyone to embrace the metric system, we've mapped the field of play using that method.

While 130 metres by 80 metres is the minimum allowed playing area of a GAA field, some under-age grades are allowed to use a smaller pitch.

A modern addition – the substitution zone – is an area at the side of the playing field, five metres either side of the centre-line: all players entering and exiting the field have to pass through this zone. (That's what is supposed to happen, anyway.)

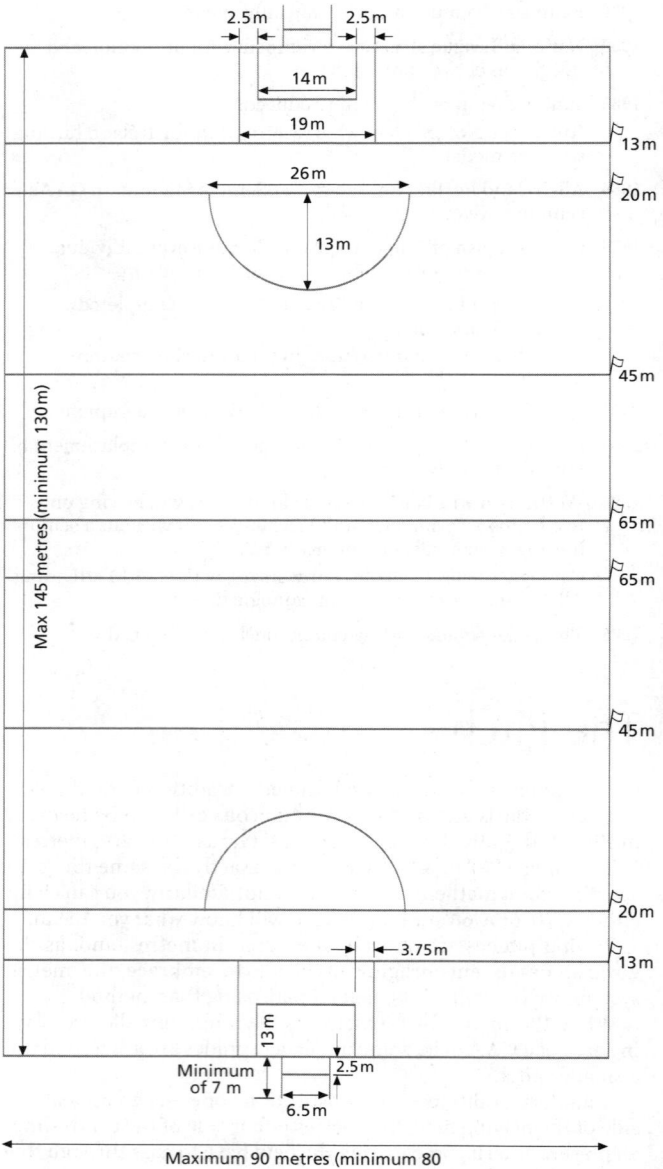

2.5m 2.5m

14m

19m

13m

26m

13m

20m

45m

Max 145 metres (minimum 130m)

65m

65m

45m

20m

3.75m

13m

13m

Minimum of 7 m

2.5m

6.5m

Maximum 90 metres (minimum 80

The Rules

It is quite common to witness even the most seasoned campaigners arguing over the rules of hurling and football. Here we list some of the most commonly misunderstood – and some of the most fundamental – rules of the games.

Basic rules that can cause confusion

- Boundary lines are part of the field of play.
- A team may start a match with 13 players, but must have 15 players (inclusive of any players sent off or taken off) by the start of the second half.
- A maximum of five substitutions is allowed in a game. However, in extra-time, a further three substitutions are allowed and both teams can start again with 15 players, even if a player was sent off in regular time (though the player who was sent off cannot come back on).
- All club and county matches – from under-16 to adult – are 60 minutes long, except inter-county senior championship and National League games, which are 70 minutes.
- If a ball hits a sideline flag it is out of play, even if it bounces back on to the playing field.
- A player who has caught the sliotar and placed it on his hurley may bring it back into his hand only once, and the sliotar may be carried in the hand for only four steps (or the time needed to take four steps).
- If a player taking a free fails to strike the sliotar, or fails to rise it off the ground, he must strike the ball on the ground immediately, otherwise an opposing player can approach. However, if a player taking a puck-out misses the sliotar, he can rise it off the ground and strike it (but not handle the sliotar again).
- If a player taking a sideline cut fails to strike the sliotar, he may make another attempt, but an opposing player may approach if he delays.
- A referee can order a player who is bleeding (or who has blood on him) off the field to receive medical attention. In these circumstances, a temporary substitution may be used.
- A player can score a goal by striking the sliotar or football in flight with the hand (as distinct from a hand-pass).
- It is a foul to jump up and down or wave the hands or a hurley while a player is taking a free (a player may hold the hurley upright, though).
- The football may be passed from one hand to the other, provided the original hand maintains contact with the ball until the change is completed.

- A goalkeeper may move along the goal-line before a penalty is struck.

Some unusual rules
- The referee can award a goal to the attacking team if the slio-tar or football was prevented from going over the line by a spectator or official.
- A player may not lift a sliotar or football off the ground using his knees.
- If the goalposts move during play, the referee may award (or deny) a score depending on which side of the posts he believes the ball would have passed had they been in their proper position.
- If a player refuses to leave the pitch after being sent off, the referee can give a three-minute warning, and then terminate the match if the offending player is still on the pitch after the time-limit elapses.
- One of the official duties of the referee is to present the ball to the captain of the winning team at the end of a provincial or All-Ireland final.
- You may not wear a hurling helmet in a football game.

All-Ireland Finals 1887–2004

For the first few years of the All-Ireland championships, counties were represented by their champion club rather than by a county side; names of the competing clubs are given in brackets below. Another early tradition was the 'away' final, in which the All-Ireland champion would play London – and win, usually. London managed a win in the 1901 away hurling final, and so we list that result to mark the one occasion when the All-Ireland champion did not win both finals.

Hurling

1887 Tipperary (Thurles) 1–1
      Galway (Meelick) 0–0
1888 Unfinished due to USA tour
1889 Dublin (Kickhams) 5–1
      Clare (Tulla) 1–6
1890 Wexford (Castlebridge) 2–2
      Cork (Aughabullogue) 1–6
      (Unfinished: Cork awarded title)
1891 Kerry (Ballyduff) 2–3
      Wexford (Crossabeg) 1–5

1892 Cork 2–4 Dublin 1–1
      (Unfinished: Cork awarded title)
1893 Cork 6–8 Kilkenny 0–2
1894 Cork 5–20 Dublin 2–0
1895 Tipperary 6–8 Kilkenny 1–0
1896 Tipperary 8–14 Dublin 0–4
1897 Limerick 3–4 Kilkenny 2–4
1898 Kilkenny 3–3 Clare 2–3
1899 Tipperary 3–12 Wexford 1–4
      (Unfinished: Tipperary awarded title)

1900	Tipperary 6–13 Galway 1–5
1901	Cork 2–8 Wexford 0–6
	(Away final: London 1–5
	Cork 0–4)
1902	Cork 1–7 Dublin 1–7
	Replay
	Cork 2–6 Dublin 0–1
1903	Cork 8–9 Kilkenny 0–8
1904	Kilkenny 1–9 Cork 1–8
1905	Cork 5–10 Kilkenny 3–13
	Refixture (due to objections)
	Kilkenny 7–7 Cork 2–9
1906	Tipperary 3–16 Dublin 3–8
1907	Kilkenny 3–12 Cork 4–8
1908	Tipperary 2–5 Dublin 1–8
	Replay
	Tipperary 3–15 Dublin 1–5
1909	Kilkenny 4–6 Tipperary 0–12
1910	Wexford 7–0 Limerick 6–2
1911	Kilkenny 3–3 Tipperary 1–1
1912	Kilkenny 2–1 Cork 1–3
1913	Kilkenny 2–4 Tipperary 1–2
1914	Clare 5–1 Laois 1–0
1915	Laois 6–2 Cork 4–1
1916	Tipperary 5–4 Kilkenny 3–2
1917	Dublin 5–4 Tipperary 4–2
1918	Limerick 9–5 Wexford 1–3
1919	Cork 6–4 Dublin 2–4
1920	Dublin 4–9 Cork 4–3
1921	Limerick 8–5 Dublin 3–2
1922	Kilkenny 4–2 Tipperary 2–6
1923	Galway 7–3 Limerick 4–5
1924	Dublin 5–3 Galway 2–6
1925	Tipperary 5–6 Galway 1–5
1926	Cork 4–6 Kilkenny 2–0
1927	Dublin 4–8 Cork 1–3
1928	Cork 6–12 Galway 1–0
1929	Cork 4–9 Galway 1–3
1930	Tipperary 2–7 Dublin 1–3
1931	Cork 1–6 Kilkenny 1–6
	Replay
	Cork 2–5 Kilkenny 2–5
	2nd replay
	Cork 5–8 Kilkenny 3–4
1932	Kilkenny 3–3 Clare 2–3
1933	Kilkenny 1–7 Limerick 0–6
1934	Limerick 2–7 Dublin 3–4
	Replay
	Limerick 5–2 Dublin 2–6
1935	Kilkenny 2–5 Limerick 2–4
1936	Limerick 5–6 Kilkenny 1–5
1937	Tipperary 3–11 Kilkenny 0–3

1938	Dublin 2–5 Waterford 1–6
1939	Kilkenny 2–7 Cork 3–3
1940	Limerick 3–7 Kilkenny 1–7
1941	Cork 5–11 Dublin 0–6
1942	Cork 2–14 Dublin 3–4
1943	Cork 5–16 Antrim 0–4
1944	Cork 2–13 Dublin 1–2
1945	Cork 7–5 Kilkenny 3–8
1946	Cork 7–5 Kilkenny 3–8
1947	Kilkenny 0–14 Cork 2–7
1948	Waterford 6–7 Dublin 4–2
1949	Tipperary 3–11 Laois 0–3
1950	Tipperary 1–9 Kilkenny 1–8
1951	Tipperary 2–14 Wexford 7–7
1952	Cork 2–14 Dublin 0–7
1953	Cork 3–3 Galway 0–8
1954	Cork 1–9 Wexford 1–6
1955	Wexford 3–13 Galway 2–8
1956	Wexford 2–14 Cork 2–8
1957	Kilkenny 4–10 Waterford 3–12
1958	Tipperary 4–9 Galway 2–5
1959	Waterford 1–17 Kilkenny 5–5
	Replay
	Waterford 3–12 Kilkenny 1–10
1960	Wexford 2–15 Tipperary 0–11
1961	Tipperary 0–16 Dublin 1–12
1962	Tipperary 3–10 Wexford 2–11
1963	Kilkenny 4–17 Waterford 6–8
1964	Tipperary 5–13 Kilkenny 2–8
1965	Tipperary 2–16 Wexford 0–10
1966	Cork 3–9 Kilkenny 1–10
1967	Kilkenny 3–8 Tipperary 2–7
1968	Wexford 5–8 Tipperary 3–12
1969	Kilkenny 2–15 Cork 2–9
1970	Cork 6–21 Wexford 5–10
1971	Tipperary 5–17 Kilkenny 5–14
1972	Kilkenny 3–24 Cork 5–11
1973	Limerick 1–21 Kilkenny 1–14
1974	Kilkenny 3–19 Limerick 1–13
1975	Kilkenny 2–22 Galway 2–10
1976	Cork 2–21 Wexford 4–11
1977	Cork 1–17 Wexford 3–8
1978	Cork 1–15 Kilkenny 2–8
1979	Kilkenny 2–12 Galway 1–8
1980	Galway 2–15 Limerick 3–9
1981	Offaly 2–12 Galway 0–15
1982	Kilkenny 3–18 Cork 1–13
1983	Kilkenny 2–14 Cork 2–12
1984	Cork 3–16 Offaly 1–12
1985	Offaly 2–11 Galway 1–12
1986	Cork 4–13 Galway 2–15
1987	Galway 1–12 Kilkenny 0–9

1988	Galway 1–15 Tipperary 0–14
1989	Tipperary 4–24 Antrim 3–9
1990	Cork 5–15 Galway 2–21
1991	Tipperary 1–16 Kilkenny 0–15
1992	Kilkenny 3–10 Cork 1–12
1993	Kilkenny 2–17 Galway 1–15
1994	Offaly 3–16 Limerick 2–13
1995	Clare 1–13 Offaly 2–8
1996	Wexford 1–13 Limerick 0–14
1997	Clare 0–20 Tipperary 2–13
1998	Offaly 2–16 Kilkenny 1–13
1999	Cork 0–13 Kilkenny 0–12
2000	Kilkenny 5–15 Offaly 1–14
2001	Tipperary 2–18 Galway 2–15
2002	Kilkenny 2–20 Clare 0–19
2003	Kilkenny 1–14 Cork 1–11
2004	Cork 0–17 Kilkenny 0–9

Football

1887	Limerick (Commercials) 1–4
	Louth (Young Irelands) 0–3
1888	Unfinished due to USA tour
1889	Tipperary (Bohercrowe) 3–6
	Laois (Portlaoise) 0–0
1890	Cork (Midleton) 2–4
	Wexford (Blues & Whites) 0–1
1891	Dublin (Young Irelands) 2–1
	Cork (Clondrohid) 1–9
1892	Dublin 1–4 Roscommon 1–0
1893	Wexford 1–1 Cork 0–1
1894	Dublin 1–1 Cork 0–6
	Replay
	Dublin 0–5 Cork 1–2
1895	Tipperary 0–4 Meath 0–3
1896	Limerick 1–5 Dublin 0–7
1897	Dublin 2–6 Cork 0–2
1898	Dublin 2–8 Waterford 0–4
1899	Dublin 1–10 Cork 0–6
1900	Tipperary 2–20 Galway 0–1
1901	Dublin 1–2 Cork 0–4
1902	Dublin 0–6 Tipperary 0–5
1903	Kerry 1–4 Kildare 1–3
	(Unfinished)
	Refixture
	Kerry 0–7 Kildare 1–4
	Replay
	Kerry 0–8 Kildare 0–2
1904	Kerry 0–5 Dublin 0–2
1905	Kildare 1–7 Kerry 0–5
1906	Dublin 0–5 Cork 0–4
1907	Dublin 0–6 Cork 0–2

1908	Dublin 0–10 Kerry 0–3
1909	Kerry 1–9 Louth 0–6
1910	Louth walkover from Kerry
	(Kerry refused to travel)
1911	Cork 6–6 Antrim 1–2
1912	Louth 1–7 Antrim 1–2
1913	Kerry 2–2 Wexford 0–3
1914	Kerry 1–3 Wexford 0–6
	Replay
	Kerry 2–3 Wexford 0–6
1915	Wexford 2–4 Kerry 2–1
1916	Wexford 3–4 Mayo 1–2
1917	Wexford 0–9 Clare 0–5
1918	Wexford 0–5 Tipperary 0–4
1919	Kildare 2–5 Galway 0–1
1920	Tipperary 1–6 Dublin 1–2
1921	Dublin 1–9 Mayo 0–2
1922	Dublin 0–6 Galway 0–4
1923	Dublin 1–5 Kerry 1–3
1924	Kerry 0–4 Dublin 0–3
1925	Galway 3–2 Cavan 1–2
1926	Kerry 1–3 Kildare 0–6
	Replay
	Kerry 1–4 Kildare 0–4
1927	Kildare 0–5 Kerry 0–3
1928	Kildare 2–6 Cavan 2–5
1929	Kerry 1–8 Kildare 1–5
1930	Kerry 3–11 Monaghan 0–2
1931	Kerry 1–11 Kildare 0–8
1932	Kerry 2–7 Mayo 2–4
1933	Cavan 2–5 Galway 1–4
1934	Galway 3–5 Dublin 1–9
1935	Cavan 3–6 Kildare 2–5
1936	Mayo 4–11 Laois 0–5
1937	Kerry 2–5 Mayo 1–8
	Replay
	Kerry 4–4 Cavan 1–7
1938	Galway 3–3 Kerry 2–6
	Replay
	Galway 2–4 Kerry 0–7
1939	Kerry 2–5 Meath 2–3
1940	Kerry 0–7 Galway 1–3
1941	Kerry 1–8 Galway 0–7
1942	Dublin 1–10 Galway 1–8
1943	Roscommon 1–6 Cavan 1–6
	Replay
	Roscommon 2–7 Cavan 2–2
1944	Roscommon 1–9 Kerry 2–4
1945	Cork 2–5 Cavan 0–7
1946	Kerry 2–4 Roscommon 1–7
	Replay
	Kerry 2–8 Roscommon 0–10

1947	Cavan 2–11 Kerry 2–7
1948	Cavan 4–5 Mayo 4–4
1949	Meath 1–10 Cavan 1–6
1950	Mayo 2–5 Louth 1–6
1951	Mayo 2–8 Meath 0–9
1952	Cavan 2–4 Meath 1–7
	Replay
	Cavan 0–9 Meath 0–5
1953	Kerry 0–13 Armagh 1–6
1954	Meath 1–13 Kerry 1–7
1955	Kerry 0–12 Dublin 1–6
1956	Galway 2–13 Cork 3–7
1957	Louth 1–9 Cork 1–7
1958	Dublin 2–12 Derry 1–9
1959	Kerry 3–7 Galway 1–4
1960	Down 2–10 Kerry 0–8
1961	Down 3–6 Offaly 2–8
1962	Kerry 1–12 Roscommon 1–6
1963	Dublin 1–9 Galway 0–10
1964	Galway 0–15 Kerry 0–10
1965	Galway 0–12 Kerry 0–9
1966	Galway 0–10 Meath 0–7
1967	Meath 1–9 Cork 0–9
1968	Down 2–12 Kerry 1–13
1969	Kerry 0–10 Offaly 0–7
1970	Kerry 2–19 Meath 0–18
1971	Offaly 1–14 Galway 2–8
1972	Offaly 1–13 Kerry 1–13
	Replay
	Offaly 1–19 Kerry 0–13
1973	Cork 3–17 Galway 2–13
1974	Dublin 0–14 Galway 1–6
1975	Kerry 2–12 Dublin 0–11
1976	Dublin 3–8 Kerry 0–10

1977	Dublin 5–12 Armagh 3–6
1978	Kerry 5–11 Dublin 0–9
1979	Kerry 3–13 Dublin 1–8
1980	Kerry 1–9 Roscommon 1–6
1981	Kerry 1–12 Offaly 0–8
1982	Offaly 1–14 Kerry 0–17
1983	Dublin 1–10 Galway 1–8
1984	Kerry 0–14 Dublin 1–6
1985	Kerry 2–12 Dublin 2–8
1986	Kerry 2–15 Tyrone 1–10
1987	Meath 1–14 Cork 0–11
1988	Meath 0–12 Cork 1–9
	Replay
	Meath 0–13 Cork 0–12
1989	Cork 0–17 Mayo 1–11
1990	Cork 0–11 Meath 0–9
1991	Down 1–16 Meath 1–14
1992	Donegal 0–18 Dublin 0–14
1993	Derry 1–14 Cork 2–8
1994	Down 1–12 Dublin 0–13
1995	Dublin 1–10 Tyrone 0–12
1996	Meath 0–12 Mayo 1–9
	Replay
	Meath 2–9 Mayo 1–11
1997	Kerry 0–13 Mayo 1–7
1998	Galway 1–14 Kildare 1–10
1999	Meath 1–11 Cork 1–8
2000	Kerry 0–14 Galway 0–14
	Replay
	Kerry 0–17 Galway 1–10
2001	Galway 0–17 Meath 0–8
2002	Armagh 1–12 Kerry 0–14
2003	Tyrone 0–12 Armagh 0–9
2004	Kerry 1–20 Mayo 2–9

Reigning Champions

All-Ireland

Football

Senior	Kerry	(Final: Kerry 1–20 Mayo 2–9)
Junior	Waterford	(Final: Waterford 2–12 Leitrim 2–9)
Under-21	Armagh	(Final: Armagh 2–8 Mayo 1–9)
Minor	Tyrone	(Final: Tyrone 0–12 Kerry 0–10)
Masters	Dublin	(Final: Dublin 2–8 Leitrim 1–10)
Tommy Murphy Cup	Clare	(Final: Clare 1–11 Sligo 0–11)

Hurling

Senior	Cork	(Final: Cork 0–17 Kilkenny 0–9)
Intermediate	Cork	(Final replay: Cork 1–16 Kilkenny 1–10)
Junior	Meath	(Final: Meath 1–10 Down 1–6)
Under-21	Kilkenny	(Final: Kilkenny 3–21 Tipperary 1–6)
Minor	Galway	(Final: Galway 0–16 Kilkenny 1–12)
Senior B	Kildare	(Final: Kildare 3–14 Mayo 3–7)
Minor B	Carlow	(Final: Carlow 3–9 Kildare 1–8)
Under-21 B	Laois	(Final: Laois 5–18 Donegal 0–8)

Leinster

Football

Senior	Westmeath	(Final replay: Westmeath 0–12 Laois 0–10)
Junior	Kildare	(Final: Kildare 0–9 Dublin 0–8)
Under-21	Kildare	(Final replay: Kildare 1–10 Dublin 0–12)
Minor	Laois	(Final: Laois 0–10 Kildare 0–6)

Hurling

Senior	Wexford	(Final: Wexford 2–12 Offaly 1–11)
Intermediate	Kilkenny	(Final: Kilkenny 3–17 Wexford 1–10)
Junior	Meath	(Final: Meath 4–14 Longford 2–7)
Under-21	Kilkenny	(Final: Kilkenny 1–16 Wexford 2–3)
Minor	Kilkenny	(Final: Kilkenny 1–15 Dublin 1–4)

Munster

Football

Senior	Kerry	(Final: Kerry 3–10 Limerick 2–9)
Junior	Waterford	(Final: Waterford 1–7 Cork 0–9)
Under-21	Cork	(Final: Cork 0–13 Kerry 0–12)
Minor	Kerry	(Final replay: Kerry 0–13 Cork 1–7)

Hurling

Senior	Waterford	(Final: Waterford 3–16 Cork 1–21)
Intermediate	Cork	(Final: Cork 1–18 Tipperary 1–9)
Under-21	Tipperary	(Final: Tipperary 1–16 Cork 1–13)
Minor	Cork	(Final: Cork 2–13 Tipperary 3–8)

Connacht

Football

Senior	Mayo	(Final: Mayo 2–13 Roscommon 0–9)
Junior	Leitrim	(Final: Leitrim 0–12 Roscommon 1–8)
Under-21	Mayo	(Final: Mayo 0–16 Roscommon 0–13)
Minor	Galway	(Final: Galway 3–10 Roscommon 2–10)

Hurling

Junior	Mayo	(Final: Mayo 1–10 Sligo 2–3)

Ulster

Football
Senior	Armagh	(Final: Armagh 3–15 Donegal 0–11)
Under-21	Armagh	(Final: Armagh 2–12 Derry 0–4)
Minor	Tyrone	(Final replay: Tyrone 0–15 Down 0–8)

Hurling
Senior	Antrim	(Final replay: Antrim 3–14 Down 0–18)
Junior	Down	(Final: Down 1–11 Fermanagh 1–9)
Under-21	Down	(Final: Down 5–8 Derry 4–7)
Minor	Antrim	(Final: Antrim 5–17 Down 3–7)

Websites

Official Gaelic Games websites

GAA	http://www.gaa.ie
Women's Football	http://www.ladiesgaelic.ie
Camogie	http://www.camogie.ie
Handball	http://www.handball.ie
Rounders	http://www.rounders.ie

Leinster
	http://leinster.gaa.ie
Carlow	http://carlow.gaa.ie
Dublin	http://www.hill16.ie
Kildare	http://kildare.gaa.ie
Kilkenny	http://kilkenny.gaa.ie
Laois	http://laois.gaa.ie
Longford	http://longford.gaa.ie
Louth	http://louthgaa.ie
Meath	http://meath.gaa.ie
Offaly	http://offaly.gaa.ie
Westmeath	http://westmeath.gaa.ie
Wexford	http://wexford.gaa.ie
Wicklow	http://wicklow.gaa.ie

Munster
	http://munster.gaa.ie
Clare	http://claregaa.ie
Cork	http://cork.gaa.ie
Kerry	http://kerry.gaa.ie
Limerick	http://limerick.gaa.ie
Tipperary	http://tipperary.gaa.ie
Waterford	http://waterford.gaa.ie

Connacht
	http://www.connachtgaa.ie
Galway	http://galwaygaa.ie
Leitrim	http://leitrimgaa.ie

Mayo	http://www.mayogaa.com
Roscommon	http://www.gaaroscommon.ie
Sligo	http://www.sligogaa.com
Ulster	http://ulster.gaa.ie
Antrim	http://www.antrimgaa.net
Armagh	http://www.armagh-gaa.com
Cavan	http://cavan.gaa.ie
Derry	http://derry.gaa.ie
Donegal	http://www.donegal-gaa.com
Down	http://www.downgaa.net
Fermanagh	http://fermanagh.gaa.ie
Monaghan	http://monaghan.gaa.ie
Tyrone	http://tyrone.gaa.ie

Alternative county websites

Dublin	http://www.dubsforum.tk
Dublin	http://www.reservoirdubs.com
Cork	http://www.rebelgaa.com
Tipperary	http://www.premierview.pro.ie
Tyrone	http://www.teamtalkmag.com
Roscommon	http://www.sheepstealers.com
Sligo	http://friendsofsligofootball.com
Armagh	http://www.orchardcounty.com

Other sites of interest

Sigerson Cup	http://www.sigersoncup.com
Gaelic Games journalists	http://www.ulstergaawriters.com
Views & humour	http://www.anfearrua.ie
Worldwide sports	http://www.setanta.com
News site	http://www.hoganstand.com
Club management system	http://www.gaelsport.com
News & views	http://www.gaelicgazette.com
Weeshie Fogarty (Radio Kerry)	http://www.terracetalkireland.com
Discussion board	http://www.gaaboard.com
For kids	http://www.cul4kidz.com
Azzurri	http://www.azzurri.ie
O'Neill's	http://www.oneills.ie
Online shop	http://www.pride.ie
Gaelic Gear	http://www.gaelicgear.com

Websites abroad

North America	http://www.nagaa.org
New York	http://www.ny-gaa.org
London	http://www.londongaa.org

Australasia	http://www.gaelicfootball.com.au
Europe	http://europe.gaa.ie
Asia	http://www.asiangaelicgames.com

How to Contact the GAA

Gaelic Athletic Association
Croke Park
Dublin 3
Tel: +353 (0)1 836 3222
Fax: +353 (0)1 855 8436
E-mail: queries@gaa.ie
Tickets: tickets@gaa.ie

Connacht Provincial Council
Clare Road
Ballyhaunis
Co. Mayo
Tel: +353 (0)94 963 0335
Fax: +353 (0)94 963 0175
E-mail:
connachtgaa@eircom.net

Leinster Provincial Council
Leinster GAA Office
Portlaoise
Co. Laois
Tel: +353 (0)502 20871
Tel: +353 (0)502 20958
Fax: +353 (0)502 20958
E-mail: leinster@gaa.ie

Munster Provincial Council
Dublin Road
Limerick
Tel: 061 493060

E-mail: munsterweb@gaa.ie
Ulster Provincial Council
St Tiernach's Park
Clones
Co. Monaghan
Tel: +353 (0)47 52380
Fax: +353 (0)47 52384
E-mail ulsterpro@ulstergaa.ie

Ladies Gaelic Football
Croke Park
Dublin 3
Tel: +353 (0)1 836 3156
Fax: +353 (0)1 836 3111
E-mail: info@ladiesgaelic.ie

Camogie
Croke Park
Dublin 3
Tel: +353 (0)1 836 4619
Fax: +353 (0)1 855 6063
E-mail: info@camogie.ie

Irish Handball
Croke Park
Dublin 3
Tel: +353 (0)1 836 4186
Fax: +353 (0)1 836 4454
E-mail: info@handball.ie

Gaelic Games Museums

GAA Museum, Croke Park

Officially opened in 1998 by the GAA President, Joe McDonagh, and the Taoiseach, Bertie Ahern, the GAA Museum – located at the Cusack Stand side of Croke Park – communicates the extraordinary history of the Gaelic Athletic Association, both on the field of play and off it.

Designed for both supporters of Gaelic Games and visitors to Ireland who may have no previous experience of the sport, the museum uses interactive exhibits, databanks, guides, videos, photographs and art to honour the players and officials who have made exceptional contributions to the national games.

The video archive includes footage of the 1939 'Thunder and Lightning' senior hurling final, contested by Cork and Kilkenny in appalling weather conditions, and the 1982 football final, when Offaly stopped Kerry's bid for five All-Ireland championships in a row.

And with Croke Park now one of the most modern sporting arenas in the world, the stadium tours – which commence from the reception area of the museum – are proving particularly popular. The guided tour lasts approximately one hour and takes you to the corporate levels, the media centre, the pitch and the dressing rooms.

The museum is open seven days a week. On match days the museum opens at the same time as the stiles.

GAA Museum
Croke Park
St Joseph's Avenue
Dublin 3

Tel: +353 (0)1 819 2323
Fax: +353 (0)1 819 2324
E-mail: gaamuseum@crokepark.ie
Website: http://www.gaa.ie/museum

Lar na Páirce, Thurles

Lar na Páirce is Tipperary's answer to the main GAA museum, though it was actually opened before the Dublin centre, in 1994. It is located in a 19th-century building on Slievenamon Road in Thurles – only yards from Liberty Square and Hayes' Hotel, where the GAA was founded in 1884. Its collection includes football boots, hurleys, footballs, sliotars, newspaper cuttings, trophies, photographs, and jerseys – many signed by legendary footballers and hurlers. Much of the memorabilia on display was donated by Sam Melbourne, a local GAA enthusiast.

Lar na Páirce
Slievenamon Road
Thurles
Co. Tipperary

Tel: +353 (0) 504 23579

3
Hurling
Championship
2005

Hurling
Championship
2005

Championship Structure

In a brave move, the GAA annual congress last year decided to overhaul the inter-county hurling championship, adopting proposals put forward by the Hurling Development Committee. The result is a format radically different from previous championship structures – and much more complicated (see below). The reasons for the changes were obvious to most hurling supporters, players and officials: too many counties were playing too few championship games, and there was an excess of one-sided ties. The HDC eventually came up with a three-tier championship, involving round-robin play followed by a knock-out tournament, which will be employed from this year until 2007. It's probably not the ideal method for running the hurling championship, and certainly won't satisfy the traditionalists, but, at the very least, the new format looks likely to be another step in the right direction.

Tier One – which will produce the All-Ireland champion – comprises the teams that competed in last year's National Hurling League Division One. Offaly can be especially thankful it wasn't the members of this season's NHL Division One that were chosen for the inaugural Tier One competition, since they were relegated from Division One at the end of the 2004 NHL season.

Ulster counties have the most credible reason for feeling aggrieved by this year's set-up, with only Antrim gaining admission to Tier One. Provision will be made if a team other than Antrim wins the season's Ulster title (see Season Diary, July 9). This potential problem does not arise in Connacht, where there is no provincial competition; Galway is the province's lone representative in Tier One.

Another potential cause for criticism is that with two sides qualifying for the All-Ireland quarter-final stage from each four-team group, the new system opens up the possibility of meaningless final-group ties at the Qualifier stage – between teams that have no chance of coming first or second, and that may not have much reason to care whether they enter the relegation play-off as a third-placed or fourth-placed team.

The new system alters the nature of the two most important provincial championships – Leinster and Munster – and further weakens the link between provincial competitions and the All-Ireland championship. The Leinster and Munster provincial championships will be contested by just five counties each: the five that will be competing in Tier One of the All-Ireland championship.

It's not necessarily a bad idea. What did Carlow gain from being beaten by 23 points by Laois in the opening round of last season's Leinster championship? One suspects the experience didn't do much for Laois hurling either. Players from counties such as Kerry, Wicklow and Carlow have been battling against all the odds in their respective provincial competitions for years, with little to show for it. This season, along with the seven other teams that took part in last season's National Hurling League Division Two, those counties will skip the provincial championships and compete in Tier Two of the hurling championship.

The provincial champions in Leinster and Munster will no longer gain automatic entry to the All-Ireland semi-finals; instead, they will enter the All-Ireland tournament at the quarter-final stage. Teams such as Waterford – who have found the long wait between the provincial final and the All-Ireland semi-final detrimental to their title ambitions – will welcome this change.

The 11 counties not entered into Tier One or Two qualify for entry to Tier Three. The winners of Tiers Two and Three will be promoted for next year's championship, while the bottom teams in Tiers One and Two will be relegated. This will mean that more teams than in past years will have something to play for.

The nebulous concept of 'weaker' counties lives on – even in Tier One – as a criterion for who gets to play two out of three qualifying group games at home. The GAA has not established seedings within the tiers, and will presumably decide which counties are 'weaker' after the draw is made. 'Weak', like 'third world', may soon have to be replaced by 'developing'; no GAA supporter wants the term associated with their own county, except, perhaps, on the eve of the Qualifier draws.

Tier One

Antrim, Clare, Cork, Dublin, Galway, Kilkenny, Laois, Limerick, Offaly, Tipperary, Waterford, Wexford

Provincial Championships

These are organized on a knock-out basis in Munster, Ulster and Leinster. There is no provincial championship in Connacht; Galway, as a member of Tier One, is the sole county from that province that will compete for the All-Ireland title. While the Munster and Leinster championships will include only Tier One members, the Ulster championship will include Antrim from Tier One, Derry and Down from Tier Two, London from Tier Three, and New York.

All-Ireland Qualifiers

Eight counties take part in the All-Ireland Qualifiers: the first-round losers in the Munster and Leinster championships (two teams), losing semi-finalists in Leinster and Munster championships (four teams), Galway and Antrim. ('Provision will be made' if a team other than Antrim wins this season's Ulster final.) Play is organized as follows:

- The eight teams are organized into two groups of four teams.
- The groups are selected by open draw, apart from the provision that there can be a maximum of two teams from any province in each group.
- Each county plays the other three teams in the same group once.
- A county designated as 'weak' (by the National Games Administration Committee) may have two home games in the group stage, provided the home venue reaches required standard (decided by the National Games Administration Committee and the National Safety Council).
- A team's finishing position in the group will be based first on points total (two points for a win, one for a draw), then scoring difference, then highest score, then result of the game(s) between counties that are level by all other measures.

All-Ireland Quarter-finals

The pairings (a draw will be required) for the All-Ireland quarter-finals are:

- Leinster champions plays runner-up in one Qualifier group.
- Munster champions plays runner-up in other Qualifier group.
- Leinster runner-up plays winner of one Qualifier group.
- Munster runner-up plays winner of other Qualifier group.

All-Ireland Semi-finals

Leinster and Munster champions (or the teams that defeated them in the quarter-final) will not be drawn against each other.

Relegation and Promotion

The third- and fourth-placed teams in Group One and Group Two of the Qualifiers will play in a relegation play-off as follows:

- Third-placed team in Group One plays fourth-placed team in Group Two.
- Third-placed team in Group Two plays fourth-placed team in Group One.
- The two losing teams play in a relegation final.
- Losing team in relegation final will be relegated to Tier Two for 2006 season.

Tier Two

Carlow, Derry, Down, Kerry, Kildare, Mayo, Meath, Roscommon, Westmeath, Wicklow

Group Stage
Ten counties eligible to participate. They are organized into two groups of five teams. Each county plays the other four teams in its group once. A team's finishing position in the group will be based first on points total (two points for a win, one for a draw), then scoring difference, then highest score, then result of the game(s) between counties that are level by all other measures.

Semi-finals
The winner of Group One plays the runner-up of Group Two and the winner of Group Two plays the runner-up of Group One.

Final
The winning team will be promoted to Tier One for the 2006 season.

Relegation and Promotion
The fourth- and fifth-placed teams in Group One and Group Two will play in a relegation play-off as follows:

- Fourth-placed team in Group One plays fifth-placed team in Group Two.
- Fourth-placed team in Group Two plays fifth-placed team in Group One.
- The two losing teams play a relegation final.
- The losing team in the relegation final will be relegated to Tier Three for the 2006 season.

Tier Three

Eleven teams are eligible to participate. They are organized into three groups (two of four teams and one of three). Each team plays the other teams in the same group once. There is a play-off between the second-placed teams in the two four-team groups. The three first-placed teams in each group plus the winner of the play-off qualify for the semi-finals. The Tier Three champion will be promoted to Tier Two for the 2006 season.

Provincial Championship Fixtures 2005

Leinster Senior Hurling Championship

Round	Date	Teams	Venue
First Reound	May 22	Laois v Dublin	Nowlan Park
Semi-finals	June 12	1st-round winner v Wexford	Croke Park
	June 12	Offaly v Kilkenny	Croke Park
Final	July 3		Croke Park

Munster Senior Hurling Championship

Round	Date	Teams	Venue
Quarter-final	May 15	Limerick v Tipperary	Semple Stadium
Semi-finals	May 22	Cork v Waterford	Semple Stadium
	June 5	QF winner v Clare	Semple Stadium or Gaelic Grounds
Final	June 26		To be confirmed

Ulster Senior Hurling Championship

Round	Date	Teams	Venue
Quarter-final	May 15	Down v London	Down venue
Semi-finals	May 22	New York v Antrim	Gaelic Park, New York
	May 22	QF winner v Derry	Derry venue
Final	June 5		Casement Park

Connacht Senior Hurling Championship

No provincial championship; Galway go straight into All-Ireland qualifying group.

Carlow squad 2004

	v **Laois** Lost 0–8,4–19
Frank Foley	●
William Hickey	●
Adrian Corcoran	●
Michael Kehoe	●
Kenneth Nolan	●
Edward Coady	●
Andrew Gaul	●
Shane Kavanagh	●
Pat Coady	●
Paul Kehoe	●
Des Murphy	●
Ronan Minchin	●
Brian Murphy	●
Karl English	●
Seamus Smithers	●
Sean Michael Murphy	●
Des Shaw	●
Paddy Coady	●
Tommy O'Shea	●
Stephen Sheil	●
Pat Fenlon	
Brian Nolan	

● Played from start   ● Substituted on

Leinster

Carlow Ceatharlach

Colours: Green, red and yellow
Stadium: Dr Cullen Park, Carlow
Capacity: 19,000
GAA clubs: 32

Leinster SHC: 0
All-Ireland SHC: 0
National Hurling League: 0
2005 Championship section: Tier Two
Last five years:

2000: Lost to Dublin and Laois, but narrowly beat Westmeath, in round-robin section of Leinster championship.

2001: Beat Westmeath and Wicklow (after a replay) but bowed out against Laois.

2002: Battled in vain against Meath in preliminary competition.

2003: Gained revenge over Meath, but subsequently lost second-round game against Laois and Qualifier tie with Kerry.

2004: Made an early exit from the Leinster championship, losing heavily to Laois.

Top player: Pat Coady A committed warrior to the cause of Carlow hurling, the St Mullin's player has backed up his determination on many occasions with skillful play and impressive accuracy, especially from dead balls.

Penguin Ireland Guide ranking (Tier Two): **9**

Some progress has been made at under-age level in the county, culminating in last year's minor B success, but with hurling giants Kilkenny on one side and Wexford on the other, it's no wonder the county's senior players have struggled to rise to championship challenges. The county barely stayed in last season's championship for the full 70 minutes, with a bored-looking Laois team registering a 23-point victory. They won't come up against quite as high-ranking a hurling side during this season's competition, but should they capitulate in the same way, they will be punished just as ruthlessly – and find themselves former members of Tier Two.

Outlook
Not the weakest side in Tier Two, which is a major consideration when you consider one of the 10 occupants will be frequenting Tier Three next year. Carlow beat Mayo in last year's National League, and may have to do it again to secure their position in the middle tier.

Dublin squad 2004

	v Westmeath Won 2-14 0-11	v Offaly Lost 1-13 2-25	v Kilkenny Lost 0-8 4-22
Gary Maguire	●	●	●
Daragh Spain	●	●	
Simon Daly	●	●	●
Aodian de Paor	●	●	●
Stephen Hiney	●	●	●
Ronan Fallon	●	●	●
Kevin Ryan	●	●	●
Carl Meehan	●	○	●
Conal Keaney	●		
David Curtin	●		
Liam Ryan	●	●	
Michael Carton	●	○	●
David O'Callaghan	●	●	●
Kevin Flynn	●	●	
David Donnelly	●		
Padraig Fleury	○	●	●
John McGuirk	○	●	
Sean O'Shea	○	●	●
Sean McCann	○		●
Brendan McLoughlin			
Manas Breathnach			○
Cormac O'Brien			○
Aiden Glennon			
Risteard Brennan			○
David Kirwan		○	○
Stuart Mullen			
Gerard O'Meara			○
Gearoid Keogh			●
Stephen Perkins		●	●
Dave Sweeney		●	
Philip Brennan		○	●
Derek O'Reilly		○	

● Played from start ○ Substituted on

Dublin Áth Cliath

Colours: Dark blue and light blue
Stadium: Parnell Park, Dublin
Capacity: 11,000
Stadium: Croke Park, Dublin
Capacity: 82,300
GAA clubs: 211

Leinster SHC: 23
    1889, 1892, 1894, 1896, 1902, 1906, 1908, 1917, 1919, 1920, 1921,
    1924, 1927, 1928, 1930, 1934, 1938, 1941, 1942, 1944, 1948, 1952, 1961
All-Ireland SHC: 6
    1889, 1917, 1920, 1924, 1927, 1938
National Hurling League: 2
    1929, 1939
2005 Championship section: Tier One
Last five years:
    2000: Defeated Carlow and Westmeath, then needed two games to overcome
    the challenge of Laois and qualify for the Leinster semi-final, where they came
    up against the might of Kilkenny.
    2001: Made an early provincial exit, narrowly losing a quarter-final clash with
    Laois.
    2002: Defeated Westmeath and Meath before losing their Leinster semi-final
    tie with Wexford. Lost heavily to Clare in qualifying round.
    2003: Defeated Westmeath in first preliminary round tie, but again needed
    two hours to defeat rivals Laois. Lost to Kilkenny in provincial semi-final and to
    Offaly in Qualifier.
    2004: Again topped Westmeath in their provincial clash, but a semi-final loss
    to Offaly was followed by an unfortunate pairing with Kilkenny, who were still
    smarting from defeat to Wexford.
Top player: Conal Keaney It's surely worth the fight to keep the dual star
playing hurling. The county missed him badly for much of last season.

Penguin Ireland Guide ranking (Tier One): **11**

Probably no one should be more grateful than Dublin for the new
championship structure, which guarantees the county several
clashes against quality opposition. Overcoming a few counties
rather easily only to wilt year after year against the first strong
hurling side they encountered was never going to be a path to
improvement. The additions of Tipperary hurling legend John
Leahy and trainer Jim Kilty can only have helped strengthen the
side for this season's campaign. Though not quite a sleeping
giant, Dublin has the ability to make huge strides in the coming
years.

Outlook
An opening tie against familiar rivals Laois in Leinster will
provide an accurate measurement of the side's immediate

prospects. Whether they enter the Qualifiers at that stage, or after the Leinster semi-final meeting with Wexford, could make all the difference, in terms of both confidence and expectation. Either way, they are second-favourites, after Laois, to be relegated from Tier One.

Kildare Cill Dara

Colour: White
Stadium: St Conleth's Park, Newbridge
Capacity: 13,000
GAA clubs: 70

Leinster SHC: 0
All-Ireland SHC: 0
National Hurling League: 0
2005 Championship section: Tier Two
Last five years:
> **2000:** Did not field a championship side.
> **2001:** Beaten by Meath by a single point in opening round of provincial championship.
> **2002:** Defeated by Westmeath in preliminary round of Leinster competition.
> **2003:** Again defeated by Westmeath, this time by a wide margin, in the opening preliminary game.
> **2004:** Unlucky to be drawn again versus Westmeath, who were made to work a little harder for victory this time.

Top player: Joe Dempsey A stalwart for the county, though his goal and point against Westmeath last season didn't make a difference to the unfavourable result.

Penguin Ireland Guide ranking (Tier Two): **8**

Hurling teams from Kildare have always found it extremely difficult to adjust to the pace of clashes with stronger hurling counties, but there is much evidence to suggest the county is on an upward curve – not least the fact the county's minor side reached last season's All-Ireland B final, while the seniors lifted the All-Ireland B trophy. They may be baby steps, but at least they're in the right direction. Tier Two hurling provides another challenge to maintain that progress – no one in the county wants that momentum to be broken by relegation to Tier Three.

Outlook
This campaign is going to be a dog-fight for Kildare's senior hurlers. While unsuccessful championship campaigns are nothing new, there's a trap-door waiting for this summer's worst Tier Two team. Kildare don't want to be standing on it at the end of the summer.

Kildare squad 2004

	v **Westmeath** Lost 1–6 to 1–18
Cormac Leahy	●
Stephen Crowe	●
Darragh Laharte	●
Brendan Maher	●
Ciarán Divilly	●
David Harney	●
Richie Hoban	●
Colm Buggy	●
John Brennan	●
Joe Dempsey	●
Eamonn Denieffe	●
Shane Joyce	●
Adrian McAndrew	●
Andy Quinn	●
Tom Carew	●
Billy White	◉
Paudie Reidy	◉
Alan Flaherty	◉
Conal Boran	◉
Alan Dunney	
Peter Beirne	
Paul Keegan	
Lorcan Shinnors	
Stewart Gleeson	
Tony Murphy	

● Played from start   ◉ Substituted on

Kilkenny squad 2004

	v Wexford Lost 1-16 2-15	v Dublin Won 4-22 0-8	v Galway Won 4-20 1-10	v Clare Drew 1-13 1-13	v Clare Won 1-11 0-9	v Waterford Won 3-12 0-18	v Cork Lost 0-17 0-9
James McGarry	●	●	●	●	●	●	●
Michael Kavanagh	●				●	●	●
Noel Hickey	●	●	●	●	●	●	●
JJ Delaney	●	●	●	●	●	●	●
Sean Dowling	●						○
Peter Barry	●	●	●	●	●	●	●
Brian Hogan	●						
Derek Lyng	●	●	●	●	●	●	●
Pat Tennyson	●			●			
John Hoyne	●		○	○	●	●	●
Henry Shefflin	●	●	●	●	●	●	●
Tommy Walsh	●	●	●	●	●	●	●
Eddie Brennan	●	●	●	●	●	●	●
Martin Comerford	●	●	●	●	●	●	●
Jimmy Coogan	●	●	●	●			
DJ Carey	○	●	●	●	●	●	●
Aiden Fogarty	○	●					
Mark Phelan		●					
Richie Mullally		●	●	●			
Ken Coogan		●	●	●	●	●	○
James Fitzpatrick		○			●	●	●
John Maher		○			○		
James Ryall		○	●	●	●	●	●
Sean Dowling		○		○	○		
Conor Phelan		○	●				○
Paddy Mullally				○			
PJ Ryan							
Eddie Mackey							
Walter Burke							
Jackie Tyrell							
Brian Phelan							
Jamie Power							

● Played from start   ○ Substituted on

Kilkenny Cill Chainnigh

Colours: Black and amber
Stadium: Nowlan Park, Kilkenny
Capacity: 26,300
GAA clubs: 41

Leinster SHC: 61
1888, 1893, 1895, 1897, 1898, 1900, 1903, 1904, 1905, 1907, 1909, 1911, 1912, 1913, 1916, 1922, 1923, 1925, 1926, 1931, 1932, 1933, 1935, 1936, 1937, 1939, 1940, 1943, 1945, 1946, 1947, 1950, 1953, 1957, 1958, 1959, 1963, 1964, 1966, 1967, 1969, 1971, 1972, 1973, 1974, 1975, 1978, 1979, 1982, 1983, 1986, 1987, 1991, 1992, 1993, 1998, 1999, 2000, 2001, 2002, 2003

All-Ireland SHC: 28
1904, 1905, 1907, 1909, 1911, 1912, 1913, 1922, 1932, 1933, 1935, 1939, 1947, 1957, 1963, 1967, 1969, 1972, 1974, 1975, 1979, 1982, 1983, 1992, 1993, 2000, 2002, 2003

National Hurling League: 11
1933, 1962, 1966, 1976, 1982, 1983, 1986, 1990, 1995, 2002, 2003

2005 Championship section: Tier One

Last five years:

2000: Defeated Dublin and Offaly to retain provincial crown. Overcame Galway in All-Ireland semi-final, then beat Offaly again in the final.

2001: Beat Offaly and Wexford to retain Leinster title, but fell to Galway in All-Ireland semi-final.

2002: Again overcame Offaly and Wexford to remain divisional kingpins, and underlined their dominance by reclaiming the Liam McCarthy Cup, defeating Tipperary and Clare along the way.

2003: Defeated Dublin and Wexford en route to the Leinster title, and Tipperary and Cork en route to another All-Ireland.

2004: Shocked by Wexford in opening championship tie, then recovered to defeat Dublin, Galway, Clare (after a replay) and Waterford to reach All-Ireland final. Surrendered crown to Cork.

Top player: Henry Shefflin Stands head and shoulders above the rest of the team, no mean feat when you consider his team-mates are giants of hurling. His value rises each season.

Penguin Ireland Guide ranking (Tier One): **2**

The witnesses to Kilkenny's effortless slaying of Galway in their third-round Qualifier tie last season could not have left Semple Stadium in any doubt as to who the 2004 All-Ireland champions would be. It remains something of a mystery why Kilkenny did not live up to these expectations. Kilkenny enter this season's championship feeling they have something to prove, and the Cats are at their most dangerous when they're wounded.

Outlook

It would be an even greater surprise than last season should Kilkenny again fail in Leinster. But your prognosticator sees another All-Ireland final defeat on the cards for Kilkenny in 2005: this time at the hands of Waterford.

Laois Laoighis

Colours: Blue and white
Stadium: O'Moore Park, Portlaoise
Capacity: 27,000
GAA clubs: 85

Leinster SHC: 3
  1914, 1915, 1949
All-Ireland SHC: 1
  1915
National Hurling League: 0
2005 Championship section: Tier One
Last five years:
  2000: Defeated Westmeath and Carlow in early stages of Leinster championship, but eventually bowed out after a replay with Dublin.
  2001: Victories over Meath and Dublin brought them to the provincial semi-final, where a much stronger Wexford team were waiting.
  2002: Lost to Meath after Leinster preliminary-round victory over Wicklow.
  2003: Again opened Leinster campaign with victory over Wicklow, then beat Carlow. Another two-leg loss to Dublin was followed by a lesson in hurling from Tipperary in Qualifiers.
  2004: Defeated Carlow and Meath before exiting Leinster competition at the hands of Offaly. A Qualifier victory over Westmeath was followed by a big loss to Clare.
Top player: **James Young** A dead-ball specialist, he kept the scoreboard workers busy last season with his consistent accuracy.

Penguin Ireland Guide ranking (Tier One): **12**

Laois played the same number of championship games last season as Cork. The quality of the opposition, however, was not comparable, and this season – though they will probably end up playing five games again – they will not come up against the likes of Carlow, Meath or Westmeath. Whether it's a blessing or a curse remains to be seen. Some believe that Tier One contains one or two teams too many, and it'll be up to the Laois players to disprove that theory. There are certainly quality hurlers in the county, just not enough of them.

Outlook
The Dublin match, in the opening round of the provincial championship, will decide much. Victory would result in a substantial boost and a date with Wexford. Defeat could signal the start of an unhappy Qualifier campaign. The spectre of relegation will be at the back of Laois supporters' and players' minds throughout this season.

Laois squad 2004	v Carlow Won 4–19 0–8	v Meath Won 1–13 0–8	v Offaly Lost 1–15 2–23	v Westmeath Won 3–13 4–5	v Clare Lost 2–15 7–19
Kevin Galvin	●	●	●	●	●
Cyril Cuddy	●	●	●	●	●
Patrick Cuddy	●	●		●	●
Michael McEvoy	●	●	●	●	●
Joe Fitzpatrick	●	●	●	●	●
Paul Cuddy	●	●	●		
Rory Conroy	●	●	●	●	
Darren Rooney	●	●	●		●
James Walsh	●	●	●	●	●
Canice Coonan	●		●	●	●
Enda Meagher	●	●	●		
Tommy Fitzgerald	●	●	●	●	●
Liam Tynan	●	●	●	●	●
Damien Culleton	●	●	●	●	●
Fran Keenan	●		●		
Eoin Browne	●	●		●	●
Cathal Brophy	●	●	●		●
Eamonn Jackman	●			●	
Alan Delaney	●			●	
Damien Walsh	●			●	●
Robert Jones		●	●	●	●
James Young		●	●	●	●
Jimmy Dunne		●	●		●
Pat Mahon		●		●	●
David Cuddy			●	●	●
Lar Mahon				●	●
Brian Campion					
Seamus Dwyer					
John Rowney					
John Joe McHugh					
Seamus Dwyer					
Patrick Mullaney					

● Played from start   ● Substituted on

Meath An Mhí

Colours: Green and gold
Stadium: Pairc Tailteann, Navan
Capacity: 29,000
GAA clubs: 153

Leinster SHC: 0
All-Ireland SHC: 0
National Hurling League: 0
2005 Championship section: Tier Two
Last five years:

2000: Did not field a championship side.

2001: Beating Kildare was the highlight of a provincial campaign that included a heavy defeat to Laois.

2002: A longer than usual championship campaign included a victory over Carlow and a shock win against Laois. Dublin then knocked them out of Leinster, and Offaly beat them in the Qualifier series.

2003: Narrowly lost provincial championship tie with Carlow.

2004: Defeated by Laois in opening round of Leinster championship.

Top player: Michael Cole A late goal three seasons ago by the forward sealed a famous win over Laois, and coming off the bench against the same opposition last season he delivered three points in an ultimately fruitless effort.

Penguin Ireland Guide ranking (Tier Two): **6**

Meath supporters, players and officials have been looking forward to this season since well before last season's fruitless campaign ended. They are the reigning junior hurling champions, but transforming that into success on the senior hurling stage won't be a simple task.

Outlook
Staying in Tier Two may be more difficult than it might at first appear to the Meath hurling faithful. None of the teams are unbeatable, but none can be taken for granted either. Still, they should be able to keep their heads above water.

Meath squad 2004

	v **Laois** Lost 0–8 1–13
Mark Brennan	●
Sean White	●
Pat Roche	●
Sean Moran	●
Diarmuid Brennan	●
Thomas Reilly	●
Sean Reilly	●
Jim Canty	●
David Donnelly	●
Evan Lynan	●
Stephen Clynch	●
Michael Burke	●
Neville Reilly	●
Mark Gannon	●
Anthony Fox	●
Michael Cole	○
Ger O'Neill	○
Padraig Donoghue	○
Joey Keena	○
Stephen Moran	
Anton O'Neill	
Sean Corrigan	
Paul Fagan	
Seamus Wallace	
Padraig Coone	
Brian Perry	
Padraig Muldoon	
Martin Horan	
Cathal Sheridan	

● Played from start   ○ Substituted on

Offaly squad 2004	v Laois Won 2–23 1–15	v Dublin Won 2–25 1–13	v Wexford Lost 1–11 2–12	v Clare Lost 2–10 3–16
Brian Mullins	●	●	●	●
Mick O'Hara	●			
Ger Oakley	●	●	●	●
David Franks	●	●	●	●
Kevin Brady	●	●		●
Niall Claffey	●	●	●	●
Colm Cassidy	●	●	●	●
Michael Cordial	●	●	●	●
Barry Whelahan	●	●	●	●
Neville Coughlan	●	●	●	●
Gary Hanniffy	●	●	●	●
Brendan Murphy	●	●	●	●
Brian Carroll	●	●	●	
Joe Brady	●	●	●	●
Damian Murray	●	●	●	●
Simon Whelahan	●	●		
Dylan Hayden	●		●	●
Barry Teehan		●	●	●
Brian Whelahan		●	●	
Rory Hanniffy		●	●	●
Shane O'Connor				
Nigel Mannion				●
Paddy Whelan				
Richie McRedmond				●
Brian Buckley				
Eoghan Franks				
Jamie Flynn				
Stephen Brown			●	●

● Played from start ● Substituted on

Offaly Uíbh Fhailí

Colours: Green, white and gold
Stadium: St Brendan's Park, Birr
Capacity: 11,000
Stadium: O'Connor Park, Tullamore
Capacity: 16,000
GAA clubs: 85

Leinster SHC: 9
  1980, 1981, 1984, 1985, 1988, 1989, 1990, 1994, 1995
All-Ireland SHC: 4
  1981, 1985, 1994, 1998
National Hurling League: 1
  1991
2005 Championship section: Tier One
Last five years:
  2000: Defeated Wexford in provincial semi-final, but collapsed under the weight of Kilkenny in decider. A Qualifier comeback witnessed wins over Derry and Cork, but Kilkenny were waiting again, this time in the All-Ireland final.
  2001: Lost heavily to Kilkenny in Leinster semi-final.
  2002: Fell to Kilkenny again at provincial semi-final stage. Had a better result against Meath in Qualifier series, but not against Tipperary in next round.
  2003: Lost to Wexford at penultimate stage of Leinster competition. Defeated Dublin and Limerick in Qualifier series before again falling to Tipperary.
  2004: Beat Laois and Dublin, but came up short in provincial decider against Wexford. Subsequently lost to Clare in round-three Qualifier.
Top player: Brian Carroll Has been putting in increasingly valuable performances for his county over the past couple of years. A regular scorer, he was missed against Clare last season.

Penguin Ireland Guide ranking (Tier One): **9**

How does Offaly keep unearthing such impressive talent? Apart from Birr, which seems to be the end of the rainbow as far as hurling ingenuity goes, last season's county final win by Coolderry – after a hard-fought battle with favourites Birr – showed that the future for Offaly continues to be bright, even if some of the county's stars are coming to the end of their careers. Although Offaly always seems to get better as the season progresses, this season much may depend on early form.

Outlook
The opening Leinster tie against Kilkenny is one no team would choose. Even a defeat, however, would leave at least three more championship games, more than enough to keep the county occupied for a while. They won't be quite good enough to advance to the All-Ireland knock-out stage.

Westmeath An Iarmhí

Colours: Maroon and white
Stadium: Cusack Park, Mullingar
Capacity: 15,000
GAA clubs: 48

Leinster SHC: 0
All-Ireland SHC: 0
National Hurling League: 0
2005 Championship section: Tier Two
Last five years:

2000: A loss to Carlow ended a disappointing provincial campaign.

2001: Again beaten by Carlow in Leinster.

2002: Defeated Kildare in Leinster preliminary tie before surrendering to Dublin.

2003: Beat Kildare again, and again lost to Dublin. Put up a decent challenge before bowing out against Kerry in Qualifier series.

2004: Comprehensively defeated Wicklow and Kildare before losing yet again to Dublin, and then to Laois in the Qualifiers.

Top player: Andrew Mitchell More often than not the key player for the county, incredibly making it into the top five of the scorers list for the championship last season with 2–25.

Penguin Ireland Guide ranking (Tier Two): **2**

Westmeath have ambitions to make the step up in inter-county senior hurling to the respectable heights of Laois and Dublin. Last season they lost against both, but weren't disgraced. The 2004 National Hurling League Division Two runners-up have strong hopes for this season's campaign, and could well pass one of their Leinster rivals going down on the way up to Tier One hurling next season.

Outlook

With no Leinster campaign to divide the players' focus, Westmeath will be looking for a strong start in Tier Two, though a step up to Tier One hurling would be too much too soon.

Westmeath squad 2004	v Wicklow Won 6-14 1-13	v Kildare Won 1-18 1-6	v Dublin Lost 0-11 2-14	v Laois Lost 4-5 3-13
Mark Briody	●	●	●	●
Dermot Curley	●	●	●	●
Brendan Murtagh	●	●	●	●
Paul Greville	●	●	●	●
Derek Gallagher	●	●	○	○
Christo Murtagh	●	○	●	
Darren McCormack	●	●	●	●
Paul Williams	●	○	○	
Ollie Devine	●	●	●	●
Ronan Whelan	●	●	●	●
Vincent Bateman	●		●	●
Andrew Mitchell	●	●	●	●
Daniel Carty	●	○	●	
John Shaw	●	●	●	●
Barry Kennedy	●	●	○	●
Brian Connaughton	○	●		○
Frank Shaw	○			
Shane McDonnell	○	●	○	●
Killian Cosgrove	○		●	●
Derek McNicholas		●		○
Jonathon Forbes		○	●	○
Niall Flannagan		○	○	
Enda Loughlin			●	●
Brian Conaty				
Donal Devine				
Tony O'Keeffe				
Pat Clarke				
Christy Fanning				
Donal Duane				
Shane Leavy				
Paddy Divilly				
Damien Kiernan				

● Played from start ○ Substituted on

Wexford squad 2004

	v Kilkenny Won 2-15 1-16	v Offaly Won 2-12 1-11	v Cork Lost 0-12 1-27
Damien Fitzhenry	●	●	●
Malachy Travers	●	●	●
Darragh Ryan	●	●	●
David O'Connor	●	●	●
Rory McCarthy	●	●	●
Declan Ruth	●	●	●
John O'Connor	●	●	●
Adrian Fenlon	●	●	●
Tomas Mahon	●	●	●
Paul Carley	●	●	●
Barry Lambert	●	●	○
Eoin Quigley	●	●	●
Michael Jordan	●	●	●
Michael Jacob	●	●	●
Rory Jacob	●	●	●
Larry Murphy	○		○
Paul Codd	○	○	●
Colm Kehoe	○		
Chris McGrath		○	○
Diarmuid Lyng			○
Keith Rossiter			○
Matty White			
Anthony O'Connell			
Pierce Donoghue			
Mick O'Leary			
Willie Doran			
Brendan O'Leary			
Donal Berry			
Rory Stafford			
MJ Furlong			

● Played from start   ○ Substituted on

Wexford Loch Garman

Colours: Purple and gold
Stadium: Wexford Park, Wexford
Capacity: 25,000
GAA clubs: 87

Leinster SHC: 20
    1890, 1891, 1899, 1901, 1910, 1918, 1951, 1954, 1955, 1956, 1960, 1962, 1965, 1968, 1970, 1976, 1977, 1996, 1997, 2004
All-Ireland SHC: 6
    1910, 1955, 1956, 1960, 1968, 1996
National Hurling League: 4
    1956, 1958, 1967, 1973
2005 Championship section: Tier One
Last five years:
    2000: Lost heavily in the Leinster semi-final to Offaly.
    2001: Fell in the provincial decider to Kilkenny, after passing Laois in semi-final. Recovered to defeat Limerick in the Qualifier series before finally surrendering to Tipperary in an All-Ireland semi-final replay.
    2002: Again lost to Kilkenny in divisional final, this time after overcoming Dublin in semi-final. Qualifier series held no better luck, an encounter with Clare ensuring a quick championship exit.
    2003: Third time unlucky, lost again to Kilkenny in Leinster final after dispatching Offaly. Defeated Waterford and Antrim to set up an All-Ireland semi-final meeting with Cork, where the Munster side needed two chances to proceed.
    2004: Defeated Kilkenny and Offaly to become eastern kingpins again, then lost to eventual champions Cork in the All-Ireland semi-final.
Top player: Adrian Fenlon The county relies on the Rapparees star to control the middle of the field and also chip in with the odd score. Last year he duly obliged, being instrumental in Wexford's successful Leinster campaign.

Penguin Ireland Guide ranking (Tier One): **6**

The pleasure of a cracking Leinster run was ruined by the side's performance in last season's All-Ireland semi-final. Bouncing back, though, is a Wexford trademark, and if they build up some momentum no one will want to be matched with them in the latter stages.

Outlook
With Laois or Dublin the opposition in the Leinster semi-final, a provincial final date – and thus, win or lose, a ticket to the All-Ireland quarter-finals – beckons. Wexford may have to pick themselves up to face a group winner from the Qualifier section.

Wicklow squad 2004

	v **Westmeath** Lost 1–13 6–14
Thomas Finn	●
Michael J O'Neill	●
Graham Keogh	●
Jeffrey Bermingham	●
Sean Kinsella	●
Michael A O'Neill	●
Trevor McGrath	●
Christy O'Toole	●
Gerry Murray	●
Joe Murphy	●
Gerry Doran	●
Chistopher Kavanagh	●
Alan Tiernan	●
Jonathan O'Neill	●
David Moran	●
Dermot Doran	●
Denis Moran	●
John Sinnott	●
Joey Driver	
Declan Finn	
Shaun Byrne	
John Keenan	
Tony Kinsella	
Adrian Keogh	

● Played from start   ● Substituted on

Wicklow Cill Mhantáin

Colours: Blue and yellow
Stadium: Aughrim
Capacity: 7,000
GAA clubs: 65

Leinster SHC: 0
All-Ireland SHC: 0
National Hurling League: 0
2005 Championship section: Tier Two
Last five years:
  2000: Did not field a championship side.
  2001: Surrendered to Carlow in replayed preliminary provincial tie.
  2002: Battled gamely before ultimately falling to Laois in early stages of Leinster championship.
  2003: Disappointingly lost again to Laois, in a more one-sided game than in previous season.
  2004: Hit for six goals against Westmeath in quick exit out of Leinster competition.

Top player: Jonathan O'Neill 'Bosco', who scored all but two points of the county's 1–13 against Westmeath last season, is crucial to his team's fortunes.

Penguin Ireland Guide ranking (Tier Two): **5**

Under the new hurling championship format Wicklow may now be spared any more unseemly exits from the Leinster championship, but it should be remembered that another Tier Two county – Westmeath – handed them their departure papers early last season, by a margin of 16 points.

Outlook
This team is better than their only championship outing last season might indicate, and should be safe in Tier Two.

Clare squad 2004

	v Waterford Lost 1-8 3-21	v Laois Won 7-19 2-15	v Offaly Won 3-16 2-10	v Kilkenny Drew 1-13 1-13	v Kilkenny Lost 0-9 1-11
Davy Fitzgerald	●	●	●	●	●
Brian Quinn	●		●	●	●
Brian Lohan	●	●	●		●
Brian O'Connell	●	○	○		
Gerry Quinn	●	●		●	●
Sean McMahon	●	●	●	●	●
Conor Plunkett	●				○
Ollie Baker	●		○	○	○
Diarmuid McMahon	●	●	●	●	●
Tony Griffin	●	●	●	●	●
Colin Lynch	●	●	●	●	●
Alan Markham	●	●	●	●	●
Niall Gilligan	●	●	●	●	●
Frank Lohan	●	●	●	●	●
David Forde	●	○	●	●	○
Tony Carmody	○	○	●	●	
David Hoey	○	●	●	●	●
Jamesie O'Connor	○	●	○	○	○
Daithi O'Connell	○	●	○	○	
Colm Forde	○	○			
Tomas Holland		●			
Ger O'Grady		●	●	●	●
Barry Murphy		○			○
Andrew Quinn			●	●	●
Connor Harrison			○		
John Reddan					●
Ger O'Connell					
Brian Lynch					
Ronan Looney					
Pat Vaughan					
Sean Moloney					
Brian Culbert					
Darragh Clancy					

● Played from start   ○ Substituted on

Munster

Clare An Clár

Colours: Yellow and blue
Stadium: Cusack Park, Ennis
Capacity: 24,000
GAA clubs: 88

Munster SHC: 6
  1889, 1914, 1932, 1995, 1997, 1998
All-Ireland SHC: 3
  1914, 1995, 1997
National Hurling League: 3
  1946, 1977, 1978
2005 Championship section: Tier One
Last five years:
  2000: Beaten in Munster semi-final by Tipperary.
  2001: Unlucky to be beaten by a single point by Tipperary, again in the provincial semi-final.
  2002: Fell yet again to Tipperary before going on a successful 'back door' run with wins over Dublin, Wexford, Galway and Waterford to reach the All-Ireland final. Kilkenny, however, proved too strong on the day.
  2003: Gained some measure of revenge for recent years, beating Tipperary in provincial quarter-final. Failed to build on that win, losing to Cork in Munster semi-final and Galway in Qualifier series.
  2004: Knocked out of Munster by Waterford. Beat Laois and Offaly in Qualifier series before falling to Kilkenny in replayed All-Ireland quarter-final.
Top player: Niall Gilligan Probably the county's most potent forward threat, the Sixmilebridge player has been growing in importance each season. Last year, he was easily Clare's tormentor-in-chief of opposition defences.

Penguin Ireland Guide ranking (Tier One): **8**

After starting out so poorly, Clare can still consider themselves rather unfortunate to have not had an August interest in last season's championship. Apart from the Waterford mauling, Anthony Daly's men made an impressive impact, and came so close to handing Kilkenny their second jolt of the season. Confidence levels were topped up and a fresh season beckons. Clare still look short of a leader in one or two vital positions, though not having to play a first-round provincial tie gives the team a little more time to decide on starting places.

Outlook

Opinion is divided in the county as to whether Limerick or Tipperary is the preferred choice in the Munster semi-final. Either way, an opening performance similar to last season's won't suffice. The Qualifier route may have its benefits, and Clare will hope for a kinder All-Ireland quarter-final draw this time.

Cork squad 2004

	v Kerry Won 4-19 1-7	v Limerick Won 1-18 2-12	v Waterford Lost 1-21 3-16	v Tipperary Won 2-19 1-16	v Antrim Won 2-26 0-10	v Wexford Won 1-27 0-12	v Kilkenny Won 0-17 0-9
Dónal Óg Cusack	●	●	●	●	●	●	●
Brian Murphy	●	●	●	●	●	●	●
Diarmuid O'Sullivan	●	●	●	○	●	●	●
Cian O'Connor	●				○	●	
Tom Kenny	●	●	●	●	●	●	●
Ronan Curran	●	●	●	●	●	●	●
Sean Óg Ó hAilpín	●	●	●	●	●	●	●
John Gardiner	●	●	●	●	●		●
Michael O'Connell	●	●	○	○	○	○	
Jerry O'Connor	●	●	●	●	●	●	●
Niall McCarthy	●	●	●	●	●	●	●
Timmy McCarthy	●	●	●	○	●	●	●
Ben O'Connor	●	●	●	●	●	●	●
Joe Deane	●	●	●	●	●	●	●
Jonathan O'Callaghan	●	●	○		○	○	
John Anderson	○				○		
Brian Corcoran	○	○	●	●	●	●	●
Paul Tierney	○						
John Brown	○				○	○	○
Brendan Lombard	○						
Wayne Sherlock		●	●	●	●	●	●
Michael Byrne		○					
Garvan McCarthy			●	●			
Kieran Murphy			○	●	●	●	●
John Paul King						○	
Pat Mulcahy						○	
Paul Morrisey							
Mark Prendergast							
Graham Callinan							
Martin Coleman							
Eamonn Collins							
James Bowles							

● Played from start   ○ Substituted on

Cork Corcaigh

Colours: Red and white
Stadium: Pairc Uí Chaoimh, Cork
Capacity: 42,000
GAA clubs: 259

Munster SHC: 48
1890, 1892, 1893, 1894, 1901, 1902, 1903, 1904, 1905, 1907, 1912, 1915, 1919, 1920, 1926, 1927, 1928, 1929, 1931, 1939, 1942, 1943, 1944, 1946, 1947, 1952, 1953, 1954, 1956, 1966, 1969, 1970, 1972, 1975, 1976, 1977, 1978, 1979, 1982, 1983, 1984, 1985, 1986, 1990, 1992, 1999, 2000, 2003

All-Ireland SHC: 29
1890, 1892, 1893, 1894, 1902, 1903, 1919, 1926, 1928, 1929, 1931, 1941, 1942, 1943, 1944, 1946, 1952, 1953, 1954, 1966, 1970, 1976, 1977, 1978, 1984, 1986, 1990, 1999, 2004

National Hurling League: 14
1926, 1930, 1940, 1941, 1948, 1953, 1969, 1970, 1972, 1974, 1980, 1981, 1993, 1998

2005 Championship section: Tier One

Last five years:

2000: Defeated Kerry, Limerick and Tipperary to claim Munster crown. All-Ireland campaign cut short by a determined Offaly team.

2001: Surprised by Limerick in Munster quarter-final, losing by a single point.

2002: Lost to Waterford in provincial semi-final, but recovered temporarily to beat Limerick before crashing out to Galway in Qualifier series.

2003: Defeated Clare and Waterford to win Munster competition. Needed two hours to account for Wexford, before falling just short in All-Ireland final battle with Kilkenny.

2004: Beat Kerry and Limerick, but surrendered provincial title to Waterford in decider. Recovered to end the campaigns of Tipperary, Antrim and Wexford before gaining revenge over Kilkenny in the All-Ireland final.

Top player: Diarmuid O'Sullivan The 'Rock' in the defence. The Rebel County's supporters love him for his no-nonsense tackling. Opposition forwards aren't quite as enamoured.

Penguin Ireland Guide ranking (Tier One): **3**

It's not a simple task to resume All-Ireland-winning form, but the Rebel County have a history of gradually changing up the gears. They certainly found the first half of their last campaign much more exacting than the second. Debate about the impact of losing Setanta Ó hAilpín was suppressed ruthlessly in the final stages of last season's championship and, now under new management, the Cork players will be keen to show they have the ability to remain at the summit.

Outlook

Cork's opening tie in the Munster championship versus Waterford – the All-Ireland champions playing the Munster champions – is mouth-watering. While Cork recovered from last season's provincial final defeat, they might not be able to repeat the trick should Waterford come out on top again this season.

Kerry Ciarraí

Colours: Green and yellow
Stadium: Fitzgerald Stadium, Killarney
Capacity: 39,000
Stadium: Austin Stack Park, Tralee
Capacity: 14,000
GAA clubs: 73

Munster SHC: 1
1891
All-Ireland SHC: 1
1891
National Hurling League: 0
2005 Championship section: Tier Two
Last five years:
  2000: Target-practice for Cork in first round of Munster championship.
  2001: Decided not to enter senior hurling championship.
  2002: Disappointingly lost semi-final of B Championship to Wicklow.
  2003: Lost in the first round of the Munster championship to Waterford, but bounced back to defeat Westmeath, Carlow and Derry in preliminary section of Wualifiers. Gave Limerick something of a fright in first-round Qualifier.
  2004: Failed to build on previous season, losing heavily to Cork in Munster then opting out of Qualifier series.
Top player: Shane Brick The Kilmoyley ace has been a vital component of Kerry's challenge each year, driving the team forward.

Penguin Ireland Guide ranking (Tier Two): 3

The new format has come a year too late for Kerry. In 2003, the Kingdom's hurlers were on something of a roll. A solid performance against Antrim in Croke Park in the National Hurling League Division Two decider was followed by an unprecedented five-game run in the championship (one more than the Kerry footballers) and ended with a creditable performance against Limerick. The new system, had it been introduced last season, might have prevented the county's visible backward step. A very poor league season was followed by the team's decision to pull out of the championship after a slaughter at the hands of Cork. It was a shame, as the team have some wonderfully talented and determined players, such as Shane Brick.

Outlook
It will probably take Kerry more than just this season to rediscover the form that once allowed them to compete against the big guns. It is inevitable, though, considering the quality in the county, that Kerry will play Tier One hurling within the next few seasons.

Kerry squad 2004	v Cork Lost 1–7 4–19
Tadhg Flynn	●
Brendan Blackwell	●
Aidan Healy	●
Andrew Keane	●
Kieran O'Sullivan	●
James McCarthy	●
Colin Harris	●
Aidan Cronin	●
Darren Young	●
Ian McCarthy	●
Shane Brick	●
Pat O'Connell	●
Erroll Tuohy	●
John Mike Dooley	●
John Egan	●
Liam Boyle	◐
Michael Lucid	◐
Joe Walsh	
Aidan Boyle	
Eamonn Fitzgerald	
Eoghan Sheehy	
Stephen Goggin	
John Fitzgerald	

● Played from start   ◐ Substituted on

Limerick squad 2004

	v Cork Lost 2–12 1–18	v Tipperary Lost 2–12 3–10
Albert Shanahan	●	
Damien Reale	●	●
TJ Ryan	●	●
Michael Cahill	●	●
Ollie Moran	●	●
Brian Geary	●	●
Peter Lawlor	●	●
Clement Smith	●	●
Mark Foley	●	●
Niall Moran	●	●
John Paul Sheahan	●	●
Michael McKenna	●	●
Andrew O'Shaughnessy	●	●
Sean O'Connor	●	●
Donncha Sheehan	●	●
Pat Tobin	◉	◉
Donal O'Grady	◉	◉
John Cahill	●	
James O'Brien	◉	
Donie Ryan	◉	
Paul O'Grady	◉	
Brian Carroll		
Eugene Mulcahy		
Pat Sheahan		
Paul O'Reilly		
Peter O'Reilly		
Maurice O'Brien		
Pat Kirby		
James Butler		
Willie Walsh		
Peter Russell		

● Played from start ◉ Substituted on

Limerick Luimneach

Colours: Green and white
Stadium: Gaelic Grounds, Limerick
Capacity: 49,500
GAA clubs: 107

Munster SHC: 18
   1897, 1910, 1911, 1918, 1921, 1923, 1933, 1934, 1935, 1936, 1940, 1955, 1973, 1974, 1980, 1981, 1994, 1996
All-Ireland SHC: 7
   1897, 1918, 1921, 1934, 1936, 1940, 1973
National Hurling League: 11
   1934, 1935, 1936, 1937, 1938, 1947, 1971, 1984, 1985, 1992, 1997
2005 Championship section: Tier One
Last five years:
   2000: Lost comprehensively to Cork in the Munster semi-final.
   2001: Gained revenge over Cork, then defeated Waterford in provincial semi-final, but found Tipperary too strong in the final. Lost narrowly to Wexford in All-Ireland quarter-final.
   2002: Lost to Tipperary in Munster semi-final and to Cork in first game of Qualifiers.
   2003: Unlucky to be beaten by Waterford in provincial semi-final. Recovered somewhat to defeat Kerry in Qualifier series, before crashing out to Offaly in next round.
   2004: Beaten by Cork and Tipperary in provincial and Qualifier competitions respectively.
Top player: **Mark Foley** The Adare player cannot be faulted for last season's disappointingly quick exits from the Munster and All-Ireland championships. The 2001 All-Star is probably more suited to the half-back line than midfield.

Penguin Ireland Guide ranking (Tier One): **7**

Pad Joe Whelahan's first season in charge was a mixture of lows and very modest highs. Despite trying to nip the dual-status issue in the bud early on, it still cast a shadow over what was ultimately a disappointing campaign. Two defeats from two games, though, disguises the progress that has been made, and if Limerick can up their game in the final ten minutes of contests this season they'll have a far more favourable balance sheet. Putting scores on the board isn't the main problem; stopping them at the other end is.

Outlook

Limerick should be looking at this season's competition with renewed determination. There is unfinished business with Tipperary and the prize for a subsequent upset over Clare would be a date on provincial final day. They should squeak through the Qualifiers to the All-Ireland quarter-finals, but probably won't go any further.

Tipperary Tiobraid Árann

Colours: Blue and gold
Stadium: Semple Stadium, Thurles
Capacity: 53,000
GAA clubs: 82

Munster SHC: 36

1895, 1896, 1898, 1899, 1900, 1906, 1908, 1909, 1913, 1916, 1917, 1922, 1924, 1925, 1930, 1937, 1941, 1945, 1949, 1950, 1951, 1958, 1960, 1961, 1962, 1964, 1965, 1967, 1968, 1971, 1987, 1988, 1989, 1991, 1993, 2001

All-Ireland SHC: 25

1887, 1895, 1896, 1898, 1899, 1900, 1906, 1908, 1916, 1925, 1930, 1937, 1945, 1949, 1950, 1951, 1958, 1961, 1962, 1964, 1965, 1971, 1989, 1991, 2001

National Hurling League: 18

1928, 1949, 1950, 1952, 1954, 1955, 1957, 1959, 1960, 1961, 1964, 1965, 1968, 1979, 1988, 1994, 1999, 2000

2005 Championship section: Tier One

Last five years:

2000: Defeated Waterford and Clare to reach Munster decider, but fell to Cork. Lost All-Ireland quarter-final tie with Galway.

2001: Beat Clare and Limerick to claim provincial crown. Defeated Wexford in an All-Ireland semi-final replay, then overcame Galway in the final.

2002: Accounted for Clare and Limerick in Munster championship, but not Waterford in the final. Recovered to defeat Offaly and Antrim, but came up short in All-Ireland semi-final against Kilkenny.

2003: Lost to Clare in first round of provincial championship. Better news in Qualifier series, beating Laois, Galway and Offaly before bowing out to Kilkenny in All-Ireland semi-final.

2004: Beaten by Waterford in provincial semi-final and Cork in third-round Qualifier. Defeated Limerick in between the two defeats.

Top player: Eoin Kelly The Premier County's scoring machine: when the Mullinahone ace has an off-day, Tipperary have an off-day. Deadly accurate from dead ball and from play. Simply irreplaceable.

Penguin Ireland Guide ranking (Tier One): **5**

Tipperary alter their appearance more often than Michael Jackson. Already, many of the young team that claimed the 2001 All-Ireland title have left, or are watching from the bench. The team hasn't appeared settled for a few seasons now, with players in positions such as centre back and midfield feeling under constant threat of being hauled off. Tipp ran into a red wall last year in Killarney and never had the look of All-Ireland contenders. If the county's modern tradition of winning just one championship every decade is to be broken, this undoubtedly talented side will have to gel, and quickly.

Outlook

Though on the apparently lighter side of the provincial draw,

Tipperary squad 2004

	v Waterford Lost 3-12 4-10	v Limerick Won 3-10 2-12	v Cork Lost 1-16 2-19
Brendan Cummins	●	●	●
Thomas Costello	●		
Philip Maher	●	●	●
Paul Curran	●	●	●
Paul Kelly	●	●	●
Diarmuid Fitzgerald	●	●	●
Eamonn Corcoran	●	●	●
Eddie Enright	●	●	
Colin Morrissey	●	●	●
Tommy Dunne	●	●	●
John Carroll	●	●	●
Benny Dunne	●	●	●
Eoin Kelly	●	●	●
John Devane	●		
Paddy O'Brien	●		
Seamus Butler	○	●	●
Martin Maher	○	●	●
Conor Gleeson	○		●
Mark O'Leary	○	○	○
Declan Fanning		●	●
Brian O'Meara		○	
Lar Corbett		○	○
Tony Scroope		○	
Noel Morris			○
Justin Cottrell			
Ken Dunne			
Shane Maher			
Noel Moloney			
Michael Phelan			
Shane Sweeney			
David Kennedy			

● Played from start   ○ Substituted on

Tipp found Limerick more than a handful last season and a similar performance against the same opponents in their opening game this season may not be sufficient. The extra games the Qualifier series offers may be a blessing in disguise.

Waterford   Port Láirge

Colours: Blue and white
Stadium: Walsh Park, Waterford
Capacity: 16,600
GAA clubs: 55

Munster SHC: 7
  1938, 1948, 1957, 1959, 1963, 2002, 2004
All-Ireland SHC: 2
  1948, 1959
National Hurling League: 1
  1963
2005 Championship section: Tier One.
Last five years:
  2000: Defeated by Tipperary in first round of provincial championship.
  2001: Lost Munster semi-final at the hands of Limerick.
  2002: Beat Cork and Tipperary to claim the Munster title before being surprised by Clare in All-Ireland semi-final.
  2003: Victories over Kerry and Limerick meant qualification for provincial decider again, but Cork won the day. Wexford rubbed salt into their wounds in Qualifier series.
  2004: Reclaimed Munster title with victories over Clare, Tipperary and Cork. Again fell short at penultimate stage of All-Ireland championship, this time against Kilkenny.
Top player: Ken McGrath There was much doubt as to whether the county could afford to lose such a forward talent when he was first handed the number six jersey. But last season he showed just how versatile he is, adding so much to the team's defence.

Penguin Ireland Guide ranking (Tier One): **1**

Supporters wearing blue and white vacated the Gaelic Grounds after last season's National Hurling League final defeat to Galway with more than a feeling of trepidation. The result inspired pundits to write off the team's chances of beating Clare the following weekend, but Waterford were in a different class in the Munster championship. Although they didn't suffer to the same extent from the long pause between the provincial title and All-Ireland semi-final as they did two years previously, the result was still the same, leaving many supporters and players wondering if their day would ever come. However, this young and talented team still has its best hurling ahead of it, and this could be the

Waterford squad 2004

	v Clare Won 3–21 1–8	v Tipperary Won 4–10 3–12	v Cork Won 3–16 1–21	v Kilkenny Lost 0–18 3–12
Stephen Brenner	●	●	●	
James Murray	●	●	●	●
Tom Feeney	●	●		
Eoin Murphy	●	●	●	●
Tony Browne	●		●	●
Ken McGrath	●	●	●	●
Brian Phelan	●	●	●	●
Dave Bennett	●	●	●	●
Eoin Kelly	●	●	●	●
Dan Shanahan	●	●	●	●
Michael Walsh	●	●	●	●
Paul Flynn	●	●	●	●
John Mullane	●	●	●	
Seamus Prendergast	●	●	●	●
Eoin McGrath	●	●	●	●
Paul O'Brien	○	○	○	○
Sean Ryan	○			
Andy Moloney	○			
Declan Prendergast		●	●	●
Brian Wall		●		
Shane O'Sullivan		○	○	○
Jack Kennedy			○	○
Ian O'Regan				●
Liam Lawlor				
Ger Quinlan				
John Wall				
John Hurney				
David O'Brien				
Denis Coffey				
Andrew Kirwan				
Wayne Hutchinson				

● Played from start   ○ Substituted on

year they bring home a cup that hasn't been seen around Waterford in 46 years.

Outlook

The toughest possible opening tie – against All-Ireland champions Cork – may not be as unwelcome as it seems. Beating the All-Ireland title holders would be a major coup, and there is now, of course, an All-Ireland Quarter-final spot awaiting whoever claims the Munster crown. It's something Waterford, considering their traditional aversion to extended periods between competitive fixtures, may yet be thankful for.

Ulster

Antrim Aontroim

Colours: Saffron and white
Stadium: Casement Park, Belfast
Capacity: 32,500
GAA clubs: 108

Ulster SHC: 43
 1900, 1901, 1903, 1904, 1905, 1907, 1909, 1910, 1913, 1916, 1924, 1925, 1926, 1927, 1928, 1929, 1930, 1931, 1933, 1934, 1935, 1937, 1938, 1939, 1940, 1943, 1944, 1945, 1946, 1947, 1948, 1949, 1989, 1990, 1991, 1993, 1994, 1996, 1998, 1999, 2002, 2003, 2004

All-Ireland SHC: 0
National Hurling League: 0
2005 Championship section: Tier One
Last five years:
 2000: Beat London easily in Ulster semi-final, then lost out narrowly to Derry in the provincial decider despite raising the white flag 19 times.
 2001: Beaten in Ulster semi-final by Down.
 2002: Defeated New York and Down to reclaim Ulster title. A late rally by Tipperary in All-Ireland quarter-final ended their interest in the championship.
 2003: Hammered London and went on to defeat Down and Derry and retain provincial title. Desperately unlucky to be beaten by Wexford in All-Ireland quarter-final.
 2004: Beat Derry to reach title decider, where – after two games with Down – the crown was secured for another season. Cork were in no mood to entertain thoughts of an upset in All-Ireland quarter-final clash.

Top player: Brian McFall An ounstanding instinctive player, the St John's star has the ability to change the course of a game in an instant.

Penguin Ireland Guide ranking (Tier One): **10**

The harsh nature of inter-county hurling has often resulted in years of slow development being shattered by one sudden bump

Antrim squad 2004	v **Derry** Won 2–14 0–12	v **Down** Drew 1–15 1–15	v **Down** Won 3–14 0–18	v **Cork** Lost 0–10 2–26
Damien Quinn	●	●	●	●
Michael McCambridge	●	●	●	●
Kieran Kelly	●	●	●	●
Brendan Herron	●	●	●	●
Johnny Campbell	●	●	●	●
Conor McKeegan	●	●	●	●
Ciarán Herron	●	●	●	
Jim Connolly	●	●	●	●
Martin Scullion	●			●
Liam Richmond	●	●		●
Calum McGuickian	●	●	●	●
Michael Herron	●	●	●	●
Liam Watson	●	●	●	●
Patrick Richmond	●	●	●	●
Brian McFall	●	●	●	●
Darren Quinn	●	●	●	●
Jonny McIntosh	●			●
Gerard Cunningham		●		●
Mickey Kettle		●	●	●
Gareth Ward			●	
Michael Magill			●	●
Ryan McGarry				
Ainle Óg Ciareallian				
Neil Reynolds				
Darren Quinn				
Patrick Cunningham				
Sean Kelly				
Niall McCallin				
Kevin McDonnell				
Phillip Curran				
Joey Scullion				
Seán Óg McFadden				
Connor Cunning				
Ciarán Connolly				

● Played from start   ● Substituted on

in the road. In 2004, Cork were that obstacle for Antrim, and this year will show whether they can sustain their recent progress, rather than tumble out of the picture like other pretenders. But while many believe the northern county brought last year's misfortune on themselves with a few ill-advised comments before the All-Ireland quarter-final, there is no doubt manager Dinny Cahill has taken this team to a new level. They have yet to slay a true giant, though Wexford and Tipperary were pushed to the edge in recent years. The new format makes it more unlikely that the county will get within touching distance of an All-Ireland final – at least in the foreseeable future.

Outlook

The Ulster championship is now a secondary concern for the county, though Antrim should still have enough to see off New York and whoever turns up on final day. It won't be anything like as comfortable in the All-Ireland Qualifier group.

Derry Doire

Colours: Red and white
Stadium: Celtic Park, Derry
Capacity: 18,000
GAA clubs: 60

Ulster SHC: 4
  1902, 1908, 2000, 2001
All-Ireland SHC: 0
National Hurling League: 0
2005 Championship section: Tier Two
Last five years:
  2000: Defeated Down in provincial semi-final and Antrim, finally, in the decider. Put up a decent challenge to Offaly in All-Ireland quarter-final.
  2001: Defeated London and Down to retain Ulster title, but again fell short at All-Ireland quarter-final stage, this time to Galway.
  2002: Bowed out of championship after losing replayed provincial semi-final with Down.
  2003: Lucky to scrape past New York, but not as fortunate against Antrim in Ulster final.
  2004: Won in London, but again couldn't overcome Antrim in provincial decider.
Top player: Geoffrey McGonigle The big Kevin Lynch's player usually has a meaningful impact on the scoreboard, both from play and frees.

Penguin Ireland Guide ranking (Tier Two): **7**

A county that cannot wait to meet the more realistic challenge presented by Tier Two hurling, Derry's form has dipped since claiming the All-Ireland B championship title in 1996 and, more

Derry squad 2004	v London Won 2-14 0-11	v Antrim Lost 0-12 2-14
Kieran Stevenson	●	●
Gregory Brunton	●	●
Liam Himphey	●	●
Michael Conway	●	●
Benny Ward	●	●
Cathal Brunton	●	●
Peter O'Kane	●	●
Ruairi Convery	●	
Pheilim Kelly	●	●
Kevin Himphey	●	●
Gregory Biggs	●	●
Gary Biggs	●	●
Danny McGrellis	●	●
Paul Hearty	●	●
Geoffrey McGonigle	●	●
Paul Doherty	○	○
Barry McGoldrick		○
Anton Rafferty		○
Michael Kirpatrick		
Daryll Connolly		
Christopher Coyle		
Neil Magill		
Aaron McCloskey		
Barry McCloskey		
Peadar Quigg		
Brendan Quigley		
Conor Quinn		
Colm McGuigan		

● Played from start   ○ Substituted on

recently, the Ulster triumphs of 2000 and 2001. The new format offers the side a chance to regroup and refocus; the first task will be to cement their place as a Tier Two power, rather than expecting to exit it at the top end.

Outlook
Awaiting the winners of Down and London in the Ulster competition will be only a slight distraction from the more attractive lure of the four Tier Two group games.

Down An Dún

Colours: Red and black
Stadium: Pairc Esler, Newry
Capacity: 19,000
GAA clubs: 70

Ulster SHC: 4
  1940, 1992, 1995, 1997
All-Ireland SHC: 0
National Hurling League: 0
2005 Championship section: Tier Two
Last five years:
  2000: Defeated New York to qualify for Ulster semi-final, but – for the third year in a row – found Derry too strong.
  2001: Again defeated New York, and qualified for final by defeating Antrim. Derry, however, were lying in wait once more.
  2002: Finally accounted for Derry, in a replayed semi-final, having already beaten London in first round. Lost the final to Antrim and exited the Qualifier series at the hands of Galway.
  2003: Lost to Antrim in Ulster semi-final.
  2004: Defeated New York, but surrendered in Ulster final replay against Antrim. Galway were again waiting in Qualifier series.
Top player: Martin Coulter Has a great ability to get goalside of defences and produce crucial scores that make the county's supporters more than grateful.

Penguin Ireland Guide ranking (Tier Two): **1**

Last year's National Hurling League Division One champions have particular reason to look forward to the new season and the revised championship format, with players such as scoring machine Paul Braniff giving the county a new confidence. Promotion is certainly within Down's reach, but will they want to be meeting the cream of hurling in 2006?

Outlook
With Antrim distracted by the chore of Tier One hurling, Down has the opportunity to cause an upset in the Ulster championship. It's Tier Two, however, that holds the biggest prize.

Down squad 2004	v New York Won 1–19 1–9	v Antrim Drew 1–15 1–15	v Antrim Lost 0–18 3–14	v Galway Lost 1–14 5–19
Graham Clarke	●	●	●	●
Liam Clarke	●	●	●	●
Stephen Murray	●	●	●	
James Hughes	●	●	●	
Simon Wilson	●	●	●	
Gary Savage	●	●	●	●
Gabriel Clarke	●	●	●	●
Andy Savage	●	●	●	●
Gerald Adare	●	●	●	●
Ger McGrattan	●	●	●	●
Paul Braniff	●			
Brendan McGourty	●	●	●	●
Martin Coulter	●	●	●	●
Gareth Johnson	●	●	●	●
Mick Braniff	●	●		●
John Convery	○	○	○	○
Emmett Trainor	○	○		
Stephen Clarke		○	○	○
Emmett Dorrian		○	○	○
Eoin Clarke		○		
Patrick Hughes			○	
Andrew Bell			○	○
Ryan Conlon				○
Richard Murray				
Daniel McCusker				
Paddy Monan				
Micheal Pucci				
Johnny McGrattan				

● Played from start   ○ Substituted on

Galway squad 2004

Galway squad 2004	v **Down** Won 5–19 1–14	v **Kilkenny** Lost 1–10 4–20
Liam Donoghue	●	●
Damian Joyce	●	●
Diarmuid Cloonan	●	●
Ollie Canning	●	●
Derek Hardiman	●	●
David Collins	●	
Fergal Moore	●	●
Fergal Healy	●	●
David Hayes	●	●
Alan Kerins	●	●
David Forde	●	●
David Tierney	●	●
Damien Hayes	●	●
Eugene Cloonan	●	●
Kevin Broderick	●	●
Mark Kerins	●	●
Tony Óg Regan	●	●
Rory Gantley	●	
Shane Kavanagh	●	
John Conway	●	
Paul Dullaghan		
Ollie Sahy		
Conor Ryan		
Declan O'Brien		
Adrian Cullinance		

● Played from start ● Substituted on

Connacht

Galway Gaillimh

Colours: Maroon and white
Stadium: Pearse Stadium, Galway
Capacity: 35,000
Stadium: Tuam Stadium, Tuam
Capacity: 30,000
GAA clubs: 86

Connacht SHC: 20
 1900, 1901, 1902, 1904, 1905, 1906, 1908, 1910, 1911, 1912, 1914, 1915, 1917, 1923, 1994, 1995, 1996, 1997, 1998, 1999
All-Ireland SHC: 4
 1923, 1980, 1987, 1988
National Hurling League: 8
 1931, 1951, 1975, 1987, 1989, 1996, 2000, 2004
2005 Championship section: Tier One
Last five years:
 2000: Defeated Tipperary in All-Ireland quarter-final, but were outclassed in next game by Kilkenny.
 2001: Defeated Derry and Kilkenny to qualify for the All-Ireland final, where they fell to Tipperary.
 2002: Big victories over Down and Cork meant a place in All-Ireland quarter-final, where they were tripped up by Clare.
 2003: Successive defeats by Clare and Tipperary prevented progress from qualifying series.
 2004: An easy victory over Down was followed by a thrashing at the hands of Kilkenny in third Qualifier round.
Top player: Eugene Cloonan Blending an outstanding talent with a uncompromising style of play, the Athenry star has made himself indispensable to Galway.

Penguin Ireland Guide ranking (Tier One): **4**

If only the Tribesmen could be stirred to acts of revenge in the same way as, say, Kilkenny. Galway are the equivalent of Spain's national soccer team, with an abundance of talent and an endless ability to fool supporters and observers into believing that a championship title is within their grasp. Last season's National League victory reinforced the opinion that the team were gearing up for a big summer campaign, yet there was hardly a Galway supporter left in Semple Stadium when the final whistle blew in their clash with Kilkenny. Galway supporters deserve better, and the county's players know they are capable of much more.

Outlook
Last season was a tale of two extremes: an easy win over Down and then a meeting with the All-Ireland champions, which

exposed, once again, the flaws in the previous format of the competition. This season, the Tribesmen are guaranteed three Qualifier ties, and should claim at least one or two knock-out ties through their performances on the field.

Mayo   Maigh Eo

Colours: Green and red
Stadium: McHale Park, Castlebar
Capacity: 35,000
GAA clubs: 52

Connacht SHC: 0
All-Ireland SHC: 0
National Hurling League: 0
2005 Championship section: Tier Two
Last five years: Did not field a championship side.
Top player: Pierce Higgins A menancing threat in the full-forward line for his
   county. Along with his brother, Keith, he led Ballyhaunis to the county title last
   year.

Penguin Ireland Guide ranking (Tier Two): **10**

Mayo are breaking new ground in hurling this season, something that will be welcomed by the brave few who have championed the game against the dominance of Gaelic football in the county. It's going to be a long and difficult struggle, however – Tier Two hurling will probably be a tougher challenge for Mayo then for any of the other nine teams.

Outlook
Should Mayo, as expected, end up in the relegation play-offs, it will come down to two matches against counties also down on their luck. A victory against either would represent a successful season.

Roscommon Ros Comáin

Colours: Blue and yellow
Stadium: Hyde Park, Roscommon
Capacity: 25,000
GAA clubs: 51

Connacht SHC: 2
1907, 1913
All-Ireland SHC: 0
National Hurling League: 0
2005 Championship section: Tier Two
Last five years: Did not field a championship side.
Top player: Colm Kelly Plays further out the field for his county, but inspired his club, Oran, from the edge of the square last season to claim the Roscommon senior hurling championship title.

Penguin Ireland Guide ranking (Tier Two): **4**

Back in the days when there was a Connacht hurling championship, Roscommon regularly provided Galway with an early summer day out. The Tribesmen would then retreat into splendid isolation before their All-Ireland semi-final date. It was the most regular mismatch of the hurling championship, and there was no doubting the detrimental effect it had on the Roscommon players. Hurling supporters in the county finally have a championship outing worth attending – at least four of them this summer, in fact. This is one of the most positive outcomes of the new format.

Outlook
There's little basis for a judgement on how the Roscommon players will handle Tier Two hurling, but the county can look at the opposition and feel confident they won't be playing in the bottom tier next season. They are likely to be comfortable in Tier Two for a while.

Hurling Championship Results Table

Munster

First Round		
Limerick		Tipperary
Replay:		

Semi-finals		
Limerick/Tipperary		Clare
Replay:		
Waterford		Cork
Replay:		

Final		
Replay:		

Ulster

Quarter-final		
Down		London
Replay:		

Semi-finals		
Down/London		Derry
Replay:		
Antrim		New York
Replay:		

Final		
Replay:		

Leinster

Quarter-final		
Laois		Dublin
Replay:		

Semi-finals		
Laois/Dublin		Wexford
Replay:		
Offaly		Kilkenny
Replay:		

Final		
Replay:		

All-Ireland Qualifiers

Group One – Round One		
Replay:		

Group Two – Round One		
Replay:		

Group One – Round Two		
Replay:		

Group Two – Round Two		
Replay:		

Group One – Round Three		
Replay:		

Group two – Round Three		
Replay:		

Group One	P	W	D	L	F	A	Pts
1							
2							
3							
4							

Group Two	P	W	D	L	F	A	Pts
1							
2							
3							
4							

All-Ireland Quarter-finals

Replay:

Replay:

Replay:

Replay:

All-Ireland Semi-finals

Replay:

Replay:

All-Ireland Final

Replay:

Relegation Play-offs

Replay:

Replay:

Relegation Final

Replay:

Tier Two

Group One – Round One

Replay:

Group Two – Round One

Replay:

Group One – Round Two

Replay:

Group Two – Round Two

Replay:

Group One – Round Three

Replay:

Group two – Round Three

Replay:

Group One – Round Four

Replay:

Group two – Round Four

Replay:

Group One – Round Five

Replay:

Group two – Round Five

Replay:

Group One	P	W	D	L	F	A	Pts
1							
2							
3							
4							
5							

Group Two	P	W	D	L	F	A	Pts
1							
2							
3							
4							
5							

All-Ireland Semi-finals
Replay:

All-Ireland Final
Replay:

Relegation Play-offs

Replay:

Relegation Final
Replay:

4
Football
Championship
2005

Football Championship 2005

Championship Structure

There is no change to the competition structures for this season's senior football championship. And why should there be? Last season was another successful summer for the Qualifier system, with teams such as Fermanagh, Derry and Dublin particularly thankful that first-round provincial losses no longer meant exit from the All-Ireland championship. A renewed determination to allow teams depleted in their respected provincial championships longer than a week to prepare for the Qualifier rounds should also help.

For the second season running there will be a secondary football competition: the Tommy Murphy Cup. Counties who are beaten in Round One or Round Two of the All-Ireland Qualifiers are eligible to participate in the competition. It is to be hoped that this season's contest will be more successful than last year's, when a raft of withdrawals meant that only three games were needed to decide the competition.

Like London, New York competes in the Connacht championship, and this year will play Galway in their first-round provincial tie. Apart from the obvious financial difficulties, tougher cross-Atlantic travel restrictions haven't exactly encouraged Irish players based in New York to take the chance of coming home to play a game, in case they can't get back across the water. So, although 17 teams fail to qualify for a provincial semi-final, only 16 actually attempt the Qualifying route. At least New York actually field a team in the provincial championship, which is more than can be said for Kilkenny.

If Kilkenny ever did field a senior football team in the championship again, one of the few advantages they would enjoy is having their opening-round Qualifier at Nowlan Park – presuming, of course, that they didn't win the Leinster title. The 'weaker county' concept – which allows home advantage in the first and second rounds of the All-Ireland Qualifiers – has been of limited benefit to the counties so designated in the football championship. The GAA has never defined how a county might rid itself of the label in the future, or just how bad a team has to become before falling into the basement grade for the first time.

Provincial Championships

These will be played on a knock-out basis in all four provinces, with the provincial winners qualifying for the All-Ireland Quarter-finals.

All-Ireland Qualifiers

Counties designated as 'weak' (by the National Games Administration Committee) shall have home advantage in Round One and Round Two – unless the home ground does not meet required standard. Home venues may be used in Round Three and Round Four, also provided they reach the necessary standard. The draw for each round may have to be adjusted to prevent counties that have already met in the provincial championship from meeting again before the All-Ireland Semi-final stage.

Round One
Involves all teams that did not qualify for their respective provincial semi-finals. Sixteen counties (assuming the non-participation of New York), eight games.

Round Two
Involves the eight winning teams from Round One against the eight defeated sides from the provincial semi-finals. Sixteen counties, eight games.

Round Three
Involves the eight winning teams from Round Two. Eight counties, four games.

Round Four
Involves the four winning teams from Round Three, each playing against one of the four defeated provincial finalists. Eight counties, four games.

All-Ireland quarter-finals
Involving the four winning teams from Round Four, each playing against one of the four provincial champions. (Provincial champions cannot meet the team they defeated in the provincial final.) Eight counties, four games.

All-Ireland semi-finals
The draw is based on a provincial rota system. This season the draw will pit the Ulster champions against the Leinster winners, and the champions of Connacht against the Munster champions – provided, of course, that the provincial winners come through the quarter-finals. If any of these teams does not come through, the team that beat them in the quarters will occupy their slot in the rota.

Provincial Championship Fixtures 2005

Leinster SFC

Round	Date	Teams	Venue
First Round	(A) May 8	Offaly v Louth	Navan
	(B) May 15	Wicklow v Kildare	Croke Park
	(C) May 15	Dublin v Longford	Croke Park
Quarter-finals	(D) May 29	Winner A v Laois	Croke Park
	(E) May 29	Winner B v Westmeath	Croke Park
	(F) June 5	Winner C v Meath	Croke Park
	(G) June 5	Carlow v Wexford	Croke Park
Semi-finals	June 19	Winner D v Winner E	Croke Park
	June 19	Winner F v Winner G	Croke Park
Final	July 17		Croke Park

Munster SFC

Round	Date	Teams	Venue
Quarter-finals	(A) May 29	Tipperary v Kerry	
	(B) May 29	Waterford v Clare	Ennis
Semi-finals	June 12	Winner B v Cork	Dungarvan or Ennis
	June 19	Winner A v Limerick	Gaelic Grounds
Final	July 10		

Ulster SFC

Round	Date	Teams	Venue
First Round	May 15	Armagh v Fermanagh	
Quarter-finals	(A) May 22	Tyrone v Down	
	(B) May 29	Cavan v Antrim	
	(C) June 5	Monaghan v Derry	
	(D) June 12	1st-round winner v Donegal	Enniskillen (if Fermanagh) or Bally-bofey (if Armagh)
Semi-finals	June 19	Winner A v Winner B	Clones
	June 26	Winner C v Winner D	Clones
Final	July 17		

Connacht SFC

Round	Date	Teams	Venue
Quarter-finals	(A) May 1	New York v Galway	Gaelic Park, New York
	(B) May 22	Leitrim v Sligo	Carrick-on-Shannon
	(C) May 29	London v Roscommon	Ruislip, London
Semi-finals	June 19	Winner C v Mayo	Dr Hyde Park
	June 26	Winner A v Winner B	Pearse Stadium or Markievicz Park
Final	July 10		

Leinster

Carlow Ceatharlach

Colours: Green, red and yellow
Stadium: Dr Cullen Park, Carlow
Capacity: 19,000
GAA clubs: 32

Leinster SFC: 1
   1944
All-Ireland SFC: 0
National Football League: 0
Last five years:
   2001: Lost to Wicklow, Wexford and Longford in preliminary stages of Leinster championship.
   2001: Beat Wicklow at second attempt before losing to Kildare. Defeated Waterford in Qualifier series, then surrendered to Sligo.
   2002: Beaten by Westmeath in preliminary round of provincial championship before collapsing to Laois by double scores in round one of Qualifier series.
   2003: Lost to Westmeath, before scoring a rare victory – over Wicklow in the Qualifiers. Tripped up against Tipperary in the next round.
   2004: Shocked Longford in first provincial round before giving Laois a good game. Down were waiting in the Qualifiers.
Top player: Simon Rea Free-taker, penalty-taker and – more often than not – top scorer from play, the Éire Óg forward is a vital cog in the Carlow machine. If only there were a few more players of his ability floating about the county.

Penguin Ireland Guide ranking: **29**

After watching London emerge victorious from the National League tie at Dr Cullen Park last season, Carlow supporters must have approached the championship campaign with justifiable apprehension. But then the county footballers went out and beat Longford in Tullamore with eight points to spare. All was

Carlow squad 2004	v Longford Won 4-15 1-16	v Laois Lost 1-7 0-15	v Down Lost 1-13 1-19
James Clarke	●	●	●
Brian Farrell	●	●	●
Stephen O'Brien	●		
Cormac McCarthy	●	●	●
Ken Walker	●		○
John Hayden	●	●	●
Joe Byrne	●	●	●
Mark Brennan	●	○	○
Thomas Walsh	●	●	○
Pat Hickey	●	●	○
Johnny Nevin	●	●	●
Mark Carpenter	●	●	●
Simon Rea	●	●	●
Sean Kavanagh	●	●	●
Brian Carberry	●	○	●
Barry English	○	●	
Brian Kelly	○	●	●
Willie Power	○	●	●
Paul Cashin		●	●
Johnny Kavanagh		○	●
David Byrne		○	●
Ray Walker		○	
John Brennan			
John Doyle			
Willie Minehin			
Willie Ryan			
Paul Kelly			
Philip Nolan			

● Played from start　　○ Substituted on

forgiven. It may be cruel to play with people's emotions, but, undeterred, the team subsequently surrendered to Down in the Qualifier series after earlier giving Laois a scare in the provincial competition. With such varied results, Carlow supporters have grown used to not knowing what to expect from their first team.

Outlook

Another surprise first-round result would be heaven on earth, but it's much less likely this season as they are facing a rejuvenated Wexford. They may have slightly better luck in the Qualifier series, depending on the draw.

Dublin Áth Cliath

Colours: Dark blue and light blue
Stadium: Parnell Park, Dublin
Capacity: 11,000
Stadium: Croke Park, Dublin
Capacity: 82,300
GAA clubs: 211

Leinster SFC: 44
1891, 1892, 1894, 1896, 1897, 1898, 1899, 1901, 1902, 1904, 1906, 1907, 1908, 1920, 1921, 1922, 1923, 1924, 1932, 1933, 1934, 1941, 1942, 1955, 1958, 1959, 1962, 1963, 1965, 1974, 1975, 1976, 1977, 1978, 1979, 1983, 1984, 1985, 1989, 1992, 1993, 1994, 1995, 2002

All-Ireland SFC: 22
1891, 1892, 1894, 1897, 1898, 1899, 1901, 1902, 1906, 1907, 1908, 1921, 1922, 1923, 1942, 1958, 1963, 1974, 1976, 1977, 1983, 1995

National Football League: 8
1953, 1955, 1958, 1976, 1978, 1987, 1991, 1993

Last five years:
2000: Beat Wexford and Westmeath to reach provincial final, where they fell to Kildare after two hours of play.
2001: Defeated Longford and Offaly to again make Leinster final, and again came up short, this time to Meath. Beat Sligo to set up All-Ireland quarter-final meeting with Kerry. Lost replay.
2002: Defeated Wexford, Meath and Kildare to win provincial title. Ended Donegal's interest in All-Ireland championship at second attempt to set semi-final date with what would prove to be the next All-Ireland champions – Armagh.
2003: Lost to Laois at Leinster semi-final stage, after first accounting for Louth. Similar story in Qualifier series, losing to Armagh after overcoming Derry.
2004: Disappointing start, losing to Westmeath, but favourable Qualifier draw resulted in wins over London, Leitrim, Longford and Roscommon. Quarter-final clash with Kerry proved a different story, though.
Top player: Alan Brogan Has emerged in a relatively short space of time as probably Dublin's most influential forward. Pushed the county's fortunes

Dublin squad 2004

	v Westmeath Lost 0-12 0-14	v London Won 3-24 0-6	v Leitrim Won 1-13 0-4	v Longford Won 1-17 0-11	v Roscommon Won 1-14 0-13	v Kerry Lost 1-8 1-15
Brian Murphy	●					
Barry Cahill	●	●	●	●	●	●
Paddy Christie	●	●	●	●	●	●
Paul Griffin	●	●	●	●	●	●
Shane Ryan	●	●	○	○	○	●
Collie Moran	●	●				
Peadar Andrews	●	●				
Ciarán Whelan	●	●	●	●	●	●
Darren Homan	●			●	●	●
Conal Keaney	●				●	●
Darren Magee	●	●	●	●	●	●
Brian Cullen	●		●	●	●	●
Alan Brogan	●	●	●	●	●	●
Jason Sherlock	●	●	●	●	●	●
Senan Connell	●	●	●	●	●	●
Ray Cosgrove	○	○	○	○		○
Coman Goggins	○	○	○	●	●	
Declan Lally	○	○	●			
Tomas Quinn	○	●	●		○	○
Stephen Cluxton		●	●	●	●	●
Declan O'Mahony		●	○			○
John McNally		●				
Paul Casey		○	●	●	●	●
David Henry		○				
Jonny McGee			●	○	○	○
Ian Robertson			○	●	●	●
Dessie Farrell			○	○	○	
Robert Boyle				○		
Paul Copeland						
Kevin Golden						
Liam Óg Ó hEineacháin						
Stephen Hiney						
Stephen O'Shaughnessy						
Niall Cooper						

● Played from start   ○ Substituted on

forward last year, only to register a below-par game against Kerry – which, not coincidentally, was Dublin's final game of the summer.

Penguin Ireland Guide ranking: **7**

Dublin were beaten last season by the eventual Leinster champions, and then by the eventual All-Ireland champions. It may not sound so bad when viewed like that, but the manner of both defeats – especially to Kerry in the All-Ireland quarter-final – won't have impressed anyone. The talent in the capital is undoubtedly there, but there are still too few on the team prepared to stand up and be counted when the going gets tough, something the new regime will have been working on. They won't always be able to count on kind Qualifier draws to recover momentum.

Outlook
Probably heading for an early showdown with old rivals Meath, and then quite possibly a Leinster final appearance. After that, if the mood isn't right, it could all end in tears again.

Kildare Cill Dara

Colour: White
Stadium: St Conleth's Park, Newbridge
Capacity: 13,000
GAA clubs: 70

Leinster SFC: 12
  1903, 1905, 1919, 1926, 1927, 1928, 1929, 1930, 1931, 1935, 1956, 1998, 2000
All-Ireland SFC: 4
  1905, 1919, 1927, 1928
National Football League: 0
Last five years:
  2000: Victory over Louth was followed by a successful replayed Leinster semifinal meeting with Offaly. A replay was also needed to emerge victorious from the final clash with Dublin. All-Ireland quarter-final ended in defeat to Galway.
  2001: Beat Carlow, then lost to Meath in provincial semi-final. Recovered to defeat Donegal by one point in Qualifier round two clash, before being on the other side of a single-point finish with Sligo.
  2002: Beat Louth and, after a replay, Offaly to qualify for Leinster final. Defeat to Dublin was followed by heavy loss to Kerry in Qualifier series.
  2003: Beat Longford and Meath to reach provincial final, but again fell at the last, this time to Laois. Lost to Roscommon in round four of Qualifiers.
  2004: Disappointing season, losing to Wexford in the provincial championship and Offaly in round one of the Qualifiers.
Top player: Glen Ryan A survivor from the successful side of 1997, when he earned an All-Star award, the attacking defender has the ability to turn games on his own. It's a quality Kildare need now more then ever.

Kildare squad 2004

	v **Wexford** Lost 0–12 0–10	v **Offaly** Lost 2–17 1–16
Enda Murphy	●	●
Brian Lacey	●	
Rob McCabe	●	●
Andrew McLoughlin	●	●
Eamonn Callaghan	●	●
Michael Foley	●	●
Karl Ennis	●	●
Killian Brennan	●	●
Dermot Earley	●	●
Dermot McCormack	●	●
John Doyle	●	●
Alan Barry	●	●
Padraig Brennan	●	
Morgan O'Sullivan	●	●
Tadgh Fennin	●	●
Padraig Hurley	●	
Anthony Rainbow	●	●
Padraig Donnelly	●	●
Glen Ryan	●	●
Terry Rossiter	●	●
Damien Hendry		●
Eamonn Fitzpatrick		●
Willie Heffernan		●
Paul Flood		
David Lyons		
Mick Wright		
James Kavanagh		
Ciarán Dempsey		
Ronan Sweeney		

● Played from start   ● Substituted on

Penguin Ireland Guide ranking: **19**

The Lilywhites are in rebuilding mode and the county's supporters will be demanding a much stronger performance in this
season's championship than what they witnessed last season.
Mick O'Dwyer was never going to be easy to replace.

Outlook
Fortunate to draw Wicklow, but Westmeath awaits the winner.
An early dip into the Qualifier pool looks likely, with the county
needing to avoid the big guns early on to restore lost confidence.

Laois Laoighis

Colours: Blue and white
Stadium: O'Moore Park, Portlaoise
Capacity: 27,000
GAA clubs: 85

Leinster SFC: 6
  1889, 1936, 1937, 1938, 1946, 2003
All-Ireland SFC: 0
National Football League: 2
  1927, 1986
Last five years:
  2000: Interest in the championship ended almost as soon as it began with
  defeat to Westmeath.
  2001: After defeating Wexford, Offaly proved too strong in the Leinster
  quarter-final. Hopes were heightened again with victory over Clare in the
  Qualifiers, but Derry emerged from the round-two tie.
  2002: Victory over Wicklow was followed by another defeat to Offaly in the
  provincial quarter-final. Big victories over Carlow and Clare in the Qualifiers
  were followed by an equally big third-round loss to Meath.
  2003: Victory over Wexford was followed by another meeting with Offaly in
  the provincial quarter-final. This time Offaly were beaten, albeit after a replay,
  and this was followed by wins over Dublin and then Kildare in the final.
  Armagh ended the Laois campaign in the All-Ireland quarter-final.
  2004: Defeated Carlow and Meath in another run to the Leinster final, where,
  after two hours, Westmeath emerged victorious. Tyrone rubbed salt into the
  wound in a round-four Qualifier.
Top player: Tom Kelly Ever-present at the heart of the defence, a player who
  mops up ball and halts opposition attacks as a matter of course. The 2002
  All-Star has been the driving force behind the county's success.

Penguin Ireland Guide ranking: **1**

Will the controversy at the end of last season be detrimental or
positive? Well, if it works for other counties, such as Cork, then
it's probably worth a try using it as a motivational tool. Pound-
for-pound Laois is the best footballing county on the island, and,
with an abundance of under-age talent being slowly assimilated

Laois squad 2004

	v Carlow Won 0-15 1-7	v Meath Won 1-13 0-9	v Westmeath Drew 0-13 0-13	v Westmeath Lost 0-10 0-12	v Tyrone Lost 2-4 3-15
Fergal Byron	●	●	●	●	●
Aidan Fennelly	●	●	●	●	●
Colm Byrne	●	●	●		
Joe Higgins	●	●	●	●	
Darren Rooney	●	●	●	●	●
Tom Kelly	●	●	●	●	●
Paul McDonald	●	●	●	●	●
Kevin Fitzpatrick	●	●	●	●	●
Noel Garvan	●	●	●	●	●
Ross Munnelly	●	●	●	●	●
Ian Fitzgerald	●	●	●	●	
Colm Parkinson	●	●	●	●	●
Brian McDonald	●	●	●	●	●
Michael Lawlor	●	●	●	●	
Chris Conway	●	●	●		
Padraig Clancy	○	○	○	○	○
Shane Cooke	○		○		○
Padraig McMahon	○				○
Garry Kavanagh			○	○	○
Paul Lawlor			○		○
Donal Brennan				●	
Donal Miller				○	○
Martin Delaney				○	
Patrick Conway				○	○
Cathal Ryan					●
Chris Bergin					○
Mark Dunne					
Michael Nolan					
Tom McDonald					
Daragh Mulhall					
Daragh McEvoy					

● Played from start   ○ Substituted on

into the senior ranks, there is no doubt they hold all the ingredients needed for future success. Regaining the heights of 2003 will not be an easy task. The aim now is not just provincial success, but a more prolonged interest in the All-Ireland Championship.

Outlook

If they emerge victorious from a likely tie with Westmeath in the Leinster semi-final, they'll be only be 70 minutes away from reclaiming the Leinster crown – and from a serious run at an even bigger prize.

Longford An Longfort

Colours: Blue and gold
Stadium: Pearse Park, Longford
Capacity: 12,000
GAA clubs: 47

All-Ireland SFC: 0
Leinster SFC: 1
   1968
National Football League: 1
   1966
Last five years:

   2000: Lost to Wexford after beating Wicklow and Carlow in the preliminary rounds of the Leinster championship.
   2001: Beat Louth, then lost to Dublin in the provincial quarter-final. The result was similar in the Qualifier against Wicklow.
   2002: Surrendered to Louth in a replay in the first round of the Leinster championship. Beat Down in Qualifier round before bowing out to Derry.
   2003: Lost in the Leinster quarter-final to Kildare, then in the Qualifier to Donegal.
   2004: A shock first-round loss to Longford was followed by a more credible Qualifier campaign, with victories over Monaghan and Waterford, before a defeat at the hands of Dublin.

Top player: Trevor Smullen The half forward has hit some brilliantly timed three-pointers – and not just on the basketball court. Has an impressive record of standing up to be counted when the county most needs him.

Penguin Ireland Guide ranking: **22**

Longford footballers like to keep the supporters guessing. Shocked by Carlow in the first round last season, a month later they bounced back against a fancied Monaghan. It's not the steady progress fans have been waiting for over the past years, and there isn't much confidence in the county of a change anytime soon.

Longford squad 2004

	v Carlow Lost 1-16 4-15	v Monaghan Won 4-15 1-17	v Waterford Won 1-14 1-5	v Dublin Lost 0-11 1-17
Gavin Tonra	●			
Donal Ledwith	●	●		
Cathal Conefrey	●	●	●	●
Shane Carroll	●	●	●	●
Enda Ledwith	●	●	●	●
David Hannify	●	●	●	●
Arthur O'Connor	●	●	●	●
Liam Keenan	●	●	●	●
Trevor Smullen	●	●	●	●
Paul O'Hara	●	●		
John Kenny	●	●		●
Paul Barden	●	●	●	●
Jamesie Martin	●			
Niall Sheridan	●	●	●	●
Padraic Davis	●	●	●	●
Stephen Lynch	○	○		
Mark Lennon	○			
Michael Kelly	○			
Damien Sheridan		●	●	●
Dermot Brady		●	●	●
Shane Mulligan		●	●	●
Declan Reilly		●	●	●
Martin Mulleady		●	●	●
David Barden		○	○	○
Brendan Burke		○	○	○
Brian Sheridan			○	
Enda Williams			○	
Fintan Coyle				
Adrian Dalton				
Michael Hussey				

● Played from start ○ Substituted on

Outlook

There is little chance of a strong Leinster campaign: an encounter with Dublin in the opening round surely means that the Qualifiers – and hopefully a generous draw – will present the county with a more achievable target.

Louth Lú

Colours: Red and white
Stadium: O'Rahilly's, Drogheda
Capacity: 7,500
GAA clubs: 51

Leinster SFC: 8
1909, 1910, 1912, 1943, 1948, 1950, 1953, 1957
All-Ireland SFC: 3
1910, 1912, 1957
National Football League: 0
Last five years:

2000: Kildare ended their interest in the Leinster championship one hour after it started.

2001: After losing to Longford in Leinster, beat Offaly and Tipperary in inaugural Qualifier competition. Westmeath emerged victorious from third-round tie.

2002: Took two games to get past Longford, then very unfortunate to fall to Kildare by a single point. Recovered to beat Monaghan at start of Qualifier series, before being unfortunate for a second time, this time against Meath.

2003: Victory over Wicklow was followed by a crushing defeat at the hands of Dublin. Respectable loss to Cavan in Qualifier series.

2004: Beaten by Wexford before surprising Antrim in the first round of the Qualifiers. Succumbed to Galway in second round after putting up a struggle.

Top player: Ollie McDonnell The Wee County's forward consistently turns in man-of-the-match performances. When he's not tapping balls over the bar he's splitting defences with accurate passes.

Penguin Ireland Guide ranking: **26**

Louth must be looking at counties such as Westmeath and Laois and thinking: 'Why them and not us?' A few years ago Louth was threatening to make a significant breakthrough, but couldn't produce the all-important giant-killing act. In the past couple of seasons, the county has fallen back so much that defeating Antrim in the Qualifier round last year was considered something of a surprise. If the slump is to be ended, Louth need some of their stalwarts to step up to the plate this season.

Outlook

Meeting Offaly in the first game gives the county something realistic to aim for. Victory is not likely, however, and a game or two in the Qualifier series may be the most they can hope for.

Louth squad 2004	v Wexford Lost 0–8 2–10	v Antrim Won 2–13 0–14	v Galway Lost 0–9 2–8
Shane McCoy	●	●	●
Simon Gerard	●	●	●
Johnny Clerkin	●	●	
Jamie Carr	●	●	●
Alan Page	●	●	●
Paudie Mallon	●	●	●
Ray Rooney	●	●	●
David Devaney	●	●	●
Paddy Keenan	●	●	●
Ray Kelly	●	●	●
Darren Clarke	●	●	●
Ollie McDonnell	●	●	●
Paddy Matthews	●	●	●
David Reid	●	●	
Raymond Finnegan	●		●
Derek Shevlin	◐	◐	◐
Aaron Hoey	◐	◐	◐
Sean O'Neill	◐		
Mark Stanfield	◐	◐	◐
Cormac Malone	◐		
Nicky McDonnell		●	●
JP Rooney		◐	◐
Sean Connor			
Colin McGuinness			
Andrew Rogan			
Paddy McGuigan			
Christy Grimes			
JJ Quigley			
David Bracken			
John Kermath			
James McDonnell			

● Played from start ◐ Substituted on

Meath squad 2004

	v Wicklow Won 2–13 1–8	v Laois Lost 0–9 1–13	v Fermanagh Lost 2–12 0–19
David Gallagher	●	●	●
Niall McKeigue	●	●	●
Darren Fay	●	●	●
Mark O'Reilly	●	●	●
Paddy Reynolds	●	●	●
Tómas O'Connor	●	●	●
Stephen McGowan	●		
Nigel Crawford	●	●	●
Anthony Moyles	●	●	●
Niall Kelly	●		●
Charles McCarthy	●	●	●
Trevor Giles	●	●	●
Evan Kelly	●	●	●
Shane McKeigue	●		●
Daithi Regan	●	●	●
Richie Kealy	●	●	
Donal Curtis	●	●	●
John Cullinane	●	●	
David Crimmins	●		●
Brian Farrell	●		
Hank Traynor		●	
Seamus Kenny		●	●
Joe Sheridan		●	●
Ollie Murphy		●	●
Graham Geraghty		●	
Damien Byrne			●
Brendan Murphy			
Adrian Kenny			
Ray Magee			
Damian Clarke			
Cormac Murphy			

● Played from start   ● Substituted on

Meath An Mhí

Colours: Green and gold
Stadium: Pairc Tailteann, Navan
Capacity: 29,000
GAA clubs: 153

Leinster SFC: 20
  1895, 1939, 1940, 1947, 1949, 1951, 1952, 1954, 1964, 1966, 1967, 1970,
  1986, 1987, 1988, 1990, 1991, 1996, 1999, 2001
All-Ireland SFC: 7
  1949, 1954, 1967, 1987, 1988, 1996, 1999
National Football League: 7
  1933, 1946, 1951, 1975, 1988, 1990, 1994
Last five years:
  2000: Quick exit from championship, losing to Offaly in Leinster quarter-final.
  2001: Defeated Westmeath, Kildare and Dublin to claim provincial crown.
  Needed two attempts to see off challenge of Westmeath once again, before
  destroying Kerry to reach All-Ireland final. No match for on-song Galway.
  2002: Again overcame Westmeath, then crashed out of Leinster championship
  to Dublin at semi-final stage. Recovered to claim victory over Louth and Laois
  before losing fourth-round Qualifier to Donegal.
  2003: Defeated Westmeath, again after a replay, but lost provincial semi-final
  meeting with Kildare. Beat Monaghan in round two of Qualifier series, then
  lost to Fermanagh.
  2004: Defeated Wicklow in Leinster quarter-final, but found Laois a much
  tougher challenge. Fermanagh again eliminated them from the Qualifier series.
Top player: Trevor Giles Still the county's talisman, the two-time player of
  the year provides a vital link between the defence and the front men. Stop him
  playing, stop Meath playing.

Penguin Ireland Guide ranking: **13**

The Meath players must hate the sight of Fermanagh. A few years
ago, a league defeat to the Ulster county was considered an
embarrassing result. No longer. Fermanagh's strong recent runs
in championship campaigns will come as little consolation to the
Meath fans who have witnessed their team being dumped out of
the All-Ireland championship by the Lakeland county in each of
the past two seasons. For many, those defeats have signalled the
end of the glory days, but the core of recent successful sides
remains. The ruthless streak that has served Meath so well in the
recent past has to be rediscovered, though, if the county is to be
feared again.

Outlook
The Leinster draw – which sets up a probable encounter with
Dublin in the quarter-final – gives Meath a chance to recapture
some of the confidence that has deserted them in recent
campaigns.

Offaly squad 2004

	v **Westmeath** Lost 0–10 0–11	v **Kildare** Won 2–17 1–16	v **Wexford** Lost 0–15 2–14
Padraig Kelly	●	●	●
Shane Sullivan	●	●	●
Conor Evans	●	●	●
Scott Brady	●	●	●
Barry Mooney	●	●	●
Cathal Daly	●	●	●
Karl Slattery	●	●	●
Ciarán McManus	●		●
James Grennan	●	●	●
Pascal Kellaghan	●	●	●
Roy Malone	●	●	●
Alan McNamee	●	●	
Colm Quinn	●	●	●
Neville Coughlan	●	●	●
Niall McNamee	●	●	●
James Coughlan	●	●	●
Mark Daly	●	●	●
Thomas Deehan	●	●	
Barry Malone	●		●
Cillian Farrell	●		
John Reynolds		●	●
John O'Neill		●	
Colin McNamara			
John Hurst			
Joe Quinn			
Matthew Mitchell			
Alan Mulhall			
Kevin Meehan			
Ciarán Kiely			
Michael Flynn			
Basil Malone			
Nigel Grennan			

● Played from start   ● Substituted on

Offaly Uíbh Fhailí

Colours: Green, white and gold
Stadium: St Brendan's Park, Birr
Capacity: 11,000
Stadium: O'Connor Park, Tullamore
Capacity: 16,000
GAA clubs: 85

Leinster SFC: 10
  1960, 1961, 1969, 1971, 1972, 1973, 1980, 1981, 1982, 1997
All-Ireland SFC: 3
  1971, 1972, 1982
National Football League: 1
  1998

Last five years:
  2000: Defeated Meath, but fell to Kildare in provincial semi-final, after forcing a replay.
  2001: Beat Laois, then lost in Leinster semi-final to Dublin. Lost disastrously to Louth in second-round Qualifier.
  2002: Defeated Laois in provincial quarter-final, but fell to Kildare after a replay. Lost to Limerick in Qualifier series.
  2003: Took Laois to second match in Leinster quarter-final, but eventually surrendered. Favourable Qualifier draw resulted in wins over London and Clare before defeat to Roscommon.
  2004: Single-point loss to Westmeath in first round of provincial championship, followed by hard-fought victory over Kildare, before Wexford ended their interest in the championship.

Top player: Ciarán McManus A player who can operate in almost any position, the former UCD football scholarship student has contributed handsomely to Offaly's fortunes over the past few years.

Penguin Ireland Guide ranking: **17**

Offaly supporters never know where they stand with their county's football team. Potential to beat almost any team is matched only by their frequent tendency to lose to poor sides. The ability is there, but sometimes, it seems, the will is not – though one of the highlights of last season's championship was the first Qualifier clash with Kildare at Newbridge, a game that sapped every ounce of energy from both teams, and from many of the supporters in attendance. And it should be remembered that Offaly were removed from the Leinster championship by only one point, and by the eventual provincial champions. As with Dublin, the early provincial exit seemed much worse at the time than it does in hindsight.

Outlook
While Offaly will be hot favourites to defeat Louth, old rivals and neighbours Laois will pose a much greater challenge and an early

entry to the Qualifier series is likely. A strong run from there, however, is not out of the question.

Westmeath An Iarmhí

Colours: Maroon and white
Stadium: Cusack Park, Mullingar
Capacity: 15,000
GAA clubs: 48

Leinster SFC: 1
  2004
All-Ireland SFC: 0
National Football League: 0
Last five years:
  2000: Defeated Laois, but ran into a wall in the form of Dublin in the provincial semi-final.
  2001: Lost to Meath twice, in the Leinster opening round and, after a replay, in the All-Ireland quarter-final. In between, chalked up victories over Limerick, Wexford (after a replay), Louth and Mayo.
  2002: Again lost to Meath in Leinster quarter-final, after opening with a victory over Carlow. Defeated Antrim, but collapsed in the face of Fermanagh in the Qualifier series.
  2003: Again opened with victory over Carlow, and yet again fell to Meath after a replay. Worse lay in store in round one of the Qualifiers, with Monaghan registering something of a surprise.
  2004: Beat Offaly, Dublin and Wexford to qualify for decider, winning first provincial title after two hours of play with Laois. Derry halted their march in next round.
Top player: Rory O'Connell A controversial season last year included a court injunction, but the midfielder's talent has never been in doubt – or at least not since an All-Star performance back in 2001.

Penguin Ireland Guide ranking: **8**

Critics of Paidí Ó Sé's appointment as team manager are now a very rare species – it's simply impossible to argue with success. Westmeath were desperately disappointed to exit the All-Ireland series so soon after claiming their first senior provincial title, but the breakthrough in Leinster made last season one supporters and players in the county will never forget. Expectations are now set at a permanent high. It's incredible but true that reaching the All-Ireland quarter-final stage once again this season will not satisfy some of the fans.

Outlook
Commitment to the cause of defending their provincial title won't be lacking, but a difficult rematch with Laois looks likely at the semi-final stage if Westmeath find an early gear. After that, who knows what the summer might hold?

Westmeath squad 2004

	v Offaly Won 0-11 0-10	v Dublin Won 0-14 0-12	v Wexford Won 2-15 1-14	v Laois Drew 0-13 0-13	v Laois Won 0-12 0-10	v Derry Lost 0-13 2-9
Gary Connaughton	●	●	●	●	●	●
James Davitt	●	●	●	●	●	●
Donal O'Donoghue	●	●	●	●	●	●
John Keane	●	●	●	●	●	●
Michael Ennis	●	●	●	●	●	●
Damien Healy	●	●	●	●	●	●
Derek Heavin	●	●	●	●	●	●
Rory O'Connell	●			●	●	●
David O'Shaughnessy	●	●	●	●	●	●
Brian Morley	●	●	●	●	●	●
Gary Dolan	●	●	●	●	●	●
Alan Mangan	●	●	●	●	●	●
Fergal Wilson	●	●		●	●	●
Dennis Glennon	●	●	●	●	●	●
Des Dolan	●	●	●	●	●	●
JP Casey	◐		◐			
Paul Conway	◐	◐	◐	◐	◐	◐
Shane Colleary	◐		◐	◐	◐	◐
Joe Fallon	◐	◐	◐	◐	◐	◐
David Kilmartin		◐		◐		
David Mitchell		◐	◐	◐		
Colin Galligan			◐			
Aidan Lennon						
Fergal Murray						
Paul Martin						
Tom Stuart-Trainer						
Russell Casey						
Aidan Canning						
James Conroy						
Damien Gavin						

● Played from start ◐ Substituted on

Wexford squad 2004

	v Louth Won 2-10 0-8	v Kildare Won 0-12 0-10	v Westmeath Lost 1-14 2-15	v Offaly Won 2-14 0-15	v Derry Lost 2-5 2-16
John Cooper	●	●	●	●	●
Colm Morris	●	●		●	
Phillip Wallace	●	●	●	●	●
Niall Murphy	●	●	●	●	●
Darragh Breen	●	●	●	●	●
David Murphy	●	●	●	●	●
George Sunderland	●	●			◐
Paddy Colfer	●	●	●	●	●
Willie Carley	●	●	●	●	●
David Fogarty	●		●	●	●
John Hudson	●	●	●		●
Redmond Barry	●	●	●	●	●
John Hearty	●	●	◐		◐
Darren Foran	●	●	●	◐	
Matty Forde	●	●	●	●	●
Leigh O'Brien	◐	◐	●	●	●
Nicky Lambert	◐	●			
Pat Forde	◐	◐	●	●	●
Jason Lawlor	◐	◐	●	●	●
Robert Hassey		◐	◐	◐	
Kieran Kennedy		◐			◐
Darren Browne			◐	●	
Poraic Curtis				◐	●
Jim D'Arcy					◐
Diarmuid Kinsella					◐
Anthony Masterson					
Gerry O'Grady					
Adrian Morrissey					
Nicky O'Sullivan					
Shane Howard					
Tom Wall					
James Holmes					
Gavin Morris					

● Played from start ◐ Substituted on

Wexford Loch Garman

Colours: Purple and gold
Stadium: Wexford Park, Wexford
Capacity: 25,000
GAA clubs: 87

Leinster SFC: 10
1890, 1893, 1913, 1914, 1915, 1916, 1917, 1918, 1925, 1945
All-Ireland SFC: 5
1893, 1915, 1916, 1917, 1918
National Football League: 0
Last five years:
   2000: Drew with Wicklow and beat Carlow in preliminary rounds in Leinster. Dublin were waiting in next round.
   2001: Exited provincial competition to Laois, then surrendered to Westmeath in first-round Qualifier after a replay.
   2002: Narrowly beaten by both Dublin and Tyrone, in the Leinster quarter-final and Qualifier round one respectively.
   2003: First-round Leinster loss to Laois, followed by equally disappointing first-round Qualifier defeat to Derry.
   2004: Defeated Louth and Kildare to make Leinster semi-final, where they lost to Westmeath. Bounced back to dump Offaly out of Qualifiers before running into a Derry side that was growing in confidence.
Top player: Matty Forde A simply outstanding talent. The county's fortunes live and die depending on the forward's mood. Scored two goals and 10 points against Offaly last season – enough, even if none of his team-mates had scored, to win the game by a point.

Penguin Ireland Guide ranking: **15**

After threatening much in recent years, Wexford finally made something of a breakthrough last season. There was a fine victory over Offaly, and the two counties that ended Wexford's campaigns – Westmeath and Derry – went on to have particularly successful summer runs.

Outlook
While Wexford may not have to hit the ground at a full run – meeting Carlow in their first game – they are unlikely to get past the semi-final. Depending on the Qualifier draw, it could still be a relatively long summer for the squad.

Wicklow squad 2004

	v Meath Lost 1–8 2–13	v Derry Lost 1–10 1–15
Robert Hollingsworth	●	●
Ciarán Hyland	●	●
Stevie Cushe	●	●
Thomas Burke	●	●
Clive Davis	●	○
Stephen Byrne	●	
Adrian Foley	●	●
Barry Sheehan	●	
Brendan Ó Hannaidh	●	●
Thomas Harney	●	●
Ronan Coffey	●	●
Alan Ellis	●	●
Tommy Gill	●	●
Tony Hannon	●	
Wayne O'Gorman	●	●
Ciarán Clancy	○	○
Donal McGillacuddy	○	
Leighton Glynn	○	●
Darragh Ó Hannaidh	○	●
Gary Doran		●
Trevor Doyle		●
Paddy Dalton		○
Barry Mernagh		○
Paul Cronin		○
Ian Burke		
Stephen Hurley		
Kieran Foley		
Anthony Nolan		
Brendan Brady		
Paul O'Riordan		
Liam Mooney		
Conor Flannery		

● Played from start   ○ Substituted on

Wicklow Cill Mhantáin

Colours: Blue and yellow
Stadium: Aughrim
Capacity: 7,000
GAA clubs: 65

Leinster SFC: 0
All-Ireland SFC: 0
National Football League: 0
Last five years:

2000: Defeated Carlow, lost to Longford and drew with Wexford in Leinster preliminary competition.

2001: Lost replayed first-round Leinster championship game to Carlow by one point. Beat Longford in Qualifier series before crashing out to Galway.

2002: Shipped too many goals to progress past Laois in opening round of provincial championship. Had an easy victory over London in Qualifier before surrendering meekly to Kerry.

2003: Crashed out of Leinster championship to Louth before equally disappointing performance against Carlow in Qualifier series.

2004: Defeated by Meath in provincial competition, then lost in a battling performance against Derry in round-one Qualifier.

Top player: Tommy Gill The county's recognized danger man for a few years now, the Rathnew forward has also tried his hand at soccer with Bray Wanderers. Wicklow quite simply could never afford to lose a player of his ability.

Penguin Ireland Guide ranking: **30**

Wicklow have tested the chaos theory and it doesn't appear to work. If the county could get everyone pulling in the same direction, the footballers would be a force to be reckoned with. But it hasn't happened, and a disastrous run of results – including pitiful displays against Louth and Carlow two seasons ago – were matched by exits to slightly better opposition last season.

Outlook

An opening-round meeting with neighbours Kildare will not have been the preferred choice, but at least it will give the county good preparation for an expected early dip in the Qualifier pool.

Munster

Clare An Clár

Colours: Yellow and blue
Stadium: Cusack Park, Ennis
Capacity: 24,000
GAA clubs: 88

Munster SFC: 2
1917, 1992
All-Ireland SFC: 0
National Football League: 0
Last five years:

2000: Beat Waterford and Tipperary en route to Munster final. Unfortunately for Clare, Kerry weren't in a generous mood.

2001: Fell to Cork in semi-final before Laois handed them a quick exit from the Qualifier series.

2002: Beat Waterford before drawing with Tipperary at Munster semi-final stage. Replay didn't go according to plan, and neither did Qualifier meeting with Laois.

2003: Heavily beaten by Limerick in provincial semi-final before again leaving the Qualifier series empty-handed after clash with Offaly.

2004: Defeated by Kerry, then registered a surprise victory over Sligo in round one of Qualifiers. Cork then ended their interest in championship.

Top player: Denis Russell Has produced more than his fair share of man-of-the-match performances for his county. A popular target-man for Clare defenders because he keeps the scoreboard regularly ticking over.

Penguin Ireland Guide ranking: **24**

The heights of 1992 are now a distant memory. However, despite playing only three championship games, Clare will not count last season as a total wash-out. Kerry were, as expected, much too strong in Munster, but a Qualifier victory over Sligo was followed by a dogged performance against Cork. If nothing else, the Sligo win demonstrated that the talent in Clare is there to be exploited – and a longer run in the Qualifier competition this season would go some way to encouraging it.

Outlook

After accounting for Waterford, Clare won't be expected to gain revenge over Cork in the provincial semi-final. Another victory, or two, in the Qualifiers is more than possible, though, depending on the luck of the draw.

Clare squad 2004	v Kerry Lost 0-9 2-10	v Sligo Won 1-15 1-7	v Cork Lost 0-11 0-15
Dermot O'Brien	●	●	●
Padraig Gallagher	●	●	●
Connor Whelan	●	●	●
Kevin Dilleen	●	●	●
Noel Griffin	●		●
Brian Considine	●	●	●
Ronan Slattery	●	●	●
David Russell (Kilkee)	●	●	●
Donal O'Sullivan	●		●
Ger Quinlan	●	●	●
Denis Russell	●	●	●
Odran O'Dwyer	●	●	●
Colin Mullen	●	●	
Enda Coughlan	●	●	●
Shaun O'Meara	●	●	●
Stephen Hickey	●	●	●
Evan Talty	●	●	
Michael O'Shea	●	●	●
Michael O'Dwyer	●	●	
David Russell (Clarecastle)	●		●
Alan Clohessy		●	●
Ciarán Considine		●	
Dara Blake		●	
Rory Donnelly			●
David McInerney			
Daragh Kelly			
Ger Tubridy			
John Moody			
Michael Maloney			
Francis O'Dea			
David Neylon			

● Played from start   ● Substituted on

Cork squad 2004

	v Kerry Lost 0–7 0–15	v Clare Won 0–15 0–11	v Fermanagh Lost 0–12 0–18
Kevin O'Dwyer	●	●	●
Sean O'Brien	●	●	●
Derrick Kavanagh	●	●	●
Noel O'Leary	●		
Eoin Sexton	●	●	●
Martin Cronin	●	●	●
Gary Murphy	●	●	●
Graham Canty	●	●	●
Diarmuid Hurley	●	●	
Alan Cronin	●	●	●
Conor McCarthy	●	●	●
Ciarán O'Sullivan	●	○	●
Colin Crowley	●	●	●
Michael Ó Croinín	●	●	○
Kevin O'Sullivan	●	○	
Nicholas Murphy	○	●	●
Kevin McMahon	○		
Michael O'Sullivan	○	○	●
Fionan Murray	○		○
Colin Corkery		●	●
Brendan J O'Sullivan		●	○
Sean Levis		○	●
Conor Brosnan		○	
Kieran O'Connor		○	
Kevin Murphy			
Noel O'Donovan			
Maurice McCarthy			
Alan O'Regan			
Padraig Griffin			
Brian O'Regan			
Paddy Nealon			
Alan Quirke			
Kieran O'Connor			
Anthony Lynch			
Philip Clifford			

● Played from start   ○ Substituted on

Cork Corcaigh

Colours: Red and white
Stadium: Pairc Uí Chaoimh, Cork
Capacity: 42,000
GAA clubs: 259

Munster SFC: 34
1890, 1891, 1893, 1894, 1897, 1899, 1901, 1906, 1907, 1911, 1916, 1923, 1928, 1943, 1945, 1949, 1952, 1956, 1957, 1966, 1967, 1971, 1973, 1974, 1983, 1987, 1988, 1989, 1990, 1993, 1994, 1995, 1999, 2002
All-Ireland SFC: 6
1890, 1911, 1945, 1973, 1989, 1990
National Football League: 5
1952, 1956, 1980, 1989, 1999
Last five years:
2000: Beat Limerick in round one of Munster competition before running into Kerry at semi-final stage.
2001: Accounted for Waterford and Clare before succumbing to Kerry in Munster final. Lost to Galway in Qualifier series.
2002: Needed two hours to defeat Kerry, and another two to beat Tipperary in the provincial final. Beat Mayo in the All-Ireland quarter-final before losing to Kerry in semi-final.
2003: Disastrous season, losing to Limerick and Roscommon in the first rounds of the Munster championship and Qualifier series respectally.
2004: Lost to Kerry before recovering to account for Clare in Qualifier clash. Croke Park and Fermanagh, however, signalled the end of Cork's season.
Top player: Colin Corkery He has never quite had the look of a modern-day GAA superstar, but appearances are deceptive. A fantastic footballer whose deadly accuracy has been invaluable to the Rebel County.

Penguin Ireland Guide ranking: **14**

Many Rebel County supporters didn't make the trip to Croke Park for their third-round Qualifier last summer, preferring instead to save their euros for a 'bigger' tie. However, the Fermanagh players – in one of the shocks of the season – saved those fans even more money, dumping Cork out of the competition. There's not much to suggest the Munster team will be any more of a championship threat this season.

Outlook
A generous draw means a Munster final appearance is almost a certainty, but winning the southern crown may represent the county's only chance of reaching the latter stages of the All-Ireland championship.

Kerry squad 2004

	v Clare Won 2-10 0-9	v Cork Won 0-15 0-9	v Limerick Drew 1-10 1-10	v Limerick Won 3-10 2-9	v Dublin Won 1-15 1-8	v Derry Won 1-17 1-11	v Mayo Won 1-20 2-9
Diarmuid Murphy	●	●	●	●	●	●	●
Tom O'Sullivan	●	●	●	●	●	●	●
Michael McCarthy	●	●	●	●	●	●	●
Aidan O'Mahony	●	●	●	●	●	●	●
Tómás Ó Sé	●	●	●	●	●	●	●
Eamon Fitzmaurice	●	●	●	●	●	●	●
Seamus Moynihan	●	●					○
Darragh Ó Sé	●	●	●	●	●	●	
William Kirby	●	●	●	○	○	●	●
Paul Galvin	●	○	●	●	●	●	●
Declan O'Sullivan	●	●			●	●	●
Eoin Brosnan	●	●	●	●	●	●	●
Colm Cooper	●	●	●	●	●	●	●
John Crowley	●	●	○	●	○	○	●
Mike Frank Russell	●	●	●	●	●	○	○
Michael Quirke	●						
Liam Hassett	○	●	●	●	○	●	●
Mark Ó Sé	○	○	●	●	●	●	●
Ronan O'Connor (F)	○						○
Dara Ó Cinnéide		○	●	●	●	○	●
Tommy Griffin			○	○		○	
John Sheahan			○		○		
Shaun O'Sullivan				○	○		
Paddy Kelly					●	○	○
Brendan Guiney							○
Kieran Cremin							
Donal Daly							
Declan Quill							
Seamus Scanlon							
Ronan O'Connor							
Brendan O'Mahony							
Noel Kennelly							
John Cronin							
Bryan Sheehan							
Ronan O'Flatharta							
Ciarán Mac Donnchaidh							

● Played from start   ○ Substituted on

Kerry Ciarraí

Colours: Green and yellow
Stadium: Fitzgerald Stadium, Killarney
Capacity: 39,000
Stadium: Austin Stack Park, Tralee
Capacity: 14,000
GAA clubs: 73

Munster SFC: 69
1892, 1903, 1904, 1905, 1908, 1909, 1910, 1912, 1913, 1914, 1915, 1919, 1924, 1925, 1926, 1927, 1929, 1930, 1931, 1932, 1933, 1934, 1936, 1937, 1938, 1939, 1940, 1941, 1942, 1944, 1946, 1947, 1948, 1950, 1951, 1953, 1954, 1955, 1958, 1959, 1960, 1961, 1962, 1963, 1964, 1965, 1968, 1969, 1970, 1972, 1975, 1976, 1977, 1978, 1979, 1980, 1981, 1982, 1984, 1985, 1986, 1991, 1996, 1997, 1998, 2000, 2001, 2003, 2004

All-Ireland SFC: 33
1903, 1904, 1909, 1913, 1914, 1924, 1926, 1929, 1930, 1931, 1932, 1937, 1939, 1940, 1941, 1946, 1953, 1955, 1959, 1962, 1969, 1970, 1975, 1978, 1979, 1980, 1981, 1984, 1985, 1986, 1997, 2000, 2004

National Football League: 17
1928, 1929, 1931, 1932, 1959, 1961, 1963, 1969, 1971, 1972, 1973, 1974, 1977, 1982, 1984, 1997, 2004

Last five years:
2000: Beat Cork and Clare to win provincial title. Needed two attempts to defeat Armagh in All-Ireland semi-final and another two to account for Galway in the final.
2001: Defeated Tipperary, Limerick and Cork en route to another Munster title. After overcoming Dublin at the second attempt, they fell to Meath in All-Ireland semi-final.
2002: Lost replayed Munster semi-final with Cork after defeating Limerick. Qualifier run threw up successful meetings with Wicklow, Fermanagh, Kildare, Galway and Cork before All-Ireland final meeting with Armagh resulted in a one-point defeat.
2003: Beat Tipperary and Limerick to win provincial crown. An All-Ireland quarter-final victory over Roscommon was followed by a heavy loss to Tyrone.
2004: Retained provincial crown with victories over Clare, Cork and, after a second attempt, Limerick. Followed wins over Dublin and Derry with All-Ireland final success again Mayo.
Top player: Seamus Moynihan They may have won last year's All-Ireland title largely without the former player of the year, but that doesn't lessen the importance of Kerry's most gifted footballer – no matter what position he plays in.

Penguin Ireland Guide ranking: **3**

Kerry players can decide the outcome of almost any match in the dressing-room before the game: if they walk on to the pitch in the right mood, no team can touch them. As last season's championship wore on and the finish-line eventually swung into view, the focus of the Kerry footballers sharpened. Dublin, Derry and Mayo played the Kingdom much too late in the summer to catch them off-guard – and Limerick missed their chance in the drawn Munster final. This team well and truly consigned the 2003 All-Ireland semi-final nightmare to the pages of history.

Outlook

After seeing off Tipperary in the first round of the Munster championship, the defending champions will have another tricky meeting with Limerick. Even if they don't retain the provincial crown, Kerry will still have a major say in the destination of the Liam McCarthy Cup at the end of the summer.

Limerick Luimneach

Colours: Green and white
Stadium: Gaelic Grounds, Limerick
Capacity: 49,500
GAA clubs: 107

Munster SFC: 1
   1896
All-Ireland SFC: 2
   1887, 1896
National Football League: 0
Last five years:

   2000: Faint hopes were quickly squashed with an early championship exit at the hands of Cork.

   2001: Beaten by Kerry in the Munster semi-final and then by Westmeath in the inaugural Qualifier series.

   2002: Again defeated by Kerry before recovering to upset Cavan in a replayed first-round Qualifier. Followed that fine win up with victory over Offaly before finally bowing out to Mayo by a single point.

   2003: Shocked Cork in first round of provincial competition before beating Clare to reach final. Kerry stood firm, however, as did Armagh in fourth Qualifier round.

   2004: Beat Tipperary and Waterford to again set up provincial decider with Kerry. Again Kerry won the crown, though a replay was needed this time. Met a Derry side that was gathering momentum in Qualifier round four.

Top player: Stephen Kelly The former International Rules player grows in importance each year for Limerick. Usually chips in with a couple of scores in every game, often vital ones.

Penguin Ireland Guide ranking: **10**

The Munster crown remains elusive, but the Treaty County is geared up for another major assault. Last season's draw with Kerry in the provincial final at the Gaelic Grounds may have been Limerick's best chance of winning the title; this season, just getting to the final will be a Herculean undertaking, as they will probably meet Kerry in the semi-final. Their Round Four defeat to Derry appeared calamitous at the time, but Derry's subsequent

Limerick squad 2004	v Tipperary Won 0–16 3–5	v Waterford Won 1–18 0–7	v Kerry Drew 1–10 1–10	v Kerry Lost 2–9 3–10	v Derry Lost 0–7 0–10
Mike Jones	●	●			
Mark O'Riordan	●	●	●	●	●
Johnny McCarthy	●	●	●	●	●
Tommy Stack	●	●	●	●	●
Conor Mullane	●	●	●	●	●
Stephen Lucey	●	●	●	●	●
Damien Reidy	●	●	●	●	●
John Galvin	●	●	●	●	●
John Quane	●	●	●	●	●
Stephen Kelly	●	●	●	●	●
Muiris Gavin	●	●	●	●	●
Michael O'Brien	●	●	●	●	●
Conor Fitzgerald	●	●	●	●	●
Eoin Keating	●	●	●	●	●
John Murphy	●	●	●	●	●
Timmy Carroll	○				
Maurice Horan	○	○			
Michael Reidy	○	○			○
Seamus O'Donnell		●	●	●	●
Padraig Browne		●			●
Stephen Lavin		○	○	○	○
Jason Stokes			●	●	●
Diarmuid Sheehy					
Colm Hickey					
Pat Ahern					
Darren Burke					
Peter O'Dea					
Darren Horan					
Stephen Fox					
Sean Kiely					

● Played from start   ○ Substituted on

defeat of Leinster champions Westmeath will have shown Limerick just how far they have progressed in a relatively short period of time.

Outlook

Meeting Kerry in the provincial semi-final might not be a bad thing – there is no better time to take on the All-Ireland champions than early in the summer. Still, a strong Qualifier run is much more likely.

Tipperary Tiobraid Árann

Colours: Blue and gold
Stadium: Semple Stadium, Thurles
Capacity: 54,000
GAA clubs: 82

Munster SFC: 9
    1888, 1889, 1895, 1900, 1902, 1918, 1920, 1922, 1935
All-Ireland SFC: 4
    1889, 1895, 1900, 1920
National Football League: 0
Last five years:

    2000: Quick and painless provincial semi-final loss to Clare.

    2001: Heavy defeat by Kerry, followed by a more disappointing loss at the hands of Louth in opening Qualifier game.

    2002: Successful replayed Munster tie with Clare set up provincial final clash with Cork. Lost chance for upset with draw in first game, then lost replay before exiting Qualifiers against Mayo.

    2003: Defeated Waterford, but ran out of luck in provincial semi-final against Kerry. Lost third-round Qualifier against Donegal after beating Carlow.

    2004: Disastrous championship season, beginning with loss to Limerick. Worse was to follow with club-versus-county row resulting in management and then players withdrawing and allowing Fermanagh a walk-over in Qualifier series.

Top player: Declan Browne A footballing giant – not just in Tipperary, but in the GAA as a whole – he can almost win a game on his own. A double All-Star winner (1998 and 2003) despite being from a 'weaker' county.

Penguin Ireland Guide ranking: **27**

What a disaster last year was. Or could it have been a blessing in disguise? Last season, after the Tipp management, and then the players, pulled out of the championship before their All-Ireland Qualifier meeting with Fermanagh, they received much criticism – not for complaining about the injustice of the situation they found themselves in, but for refusing to accept the inequality that exists between hurling and football. Hostilities may have ceased, but it may yet turn out to be a temporary ceasefire.

Tipperary squad 2004

	v **Limerick** Lost 3–5 0–16
Brian Enright	●
Benny Hahessy	●
Sean Collum	●
Niall Curran	●
Robbie Costigan	●
Damien Byrne	●
Glen Burke	●
Fergal O'Gallaghan	●
Kevin Mulryan	●
Liam England	●
Aidan Fitzgerald	●
Micheál Webster	●
Paul Cahill	●
Declan Browne	●
Damien O'Brien	●
John Paul Looby	●
Patrick Halley	●
Liam Cronin	●
James Williams	●
David Byrne	●
Paul Fitzgerald	
Tony Doyle	
Niall Fitzgerald	
Eamonn Hanrahan	
Cian Maher	
Willie Ryan	
Niall Sheehan	

● Played from start   ● Substituted on

Outlook
First-round meeting with Kerry? Terrific. After last season's shambles, Tipp deserve some luck in the Qualifiers – a victory or two would heal some wounds.

Waterford Port Láirge

Colours: Blue and white
Stadium: Walsh Park, Waterford
Capacity: 16,600
GAA clubs: 55

Munster SFC: 1
1898
All-Ireland SFC: 0
National Football League: 0
Last five years:

2000: Whatever interest existed quickly evaporated after first-round Munster meeting with Clare.

2001: Heavy defeat to Cork in provincial championship, followed by ultimately fruitless battle with Carlow in Qualifier series.

2002: Ran Clare close in Munster competition and Roscommon a little less close in Qualifier round one.

2003: Tipperary's turn to end their interest in Munster, before a wounded and dangerous Armagh inflicted a cruel hammering in first-round Qualifier.

2004: Ran into a confident Limerick side in provincial competition and a Longford team with something to prove in Qualifier round.

Top player: Kieran Connery The young Clashmore player is a star in the making. Played at corner back for the county in the minor championship only two years ago, before establishing himself as a first-team member of the senior squad last season.

Penguin Ireland Guide ranking: **31**

It is for teams such as Waterford that the GAA created the Tommy Murphy Cup. The Waterford senior footballers need games, not the easy option of spurning the secondary competition, as they did last season. Two years ago, in a first-round Qualifier, the county played the then All-Ireland champions Armagh – who were smarting from being dumped out of the Ulster championship – and received a 19-point drubbing. Last season, at the same stage, Waterford went to Pearse Stadium in Galway and finished nine points adrift of Longford. Progress? Well, at least under-age success is starting to seep through to the senior stage. Still, it's hard to see the county reaching the second round of the Qualifiers.

Outlook
Won't be afraid of Clare, though it would be a major upset if they were to win. A few years shy of producing a giant-killing side.

Waterford squad 2004

	v Limerick Lost 0–7 1–18	v Longford Lost 1–5 1–14
Paul Houlihan	●	●
John Moore	●	●
Eddie Rockett	●	●
Trevor Costelloe	●	●
Conan Watt	●	
Thomas Dunphy	●	●
Niall Hennessy	●	●
Karl O'Keeffe	●	●
Andy Hubbard	●	●
John Hearne	●	●
Mick Aherne	●	
John Coffey	●	
Liam Ó Loináin	●	●
Shane Walsh	●	
Ger Power	●	●
Kieran Connery	◐	◐
Billy Harty	◐	◐
Tony Whelan	◐	
Paul Ogle	◐	◐
Lee Hayes	◐	◐
William Kavanagh		●
Peter Queally		●
Niall Curran		●
Connie Power		◐
Tómás Wall		
David Hickey		
Michael Crotty		
Shane Dower		
Lee Quilty		
Sean Fleming		
Tommy Power		
David Whelan		

● Played from start　◐ Substituted on

Antrim squad 2004

	v Donegal Lost 1–9 1–15	v Louth Lost 0–14 2–13
Sean McGreevy	●	●
Niall Ward	●	●
Colm Brady	●	●
Tony Convery	●	●
Gearoid Adams	●	●
Sean Kelly	●	●
Anto Finnegan	●	●
Joe Quinn	●	●
Mark McCrory	●	●
Martin McCarry	●	●
Kevin Brady	●	●
Kevin McGourty	●	●
Paul Doherty	●	
Darren O'Hare	●	●
Kevin Madden	●	●
Mark Dougan	○	○
James Marron	○	●
John McKeever	○	○
Kevin Murray	○	○
Kevin Niblock		○
Andrew McClean		○
Chris Lynch		
Gavin Brown		
Owen O'Neill		
Niall Scullion		
Sean O'Hagan		
Conor McGoldrick		
Daryl Martin		
Hugh McKay		
Peter McCann		

● Played from start   ○ Substituted on

Ulster

Antrim Aontroim

Colours: Saffron and white
Stadium: Casement Park, Belfast
Capacity: 32,500
GAA clubs: 108

Ulster SFC: 10
   1900, 1901, 1908, 1909, 1910, 1911, 1912, 1913, 1946, 1951
All-Ireland SFC: 0
National Football League: 0
Last five years:
   2000: Sensationally beat Down in first round and took Derry to a replay at semi-final stage before eventually succumbing.
   2001: Lost twice to Derry, initially in first round of provincial championship, and then in Round Two of Qualifier series. In between, they beat Leitrim by two points.
   2002: Squashed by Derry in quarter-final by ten points, before bowing out to Westmeath by just one in Round One of the Qualifier series.
   2003: After overcoming Cavan, they were stopped at Ulster semi-final stage by eventual All-Ireland champions Tyrone. Unlucky to then meet reigning All-Ireland champions Armagh in Qualifier series, losing by only three points.
   2004: Disappointing season, losing not only to Donegal in Ulster, but also to an unfancied Louth in Qualifier series.
Top player: Gearoid Adams One of the county's most consistent performers. If the breakthrough of a few years ago is to be repeated, supporters know it is players such as the St John's defender that will deliver it.

Penguin Ireland Guide ranking: **25**

When will Antrim realize their full potential? Club rivalry has dragged the county down for years, and certainly contributed to the team's inability to take advantage of the significantly better results on the field at the turn of the century – though that wouldn't be difficult, considering that Antrim didn't actually win a single senior football championship game during the 1990s. With Ulster football at such a high level, the Qualifier series is the perfect avenue for Antrim to make big strides. They must do better than last season, when they lost to Louth in the opening round.

Outlook
A respectable defeat against Cavan in the Ulster quarter-final would set the county up for a longer Qualifier series campaign than usual – though, again, that wouldn't be particularly difficult.

Armagh squad 2004	v Monaghan Won 2–19 0–10	v Cavan Won 0–13 0–11	v Donegal Won 3–15 0–11	v Fermanagh Lost 0–11 0–12
Paul Hearty	●	●	●	●
Enda McNulty	●	●	●	●
Francie Bellew	●	●	●	●
Andy Mallon	●	●	●	●
Aidan O'Rourke	●	●	●	●
Kieran Hughes	●	●	●	●
Andrew McCann	●	●	◐	◐
Phillip Loughran	●		●	
Paul McGrane	●	●	●	●
Paddy McKeever	●	●	●	●
Tony McEntee	●	●	●	●
Oisín McConville	●	●	●	◐
Stephen McDonnell	●	●	●	●
Ronan Clarke	●	●	●	●
Martin O'Rourke	●	●		
Brian Mallon	◐	◐	◐	◐
Kevin McElvanna	◐	◐		◐
Stephen Kernan	◐			
John Toal		●	◐	●
Diarmuid Marsden		◐	●	●
Kieran McGeeney		◐	●	●
Justin McNulty			◐	
John McEntee			◐	
Phillip Loughran				
Ciarán McKinney				
Jean Paul Donnelly				
Aaron Kernan				
Paul McCormack				
Malachy Mackin				
Paul Watters				
Ciarán McKeever				

● Played from start   ◐ Substituted on

Armagh Ard Mhacha

Colours: Orange and white
Stadium: Athletic Grounds, Armagh
Capacity: 18,000

Ulster SFC: 11
  1890, 1902, 1950, 1953, 1977, 1980, 1982, 1999, 2000, 2002, 2004
All-Ireland SFC: 1
  2002
National Football League: 0
Last five years:
  2000: Beat Tyrone, Fermanagh (by one point) and Derry (also by one) to claim Ulster title. Kerry needed two games and extra-time at All-Ireland semi-final stage to halt their march.
  2001: Lost to Tyrone, before recovering to defeat Monaghan and Down in Qualifiers. Galway edged their clash, however, by one point.
  2002: Needed two games to defeat Tyrone, but only two more (against Fermanagh and Donegal) to reclaim Ulster title. A replay was needed to account for Sligo in All-Ireland quarter-final, and then a single point win over Dublin was followed by a similar one-point victory in All-Ireland final over Kerry.
  2003: Dumped into Qualifiers by Monaghan, then staged an impressive comeback to beat Waterford, Antrim, Limerick, Dublin, Laois and Donegal to make a second successive All-Ireland final appearance. Tyrone, however, were not to be denied their day.
  2004: Beat Monaghan, Cavan and Donegal to emerge undefeated in Ulster Championship. But then tripped up by Ulster opposition – Fermanagh – in All-Ireland quarter-final.
Top player: Steven McDonnell In a county that has an embarrassment of riches when it comes to talented forwards, he's still head and shoulders above his team-mates. It's a rare game when the double All-Star winner doesn't hit the target at least a couple of times.

Penguin Ireland Guide ranking: **2**

The only task harder than getting to the top is staying there. The 2002 All-Ireland champions have found the past couple of seasons progressively tougher, falling short against Tyrone two years ago in the All-Ireland final, and, surprisingly, to Fermanagh in the All-Ireland quarter-final last season. Despite this, apart from Kerry, no other team on the island has such strength in depth – and the need to atone for last season's shock exit will be occupying the mind of every squad member throughout this summer's campaign.

Outlook
Winning Ulster has never been more difficult. To do so, Armagh will need to defeat Fermanagh first, then Donegal in the quarter-final; after that, the likes of Derry and Tyrone might still lie in their path. Probably no other team has the ability to win all those

games, though. If Armagh can do it, what lies ahead in the All-Ireland championship will probably look easy in comparison.

Cavan An Cabhán

Colours: Blue and white
Stadium: Breffni Park, Cavan
Capacity: 20,000
GAA clubs: 59

Ulster SFC: 38
1891, 1903, 1904, 1905, 1915, 1918, 1919, 1920, 1922, 1923, 1924, 1925, 1926, 1928, 1931, 1932, 1933, 1934, 1935, 1936, 1937, 1939, 1940, 1941, 1942, 1943, 1944, 1945, 1947, 1948, 1949, 1952, 1954, 1955, 1962, 1967, 1969, 1997

All-Ireland SFC: 5
1933, 1935, 1947, 1948, 1952

National Football League: 1
1948

Last five years:
2000: Early exit in provincial championship, coming up against a much too strong Derry team.
2001: Beat Down and Monaghan on the way to Ulster final appearance, where they lost to Tyrone before meeting and losing to Derry in Qualifiers.
2002: Lost to Donegal, then engaged in two closely contested clashes with Limerick, eventually emerging on the wrong side.
2003: Shocked by Antrim in quarter-final. Recovered to account for Louth, before Fermanagh stepped in to end their interest in the championship.
2004: Needed two hours to defeat Down before running into Armagh's march to Ulster title. Then walked into a Derry side gearing up for an even stronger run.

Top player: Jason O'Reilly Has an ability to kick points from all angles and an impressive confidence that allows the Belturbet forward to go for goal when the opportunity arises, as teams such as Down have found out all too often.

Penguin Ireland Guide ranking: **21**

Fermanagh must be viewed with particular envy by Cavan supporters: it was not that long ago that Cavan was considered by many to be the new force in Ulster football. Alas, it has not worked out that way, and the county continues to struggle to gain a foothold in the upper levels of the game. Last season produced more highs than lows, but still can hardly be considered a success. In fact, the team's genuine potential was most evident in defeat, with Cavan running Armagh very close in the provincial semi-final. While the Derry defeat looked better in hindsight, rather than the misadventure it appeared on the day, the county's supporters will demand much more from their side in this campaign.

Cavan squad 2004	v Down Drew 1–13 1–13	v Down Won 3–13 2–12	v Armagh Lost 0–11 0–13	v Derry Lost 2–9 0–25
Eoghan Elliott	●	●	●	●
Eamonn Reilly	●	●		●
Darren Rabbitte	●	●	●	●
Paul Brady	●	●		
Anthony Forde	●	●	●	●
Trevor Crowe	●	●	●	●
Anthony Gaynor	●	●	●	●
Pearse McKenna	●	●	●	
Cathal Collins	●	●	●	●
Larry Reilly	●	●	●	●
Michael Lyng	●	●	●	●
Mark McKeever	●	●	●	●
Gerald Pearson	●	●	●	●
Jason O'Reilly	●	●	●	●
Seanie Johnston	●	●	●	●
Karl Crotty	◐	◐	◐	◐
Peter Reilly	◐	◐	◐	
Rory Donohoe		◐	◐	◐
Sean Brady		◐		
Dermot McCabe			◐	◐
Michael Bride			◐	◐
Shane Cole			◐	◐
Michael Hannon				◐
Nicholas Walsh				◐
Aaron Donohoe				
Andrew Coleman				
Sean Maguire				
Finbar O'Reilly				
Ciarán McGovern				
Seanie Smith				
Edward Jackson				
James Reilly				

● Played from start ◐ Substituted on

Outlook

Cavan are on the lighter side of the Ulster draw, but it's one that still includes Tyrone. While Antrim should be accounted for, the county will probably have to seek their fortune through the Qualifier series.

Derry Doire

Colours: Red and white
Stadium: Celtic Park, Derry
Capacity: 18,000
GAA clubs: 60

Ulster SFC: 7
1958, 1970, 1975, 1976, 1987, 1993, 1998
All-Ireland SFC: 1
1993
National Football League: 5
1947, 1992, 1995, 1996, 2000
Last five years:
2000: Beat Cavan in first round of provincial competition, and needed a replay to end Antrim's interest at semi-final stage. Lost to Armagh in final.
2001: Beat Antrim, but lost to Tyrone at semi-final stage. Had to defeat Antrim again, this time in Qualifiers, and then Cavan, Laois and Tyrone to qualify for All-Ireland semi-final. Opponents Galway, though, were in no mood to lose.
2002: Lost to Donegal in provincial semi-final, after first accounting for Antrim. Beat Longford in Qualifiers, then lost to Tyrone.
2003: Lost to eventual All-Ireland champions Tyrone after a replay. Beat Wexford in Qualifiers before shipping too many goals against Dublin.
2004: Went on a fantastic Qualifier run after losing to Derry in Ulster championship, beating Wicklow, Cavan, Wexford, Limerick and Westmeath. Kerry, however, stopped them in the All-Ireland semi-final.
Top player: Enda Muldoon A player who becomes more and more important to his team's success as the summer wears on. His ability to find the target under pressure has sent supporters home singing the Ballinderry man's praises on more then a few occasions.

Penguin Ireland Guide ranking: **9**

The Derry players took their supporters on a roller-coaster ride last season, with even their home victory over Cavan early in the Qualifier series considered something of a surprise. Almost two months later, remarkably, the team was on the cusp of an All-Ireland final appearance. This season, Derry supporters have good reason to view the championship with renewed hope.

Outlook

While Monaghan cannot be taken for granted, Derry supporters will not settle for anything less than a provincial semi-final date. An early entry to the Qualifiers series is likely, but so is another strong run from there.

Derry squad 2004

	v Tyrone Lost 1-6 1-17	v Wicklow Won 1-15 1-10	v Cavan Won 0-25 2-9	v Wexford Won 2-16 2-5	v Limerick Won 0-10 0-7	v Westmeath Won 2-9 0-13	v Kerry Lost 1-11 1-17
Barry Gillis	●	●	●	●	●	●	●
Sean Marty Lockhart	●	●		●	●	●	●
Niall McCusker	●	●	●	●	●	●	●
Padraig Kelly	●	●	●	●	●	●	●
Padraig O'Kane	●		●	●			
Kevin McGuckin	●	●		●	●	●	●
Francis McEldowney	●	●	●	●	●	●	●
Fergal Doherty	●	●	●	●	●	●	●
Patsy Bradley	●	●	●	●	●	●	●
Conleth Gilligan	●	●	●	●	●	●	●
Enda Muldoon	●		●	●	●	●	○
Johnny McBride	●	●	●	●		●	●
Jim Kelly	●	●					
Paddy Bradley	●	●	●	●	●	●	○
Paul McFlynn	●		●	●	●	●	●
Ryan Lynch	○						
James Donaghy	○	○	○	○	○	○	○
Johnny Bradley	○		○	○	○	○	○
Gerard O'Kane		●	●	●	●	●	●
Conleth Moran		●	●	●	●	●	●
Eamon Burke		●		●		●	●
Fergal McEldowney		○					
Dominic McIvor			○				
Gavin Donaghy					○	○	○
Mark Lynch					○		○
Kevin McCloy							
Michael Conlan							
Paul Wilson							
Dermot Scullion							
Ciarán Mullan							
Conor McWilliams							
Conor O'Brien							

● Played from start   ○ Substituted on

Donegal squad 2004

	v Antrim Won 1-15 1-9	v Tyrone Won 1-11 0-9	v Armagh Lost 0-11 3-15	v Fermanagh Lost 0-12 1-10
Paul Durcan	●	●	●	●
Niall McCready	●	●	●	●
Raymond Sweeney	●	●	●	●
Damien Diver	●	●	●	
Eamonn McGee	●	●	●	
Barry Monaghan	●	●	●	●
Kevin Cassidy	●			○
Brendan Boyle	●	●	●	●
Brian McLoughlin	●	●		
Christy Toye	●	●	●	○
Michael Hegarty	●	●	●	●
Shane McDermott	●	○	●	○
Colm McFadden	●	●	●	●
Adrian Sweeney	●	●	●	●
Brendan Devenney	●	●	●	●
Paul McGonigle	○		○	●
Karl Lacy	○		○	●
Shane Carr	○	●	●	●
Brian Roper	○	●	●	●
Steven Cassidy		○		○
John Gildea		○	○	●
Rory Kavanagh		○	○	
John Haran			○	○
Noel McGinley				●
Barry Dunnion				○
Sean Sweeney				
Jim McGuinness				
Johnny McCafferty				
Neal Gallagher				
Dessie McNamara				
Conal Dunne				
Eamon Reddin				

● Played from start   ○ Substituted on

Donegal Dún na nGall

Colours: Green and gold
Stadium: Mac Cumhaill Park, Ballybofey
Capacity: 17,500
GAA clubs: 63

Ulster SFC: 5
1972, 1974, 1983, 1990, 1992
All-Ireland SFC: 1
1992
National Football League: 0
Last five years:

2000: Maintained only flashing interest in championship, losing to Fermanagh in Ulster's first round.

2001: Fermanagh again got the better of the county, though this time only after a replay. Revenge was immediate, though, with Fermanagh defeated at the start of the Qualifier series, before Kildare won the second-round tie.

2002: Defeated Cavan, Down and Derry to reach provincial final, where they lost to Armagh. Beat Meath in Qualifier round four before surrendering to Dublin in All-Ireland quarter-final, though only after a replay.

2003: Lost to Fermanagh in quarter-final, before going on a run through the back door – defeating Longford, Sligo, Down, Tipperary and, after a second attempt, Galway. Armagh proved a hurdle too high, however, in the All-Ireland semi-final.

2004: Wins over Antrim and Tyrone in Ulster promised much. However, a crushing defeat to Armagh in the provincial final (held in Croke Park) was followed by a surprising Qualifier loss to Fermanagh on more familiar ground – back in Clones.

Top player: Kevin Cassidy A player who doesn't take the 'back' in 'wing-back' all that seriously, preferring to get forward at timely opportunities. It's a quality that secured the young Gweedore man an All-Star three years ago.

Penguin Ireland Guide ranking: **12**

A few years ago Fermanagh dreaded meeting Donegal; now it's Donegal who must be sick of playing their neighbours, having lost to them two championship seasons in a row. Last year started brightly for Donegal, with a surprise victory over Tyrone the highlight of their Ulster campaign. It remains to be seen if the county can bounce back from the subsequent disappointments.

Outlook
A probable clash with Armagh will more than likely dump them into round one of the Qualifier series, but Donegal has the talent to embark on a summer run.

Down squad 2004

	v Cavan Drew 1–13 1–13	v Cavan Lost 2–12 3–13	v Carlow Won 1–19 1–13	v Tyrone Lost 0–10 1–15
Michael McVeigh	●	●	●	●
Michael Higgins	●			●
Alan Molloy	●	●	●	●
Adrian Scullion	●	●	●	●
John Clarke	●	●	●	●
Martin Cole	●	●	●	●
Sean Farrell	●	●	●	●
Brendan Coulter	●	●	●	●
Gregory McCartan	●	●	●	●
Liam Doyle	●		●	●
Shane Ward	●	●	●	●
Ronan Sexton	●	●	●	●
Eoin McCartan	●	●	●	
Dan Gordon	●	●	●	●
Danny Hughes	●	●	●	●
John Lavery	●	●		
Colin McCrickard	●		●	●
Aidan O'Prey	●	●	●	●
Brendan Grant		●	●	●
Ronan Murtagh		●	●	●
Ambrose Rodgers		●		
Aidan Brannigan			●	
Stephen Kearney			●	
Sean Ward				●
Aidan Fagan				●
Brendan McVeigh				
Aodhan Shields				
Kevin McGuigan				
Peter Turley				
Kalum King				
Joe Doran				
Brendan Ward				

● Played from start ● Substituted on

Down An Dún

Colours: Red and black
Stadium: Pairc Esler, Newry
Capacity: 19,000
GAA clubs: 70

Ulster SFC: 12
 1959, 1960, 1961, 1963, 1965, 1966, 1968, 1971, 1978, 1981, 1991, 1994
All-Ireland SFC: 5
 1960, 1961, 1968, 1991, 1994
National Football League: 4
 1960, 1962, 1968, 1983
Last five years:
 2000: A disaster of a season, losing to Antrim in their first outing in the Ulster championship.
 2001: The introduction of the Qualifier series only meant there were to be two losses, instead of one. After falling narrowly to Cavan, they had the misfortune to meet Armagh in the first round of the Qualifiers.
 2002: Easily defeated by Donegal in the Ulster quarter-final. They had no better luck in the Qualifier series, losing to Longford.
 2003: Beat Monaghan and Fermanagh en route to Ulster final, where they fell to Tyrone in a replay. A strong Donegal team was waiting in the Qualifiers.
 2004: Finished on losing side after two games with Cavan in provincial championship. Had more luck against Carlow, before running into a determined Tyrone.

Top player: Brendan Coulter Covers the entire playing field. Has managed to hit the back of the net on a number of vital occasions – including four times in five championship matches last season – despite usually lining out at midfield.

Penguin Ireland Guide ranking: **18**

It's been quite a while since Down were considered the giants of Ulster football. The rise and rise of other counties – particularly Tyrone and Armagh – in the province has caused a visible depreciation in the county's status. A revival was briefly signalled two years ago when Down reached the provincial decider, only for the team to collapse in the replayed tie against a team that had a different crown in their sights: the All-Ireland title. Since that loss to Tyrone, the fortunes of the county have floated perilously above the waterline, with the hard-fought victory over Cavan the highlight of a disappointing 2004 championship campaign.

Outlook
A very early move into the Qualifier series is probably inevitable as Tyrone are still performing at a higher level. If they regroup quickly, the championship campaign need not be a short one.

Fermanagh squad 2004

	v Tyrone Lost 0-12 1-13	v Meath Won 0-19 2-12	v Cork Won 0-18 0-12	v Donegal Won 1-10 0-12	v Armagh Won 0-12 0-11	v Mayo Drew 0-9 0-9	v Mayo Lost 1-8 0-13
Niall Tinney	●	●	●	●	●	●	●
Niall Bogue	●	●	●	●	●	●	●
Barry Owens	●	●	●	●	●	●	●
Hugh Brady	●	●	○	○	○	○	○
Raymond Johnston	●	●	●	●	●	●	●
Shane McDermott	●	●	●	●	●	●	●
Damian Kelly	●		○	○			
Marty McGrath	●	●	●	●	●	●	●
Liam McBarron	●	●	●	●	●	●	○
Eamonn Maguire	●	●	●	●	●	●	●
James Sherry	●	●	●	●	●	●	○
Mark Little	●	●	●	●	●	●	●
Ciarán O'Reilly	●	●	●	●	●	●	●
Stephen Maguire	●	●	●	●	●	●	●
Colm Bradley	●	●	●	●	●	●	●
Peter Sherry	○	○	○	○	●	●	●
Mark Murphy	○			○		○	
Darragh McGrath	○	○		○	○		
Declan O'Reilly		○	●	●			○
Ryan McCluskey		○	●	●	●	●	●
Eamonn Sherry		○					
Shane Goan		○		○			
Ciarán Boyle		○					
Tom Brewster			○	○	○	○	●
Sean Curry							
Gary Maguire							
Declan Deazley							
Sean Boyle							
Kieran Donnelly							
Ronan Gallagher							
Fergal Murphy							

● Played from start   ○ Substituted on

Fermanagh Fear Manach

Colours: Green and white
Stadium: Brewster Park, Enniskillen
Capacity: 18,000
GAA clubs: 50

Ulster SFC: 0
All-Ireland SFC: 0
National Football League: 0
Last five years:

2000: Beat Monaghan and Donegal in early stages of Ulster championship. One-point loss to Armagh at semi-final stage.

2001: Two games against Donegal finally resulted in victory. However, subsequent quarter-final loss to Monaghan was followed by cruel Qualifier exit at hands of Donegal.

2002: Lost to Armagh in provincial semi-final after first beating Monaghan. Impressive win over Westmeath in Qualifier series followed by heavy loss to Kerry.

2003: Defeated Donegal, but stopped by Down at semi-final stage. Embarked on Qualifier run that included victories over Cavan, Mayo and Meath. All-Ireland quarter-final loss to Tyrone.

2004: Season started with defeat to Tyrone in the provincial championship. However, an incredible Qualifier run ensued – started by a walk-over from Tipperary – with victories over Meath, Cork, Donegal and Armagh. After two hours of football, Mayo edged them to reach the All-Ireland final.

Top player: Tom Brewster A gifted forward the county simply couldn't afford to lose – though they did for a short while last season. A genius is always worth waiting for. Last season brought a new meaning to the term 'super sub'.

Penguin Ireland Guide ranking: **6**

A flash in the pan? After the 2003 championship, there were many who considered the county's championship run – which included victories over Donegal, Cavan, Meath and Mayo – to be just that. But the team that likes to embarrass pundits produced an even more surprising and successful campaign last year. Could it be that the secret of championship success is a high rate of player turnover? Probably not, though Fermanagh seem to be providing plenty of evidence to the contrary. With the return in 2005 of a few players who have been absent for a season or two, suddenly the county has an embarrassment of riches.

Outlook

Fermanagh's dubious reward for last season is an opening tie against Armagh. It would be a mammoth task to emerge unscathed from Ulster, but the county seems more comfortable in the Qualifier series anyway.

Monaghan Muineachán

Colours: White and blue
Stadium: St Tiernach's Park, Clones
Capacity: 36,000
GAA clubs: 50

Ulster SFC: 13
 1888, 1906, 1914, 1916, 1917, 1921, 1927, 1929, 1930, 1938, 1979, 1985, 1988

All-Ireland SFC: 0

National Football League: 1
 1985

Last five years:
 2000: Beaten by Fermanagh in first-round Ulster championship tie.
 2001: Gained revenge by dumping Fermanagh out of provincial championship, but couldn't build up any momentum, losing to Cavan in Ulster semi-final and Armagh in Qualifier series.
 2002: Came out on the wrong side of a clash with Fermanagh in Ulster, then had an equally poor result against Louth in first-round Qualifier.
 2003: Shocked All-Ireland champions Armagh, but then fell to Down in Ulster quarter-final. Recovered to defeat Westmeath, but couldn't repeat the feat against Meath in second-round Qualifier.
 2004: Heavily defeated by an Armagh side still smarting from the previous year, and luck didn't change in first-round Qualifier against Longford.

Top player: Thomas Freeman Well established now as the county's main threat going forward, which means opposition defenders are aware of his talent and pay him particularly close attention.

Penguin Ireland Guide ranking: **23**

The performances of 2003 – which included the defeat of the All-Ireland champions, Armagh – are now a distant memory. Last season, more or less the same team exited the provincial and Qualifier competitions in quick and brutal fashion, leaving supporters, players and officials at a loss to explain the collapse.

Outlook
Monaghan will pose an extremely difficult opening opponent for Derry, but then there are few 'handy' ties left in Ulster. Depending on the draw, some salvation can be sought from the Qualifiers.

Monaghan squad 2004	v Armagh Lost 0–10 2–19	v Longford Lost 1–17 4–15
Glen Murphy	●	●
Gary McQuaid	●	●
James Coyle	●	●
Edmund Lennon	●	●
Dermot Duffy	●	●
Dick Clerkin	●	●
Vincent Corey	●	●
Jason Hughes	●	○
Eoin Lennon	●	●
Paul Finlay	●	●
Thomas Freeman	●	●
Dessie Mone	●	○
Kieran Tavey	●	○
Raymond Ronaghan	●	○
Damien Freeman	●	●
Rory Woods	○	●
John Paul Mone	○	●
Dermot McDermott	○	
James Conlon	○	
Nicholas Corrigan	○	●
Padraig McKenna		●
Michael Slowey		○
Damian Larkin		○
Paul McElroy		
Dermot McArdle		
Rory Treanor		
Francis Doogan		
Colm Flanagan		
Francis Markey		
Mark Duffy		
Rory Mone		

● Played from start ○ Substituted on

Tyrone squad 2004

	v Derry Won 1–17 1–6	v Fermanagh Won 1–13 0–12	v Donegal Lost 0–9 1–11	v Down Won 1–15 0–10	v Galway Won 1–16 0–11	v Laois Won 3–15 2–4	v Mayo Lost 1–9 0–16
John Devine	●	●	●			○	
Ryan McMenamin	●	●	●	●	●	●	●
Conor Gormley	●	●	●	●	●	●	●
Ciarán Gourley	●	●	●	●	●	○	●
Brendan Donnelly	●						
Gavin Devlin	●	●					
Philip Jordan	●	●	●	●	●	●	●
Colin Holmes	●	●	○				
Sean Cavanagh	●	●	●	●	●	●	●
Brian Dooher	●	●	●	●	●	●	●
Brian McGuigan	●	●	●	●	●	●	○
Enda McGinley	●		○				
Mark Harte	●	●	●	●		●	●
Kevin Hughes	●	●	●	●	●	●	●
Colm McCullagh	●	●		○			○
Joe McMahon	○	●	●	●	●	●	●
Stephen O'Neill	○	●	●	●	●	●	●
Eoin Mulligan		●	●				
Gerard Cavlan		○	●	●	●	●	●
Michael Coleman		○			●		
Shane Sweeney			●	●	●	●	●
Michael McGee			○			●	●
Pascal McConnell				●	●	●	●
Owen Mulligan				●	●	●	●
Peter Canavan					○		○
Leo Meenan					○		
Barry Collins					○	○	
Chris Lawn					○		
Dermot Carlin							○

● Played from start   ○ Substituted on

Tyrone Tír Eoghain

Colours: White and red
Stadium: Healy Park, Omagh
Capacity: 18,000
GAA clubs: 68

Ulster SFC: 10
  1956, 1957, 1973, 1984, 1986, 1989, 1995, 1996, 2001, 2003
All-Ireland SFC: 1
  2003
National Football League: 2
  2002, 2003
Last five years:
  2000: First-round Ulster championship defeat to Armagh.
  2001: Gained revenge against Armagh before beating Derry and Cavan to claim provincial title. Derry gained revenge of their own in All-Ireland quarter-final.
  2002: Lost to Armagh in Ulster quarter-final replay. More success in Qualifiers, beating Wexford, Leitrim and Derry before falling to Sligo in round four.
  2003: Needed five matches – two against Derry, one with Antrim and two against Down – to claim Ulster title. No such problems in All-Ireland championship, with straightforward victories over Fermanagh, Kerry and Armagh to claim the biggest prize in football.
  2004: Claimed scalps of Derry and Fermanagh before losing to Donegal in Ulster semi-final. Got back on track with wins over Down, Galway and Laois before Mayo stoped them in the All-Ireland semi-final.
Top player: Owen Mulligan Not happy with having just one supremely talented forward, the county fashioned another in the mould of Peter Canavan. When he's on form, he's untouchable.

Penguin Ireland Guide ranking: **5**

It was always going to be difficult to repeat the achievement of 2003. The tragic loss of Cormac McAnallen was, of course, felt on the pitch as well as off it, and Tyrone struggled to build up the kind of momentum that had helped them steamroll sections of the previous season's championship. Nonetheless, the team possesses the firepower and support staff to challenge for the All-Ireland title once more.

Outlook
Ulster is there for the taking and Tyrone know it: Armagh, Fermanagh, Donegal and Derry are all on the opposite side of the draw, so an appearance in the final is more than likely. After that, Tyrone's fortunes will depend on the team's ability to rediscover its ruthless streak.

Galway squad 2004

	v London Won 8-14 0-8	v Mayo Lost 1-9 0-18	v Louth Won 2-8 0-9	v Tyrone Lost 0-11 1-16
Brian O'Donoghue	●	●	●	●
Barry Dooney	●	●	●	
Kieran Fitzgerald	●	●	●	●
Clive Monaghan	●			
Declan Meehan	●	●	●	●
Paul Clancy	●	●	●	●
Seán Óg de Paor	●			
Joe Bergin	●	●	●	●
Seán Ó Domhnaill	●	●		●
Tommy Joyce	●	●	●	○
Michael Donnellan	●	●	●	●
John Devane	●	○	○	●
Micheal Meehan	●	●	●	●
Padraic Joyce	●	●	●	●
Nicky Joyce	●			○
Matthew Clancy	○	●	●	●
Derek Savage	○	●	●	●
Michael Comer	○	●		
Noel Meehan	○		○	○
Damian Burke	○	○	○	●
Tomas Meehan		●	●	●
Kevin Walsh		○	●	
Gary Fahy			●	●
Darren Mullahy				○
Alan Keane				
Lorcan Colleran				
David Ward				
Richard Fahey				

● Played from start ○ Substituted on

Connacht

Galway Gaillimh

Colours: Maroon and white
Stadium: Pearse Stadium, Galway
Capacity: 35,000
Stadium: Tuam Stadium, Tuam
Capacity: 30,000
GAA clubs: 86

Connacht SFC: 42
1900, 1903, 1911, 1913, 1917, 1919, 1922, 1925, 1926, 1933, 1934, 1938, 1940, 1941, 1942, 1945, 1954, 1956, 1957, 1958, 1959, 1960, 1963, 1964, 1965, 1966, 1968, 1970, 1971, 1973, 1974, 1976, 1982, 1983, 1984, 1986, 1987, 1995, 1998, 2000, 2002, 2003

All-Ireland SFC: 9
1925, 1934, 1938, 1956, 1964, 1965, 1966, 1998, 2001

National Football League: 4
1940, 1957, 1965, 1981

Last five years:
2000: Accounted for New York, Sligo and Leitrim to win Connacht title. After passing the challenge of Kildare, Kerry proved too tough – albeit after a replay.
2001: Shocked by Roscommon in the provincial first round. Went on a successful Qualifier campaign, beating Wicklow, Cork, Armagh, Roscommon and Derry, before claiming the Sam Maguire Cup with victory over Meath.
2002: Defeated Roscommon, Mayo and Sligo to win provincial crown. Caught at All-Ireland quarter-final stage by Kerry steamroller.
2003: Claimed a second Connacht title in a row, beating Roscommon, Leitrim and Mayo en route. Lost to Donegal in replayed All-Ireland quarter-final.
2004: Lost to Mayo after easy preliminary tie with London. A Qualifier victory over Louth was followed by defeat in round three to Tyrone.
Top player: Padraic Joyce Irreplaceable – for club, county and country. Made a surprise return for Killererin to win the county final last October and was subsequently captain of the International Rules squad.

Penguin Ireland Guide ranking: **11**

With John O'Mahony no longer at the helm, many have been tempted to write obituary notes to mark the end of the county's glory years. However, Galway still possesses a frighteningly talented side, and although their neighbours to the north are muscling in on Galway's provincial domination, there is certainly the talent to embark on a long summer run this season. Many of the seasoned players will not want last season's rather unseemly exit at the hands of Mayo and Tyrone to be their last hurrah.

Outlook
Another appearance in the provincial decider looks more

than likely for this team, and they will be determined not to repeat last season's performance. After that, it's just a hop, skip and a jump to All-Ireland final day. That doesn't sound hard, does it?

Leitrim Liatroim

Colours: Green and gold
Stadium: Sean Mac Diarmada, Carrick-on-Shannon
Capacity: 13,500
GAA clubs: 33

Connacht SFC: 2
1927, 1994
All-Ireland SFC: 0
National Football League: 0
Last five years:
2000: Defeated Roscommon in semi-final, but it was to be Galway's provincial title.
2001: Beaten by Galway in provincial first round and Antrim in Qualifier first round.
2002: Beat London, but lost to Sligo in Connacht semi-final. Unfortunately, Tyrone were lying in wait in the Qualifiers.
2003: Defeated New York, then bowed out to Galway in provincial semi-final. Desperately unlucky to fall to Roscommon in round two of Qualifier series.
2004: Took Roscommon to a second game in the Connacht championship before eventually surrendering. Dublin were in no mood to entertain an upset in their Qualifier clash.
Top player: Michael Foley In a inter-county squad not renowned for its scoring forwards, Foley is a godsend. Supporters have come to realize their team's performances depend very much on his performances.

Penguin Ireland Guide ranking: **28**

It's over ten years now since bonfires last burned throughout the county after the Connacht final. While there may not be much reason for tyres to start disappearing from farms in the county again any time soon, the current team has shown some of the confidence and ability of that 1994 side. Last season the players were desperately unlucky not to reach the provincial decider, with Roscommon needing two games to progress. And, in the Qualifier series, Leitrim was unlucky to draw a Dublin side that was still smarting from their Leinster exit.

Outlook
If Leitrim begin their championship campaign with the same confidence as last season, then Sligo may soon have another reason to feel sorry for themselves. Either way, though, with Galway waiting in the semi-finals the Qualifier series beckons. Leitrim deserve a better draw this season.

Leitrim squad 2004

Player	v Roscommon Drew 1-10 0-13	v Roscommon Lost 0-5 1-9	v Dublin Lost 0-4 1-13
Gareth Phelan	●	●	●
Dermot Reynolds	●	●	●
John McKeon	●	●	
Michael McGuinness	●	●	●
Niall Gilbane	●	●	●
Seamus Quinn	●	●	●
Barry Prior	●	●	●
Declan Maxwell	●	●	
Chris Carroll	●	●	●
John Goldrick	●	●	
Jimmy Guckian	●	●	●
Colin Regan	●	●	●
Donal Brennan	●	●	
Fintan McBrien	●	●	●
Michael Foley	●	●	●
Shane Canning	○	○	○
Pat Farrell	○	○	○
Noel Doonan	○		○
Dermot Kennedy		○	
Brendan Brennan		○	
Padraig Flynn			●
James Clancy			●
John McGuinness			●
Philly McGuinness			○
Declan Gilhooley			○
Ende Lyons			
Donnacha Lynch			
Padraig McGarry			
John Cullen			
David Duignan			
Barry McWeeney			
John McWeeney			

● Played from start   ○ Substituted on

Mayo Maigh Eo

Colours: Green and red
Stadium: McHale Park, Castlebar
Capacity: 35,000
GAA clubs: 52

Connacht SFC: 40
1901, 1902, 1904, 1906, 1907, 1908, 1909, 1910, 1914, 1916, 1918, 1920, 1921, 1923, 1924, 1929, 1930, 1931, 1932, 1935, 1936, 1937, 1939, 1948, 1949, 1950, 1951, 1955, 1967, 1969, 1981, 1985, 1988, 1989, 1992, 1993, 1996, 1997, 1999, 2004

All-Ireland SFC: 3
1936, 1950, 1951

National Football League: 11
1934, 1935, 1936, 1937, 1938, 1939, 1941, 1949, 1954, 1970, 2001

Last five years:
2000: Surprisingly short season as Sligo emerged victorious from their first-round tie in Connacht.
2001: Better result against Sligo this time, but narrowly lost to Roscommon in the provincial final. Also beaten by Westmeath in Qualifier round four.
2002: Galway won Connacht semi-final clash. Better news in Qualifiers, beating Roscommon, Limerick and Tipperary before falling to Cork.
2003: Defeated Sligo, but again lost to Galway, this time in the provincial final. Worse news in Qualifiers, losing to Fermanagh in round four.
2004: Accounted for New York, Galway and Roscommon to claim provincial title. An impressive win over Tyrone was followed by a more laboured victory over Fermanagh, in a replay, to reach the All-Ireland final. Surrendered rather meekly to Kerry.

Top player: Ciarán McDonald How Mayo supporters rejoiced when the Crossmolina star decided to rejoin the county set-up last summer. He was instrumental in the county's long march to an ultimately unsuccessful All-Ireland final appearance.

Penguin Ireland Guide ranking: **4**

If only points were handed out for effort. The re-enlisting of Ciarán McDonald last summer was crucial to Mayo's long run to the All-Ireland final, but it was far from the full story – every single line looked stronger and more cohesive. Fermanagh almost slipped past the Connacht side – as they had in the Qualifier series the year before – but, apart from that drawn All-Ireland semi-final, there was little to suggest Mayo would concede so quickly in the decider. It may be hard to pick up where you left off after winning the All-Ireland final, but it is even harder after losing one.

Outlook
Mayo roared into life last season in the Connacht championship and many will be watching how they kick off this championship season.

Mayo squad 2004

Legend: ● Played from start ○ Substituted on

	v New York Won 3–28 1–8	v Galway Won 0–18 1–9	v Roscommon Won 2–13 0–9	v Tyrone Won 0–16 1–9	v Fermanagh Drew 0–9 0–9	v Fermanagh Won 0–13 1–8	v Kerry Lost 2–9 1–20
Peter Burke	●			●	●	●	●
Dermot Geraghty	●					○	●
Pat Kelly	●	○	○	○	●	●	●
Gary Ruane	●	●	●	●	●	●	●
Fergal Costello	●	●	●	●			
Declan Sweeney	●		○	○			
James Nallan	●	●	●	●		●	●
David Heaney	●	●	●	●	●	●	●
David Brady	●	○	●	●	●	○	○
James Gill	●	●	●	●	●	●	●
Alan Dillon	●	●	●	●	●	●	●
Andy Moran	●	○	○	○	○		○
Conor Mortimer	●	●	●	●	●	●	●
Brian Malloney	●	●	●	●	●	●	●
Marty McNicholas	●	●			○		
Austin O'Malley	○		○	○		○	
Ronan McGarrity	○	●	●	●	●	○	○
Michael Moyles	○						
Peader Gardiner	○	○	○	●	●	●	●
Gary Mullins	○	●	●		○		
Fintan Ruddy		●	●				
Conor Moran		●	●	●	●	●	○
Ciarán McDonald		●	●	●	●	●	●
Trevor Mortimer		●	●	●	●	●	●
Fergal Kelly						●	●
Damien Munnelly						○	
Michael Conroy							○
Pat Nevin							○
Liam O'Malley							
Brian Ruane							
Ronan McNamara							
Billy Joe Padden							
Alan Costello							
Michael Conroy							
David Clarke							
Gary Mullins							

● Played from start   ○ Substituted on

Roscommon squad 2004

	v Sligo Drew 1–10 0–13	v Sligo Won 2–16 1–15	v Leitrim Drew 0–13 1–10	v Leitrim Won 1–9 0–5	v Mayo Lost 0–9 2–13	v Dublin Lost 0–13 1–14
Shane Curran	●	●	●	●	●	●
John Whyte	●	●	●	●	●	●
Mike Ryan	●	●	●	●	●	●
John Nolan	●	○	●	●	●	
David Casey	●	○	●	●	●	●
Francie Grehan	●	●	●	●	●	●
John Rogers	○	●	○	○	○	○
Seamus O'Neill	●	○	●	●	●	●
Stephen Lohan	●	●	●	●	●	●
Gary Cox	●	●	●	●		
Nigel Dineen	●	●	●		○	●
Derek Connellan	●	○		●	○	
Ger Heneghan	●	●	●	●	○	●
Karl Mannion	●	●	●	●	●	○
Frankie Dolan	●	●	●	●	●	○
Paul Noone	○	●				
John Tiernan	○	○	○	○	●	○
Jarlath Egan	○					
Brian Higgins	○	●	●	○		○
Johnaton Dunning	○	○	●	●		
Andy McPadden		○	●		●	●
Eamon Towey		○		●		●
John Hanley			○	●	●	●
David O'Connor				○		
Rai Cox					○	●
Darren Lennon						
Paddy O'Connor						
Gerry Lohan						
Enda Kenny						
Mark O'Carroll						

● Played from start   ○ Substituted on

Roscommon Ros Comáin

Colours: Blue and yellow
Stadium: Hyde Park, Roscommon
Capacity: 25,000
GAA clubs: 51

Connacht SFC: 19
1905, 1912, 1915, 1943, 1944, 1946, 1947, 1952, 1953, 1961, 1962, 1972, 1977, 1978, 1979, 1980, 1990, 1991, 2001
All-Ireland SFC: 2
1943, 1944
National Football League: 1
1979
Last five years:
2000: Easy victory over London in opening round, followed by surprise loss to Leitrim in Connacht semi-final.
2001: Defeated Galway, New York and Mayo to claim provincial title. Came unstuck in All-Ireland quarter-final in second meeting with Galway.
2002: Lost to Galway in Connacht, then beat Waterford in Qualifiers before succumbing to Mayo.
2003: Again defeated by Galway, before a successful Qualifier run with victories over Cork, Leitrim, Kildare and Offaly. All-Ireland quarter-final meeting with Kerry proved a finishing note, however.
2004: Needed four matches – two with Sligo and two with Leitrim – to reach provincial decider. Loss to Mayo there, quickly followed by round-four Qualifier defeat to Dublin.
Top player: Frankie Dolan A supremely accurate footballer, whether from free-kicks or from play. When team-mates playing in defence win the ball and look up the field, it's this talented forward they usually aim for.

Penguin Ireland Guide ranking: **16**

Roscommon is one of the more unpredictable sides in the championship, and seems to enjoy keeping supporters guessing. There is the side with the ability to dump strong teams, such as Cork and Offaly, out of the championship, as they did in 2003 – but there's also the squad that has trouble dispatching the likes of Leitrim. Tommy Carr has worked hard to instil the missing quality of ruthlessness into his team.

Outlook
While London will ease the county rather gently into the new championship season, the subsequent game against Mayo will be a titanic challenge – and one that will provide an accurate indicator of the team's realistic ambitions for the season.

Sligo squad 2004

	v Roscommon Drew 0–13 1–10	v Roscommon Lost 1–15 2–16	v Clare Lost 1–7 1–15
Philip Greene	●	●	●
Noel McGuire	●	●	●
Patrick Naughton	●		
Brendan Philips	●	●	
Johnny Martyn	●	●	●
Michael Langan	●	●	●
Philip Gallagher	●		
Gary Maye	●		
Sean Davey	●	●	●
Kieran Quinn	●	○	●
Mark Breheny	●	●	○
Eamonn O'Hara	●	●	●
Dessie Sloyan	●	●	●
Michael McNamara	●	●	●
Gerry McGowan	●	●	○
Padraig Doohan	○	●	●
Brian Curran	○	●	●
Philip Neary	○		
Jonathon Davey	○	○	○
David Durkin		●	○
Paul Taylor		●	●
Dara McGarty		○	●
Paul Durcan		○	○
Neil Carew			●
Nigel Clancy			●
Jeffrey Durcan			
Adrian Marren			
John McPartland			
Tommy Brennan			
Tony Taylor			
Colin Neary			

● Played from start   ○ Substituted on

Sligo Sligeach

Colours: Black and white
Stadium: Markievicz Park, Sligo
Capacity: 13,000
GAA clubs: 51

Connacht SFC: 2
  1928, 1975
All-Ireland SFC: 0
National Football League: 0
Last five years:
  2000: Defeated Mayo, but lost heavily in Connacht semi-final to Galway.
  2001: Mayo gained revenge in provincial semi-final. Qualifier victories were gained over Carlow and Kildare before Dublin proved a bridge too far.
  2002: Defeated Sligo and Leitrim before falling to Galway in provincial decider. Bounced back with impressive victory over Tyrone and draw with soon-to-be All-Ireland champions Armagh, before bowing out in replay.
  2003: Lost to Mayo in provincial semi-final, after beating London. Lost in first-round Qualifier to Donegal.
  2004: Made Roscommon play two hours of football before allowing them to pass. Clare didn't find it quite so difficult in round-one Qualifier meeting.
Top player: Eamonn O'Hara The great white hope of Sligo football. It is no exaggeration to say that almost every attacking move goes through the half forward. Often worth the admission fee on his own.

Penguin Ireland Guide ranking: **20**

The last two campaigns have been an unmitigated disaster, culminating in a collapse in Ennis last June in the first round of the Qualifier series. For a team that took Armagh to a replay in 2002, it was a major backward step – and last season's public row over the county's participation in the secondary competition, the Tommy Murphy Cup, hasn't helped either. Supporters will be justifiably confused as to whether they should view this season with hope or trepidation.

Outlook
The county's losing streak in the championship should end when they meet Leitrim, but Galway will probably knock them into the Qualifiers.

London Londain

Colours: Green and white
Stadium: Emerald Grounds, Ruislip
Capacity: 5,000
GAA clubs: 38

Provincial SFC: 0
All-Ireland SFC: 0
National Football League: 0
Last five years

2000: Proved no match for Roscommon in the first round of provincial competition.

2001: The Foot and Mouth outbreak in England meant their game with Mayo, due to be played in Ruislip at the end of May, was called off.

2002: Lost Connacht quarter-final to Leitrim and then Qualifier series tie with Wicklow.

2003: Beaten by Sligo and Offaly in Connacht championship and Qualifier competition respectively.

2004: Galway registered eight goals at Ruislip. In the Qualifier series it was target practice for Dublin at Parnell Park.

Top player: Barry McDonagh A fixture in the London team for years, despite the high turnover of squad members. The Tír Chonaill Gaels player was missed against Dublin last season.

Penguin Ireland Guide ranking: **32**

Although years of economic prosperity in Ireland have stifled the flow of players to London, the city has managed to continue participating in the football league and championship. The level of commitment shown by some of the players and officials – apart from the tricky logistics of playing so many games against Irish counties – is simply phenomenal. That commitment was well rewarded last season when they overcame Carlow in their league tie at Dr Cullen Park, the city's first league win in four years. A small victory, perhaps, but certainly not undeserved.

Outlook

After the Roscommon game, London will not want to be matched with a high-profile team in the first Qualifier round again: playing Dublin last year was all well and good, but a more beatable team would be preferable.

London squad 2004	v Galway Lost 0-8 8-14	v Dublin Lost 0-6 3-24
Gary McEvoy	●	
Charlie Harrison	●	●
Damien McKenna	●	●
Shaun Murphy	●	●
Aidan McLarnon	●	●
John Niblock	●	●
Karl Scanlon	●	○
Gary Kane	●	●
Paddy Quinn	●	●
Scott Doran	●	●
Fergus McMahon	●	●
Brendan Egan	●	●
Patrick Lynott	●	●
Daragh Kineavey	●	●
Barry McDonagh	●	
Seamus Byrnes	○	○
Gordan Weldon	○	●
Morgan Drea	○	
Teu Ó hAilpín	○	○
Michael Lillis	○	●
Brian McGonigle		●
Ciarán Slane		○
Fergal Hoban		
Padraig Donoghue		

● Played from start   ○ Substituted on

New York squad 2004

	v **Mayo** Lost 1–8 3–28
Eunan Doherty	●
Dermot Costello	●
Paul O'Connor	●
Pa Murphy	●
Martin Sloey	●
Kevin Newell	●
David Callaghan	●
Kenny O'Connor	●
Jason Killeen	●
Shane McInerney	●
Eric Bradley	●
Bingo O'Driscoll	●
Kevin Lilly	●
Shane Russell	●
Brian Newman	●
Gary Dowd	●
Jamie Shaw	●
Paul Higgins	●
Mark Dobbin	●
Evan Byrne	
Danny O'Sullivan	
Mike Keaveney	
Eddie Greenan	
Paul Murray	
John Walsh	
Rory O'Neill	
Paddy Harrington	
Tadhg Foley	
Kevin Fitzgerald	
Barry Annette	

● Played from start ● Substituted on

New York

Colours: White and blue
Stadium: Gaelic Park
Capacity: 6,500
GAA clubs: 50

Provincial SFC: 0
All-Ireland SFC: 0
National Football League: 0
Last five years:

2000: First-round loss to Connacht kingpins Galway.
2001: Fell to Roscommon in provincial quarter-final. Didn't enter Qualifier series.
2002: Another Connacht quarter-final meeting didn't go to plan, this time against Sligo.
2003: Desperately unlucky to maintain losing streak in Connacht championship, as Leitrim scrapped through.
2004: Unfortunate to come up against a Mayo side intent on a long campaign.

Top player: Bingo O'Driscoll An important part of the team that so very nearly shocked Leitrim two years ago at Gaelic Park. Unfortunately last year, against Mayo, the forward could do little about the result.

Penguin Ireland Guide ranking: **33**

With a potential pick of around 20 million people, you'd think New York would have a better record in the football championship. Last year, major controversy enveloped the domestic football championship in the city, but there are still ambitious plans to move to a new stadium and to develop the game in other ways.

Outlook
Due to time and travel difficulties, New York can't avail of the second chance offered by the Qualifier system. So they will only get one outing again this season – against Galway.

Football Championship Results Table

Munster

First Round		
Tipperary		Kerry
Replay:		
Waterford		Clare
Replay:		

Semi-finals		
Tipperary/Kerry		Limerick
Replay:		
Waterford/Clare		Cork
Replay:		

Final		
Replay:		

Connacht

First Round		
Galway		New York
Replay:		
London		Roscommon
Replay:		
Leitrim		Sligo
Replay:		

Semi-finals		
Galway/New York		Leitrim/Sligo
Replay:		
London/Roscommon		Mayo
Replay:		

Final		
Replay:		

Ulster

First Round		
Armagh		Fermanagh
Replay:		

Quarter-finals		
Tyrone		Down
Replay:		
Cavan		Antrim
Replay:		
Monaghan		Derry
Replay:		
Armagh/Fermanagh		Donegal
Replay:		

Quarter-finals		
Tyrone/Down		Cavan/Antrim
Replay:		
Monaghan/Derry		Armagh/Fermanagh/Donegal
Replay:		

Final		
Replay:		

Leinster

First Round		
Offaly		Louth
Replay:		
Wicklow		Kildare
Replay:		

Dublin		Longford
Replay:		

Quarter-finals

Offaly/Louth		Laois
Replay:		

Wicklow/Kildare		Westmeath
Replay:		

Dublin/Longford		Meath
Replay:		

Carlow		Wexford
Replay:		

Quarter-finals

Offaly/Louth/Laois		Wicklow/Kildare/Westmeath
Replay:		

Dublin/Longford/Meath		Carlow/Wexford
Replay:		

Final

Replay:		

All-Ireland Qualifiers

Round One

Round Two

Round Three

Round Four

All-Ireland Quarter-finals

Replay:

Replay:

Replay:

Replay:

All-Ireland Semi-finals

Replay:

Replay:

All-Ireland Final

Replay:

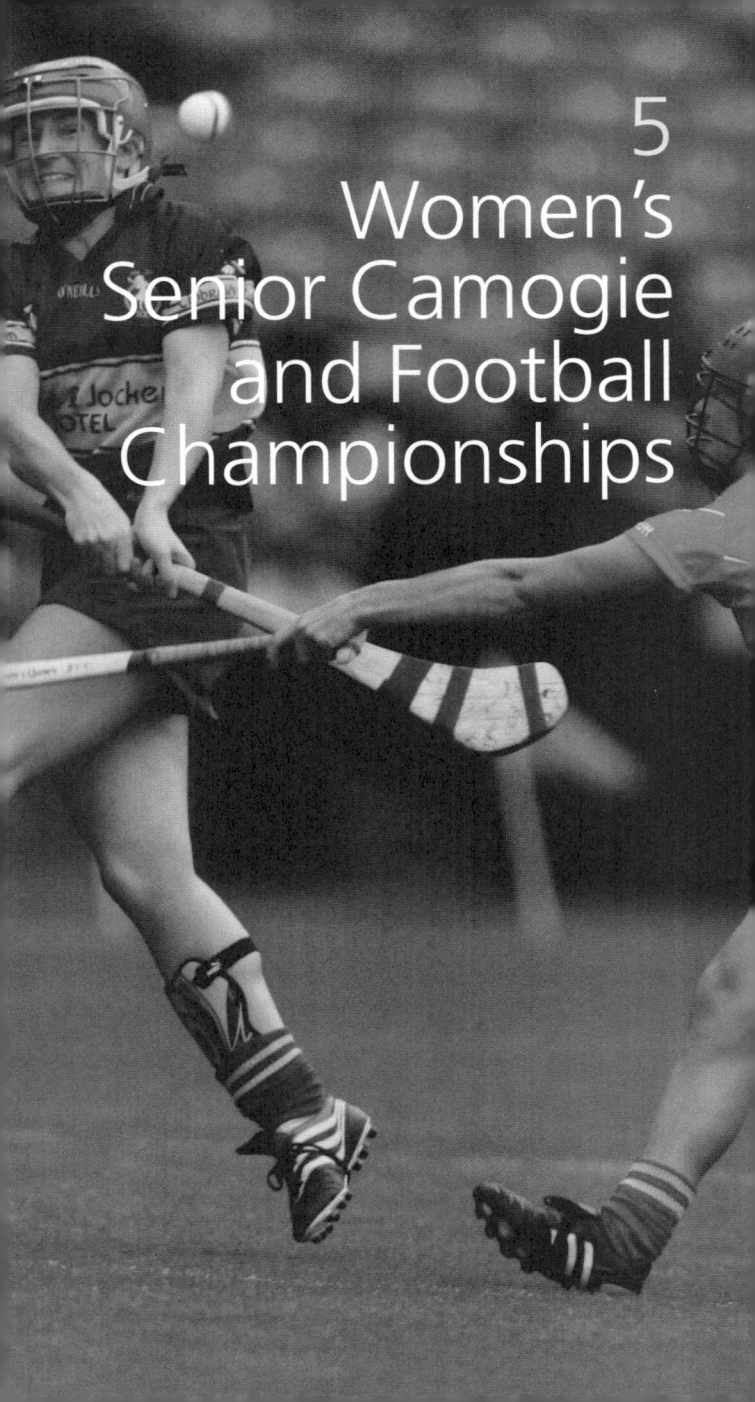

5
Women's Senior Camogie and Football Championships

5
Women's Senior Camogie and Football Championships

Camogie 2005

One hundred not out. Last September, over 2,000 kids formed 'C100' on the pitch in Croke Park in front of 24,500 spectators on the day of the All-Ireland junior and senior camogie finals. It was to commemorate the 100th anniversary of the first public camogie game, which was played in Navan; and it also happened to be the 70th anniversary of the first camogie final to be played in Croke Park.

More importantly, though, the event was a celebration of the direction the game is heading: up. Attendances are up, the numbers of matches and members are up, revenue is up. Of course, costs are up too, but such is the price of ascendancy. Camogie enters its second century in a justifiably confident mood.

Success breeds success. All well and good – unless your county is not one of the the ones recording the victories. Inter-county triumphs – especially senior ones – bring with them a proportional increase in profile and interest. More girls start playing the game, which results in a bigger pool for under-age county selectors to choose from. Standards rise. Such is the recent story of camogie in Tipperary: six years, five senior All-Ireland titles. The county's conveyor belt is moving steadily. Future stars are knocking tennis balls against the gable ends of houses. There's no point in waiting for the Premier County's current strength to dissipate. The challenge is for other counties to come up to the same standard.

There is evidence that it's happening. Tipperary left Kilkenny grounds twice last season knowing they had ridden their luck. A two-point victory over Kilkenny was followed by a similar result against Wexford in the All-Ireland semi-final. Tipperary could count themselves lucky they reached the decider at all. But when they did, they again showed their class against a battling but rather overwhelmed Cork side.

This year, the challenge for every team is to build on what they already have. While sides such as Limerick, Antrim and Derry have been visibly improving in recent years, other counties are struggling to keep pace, never mind catch up.

Can Kilkenny and Cork make the short step back up the class and reclaim the ultimate crown in camogie? Will Wexford make the breakthrough they threatened last year? Can the current minor and intermediate champions, Galway, claim a major scalp at the senior grade?

For the challengers the first target is obvious. Beat Tipperary and an inevitable upswing in interest, energy and profile will follow. Simple. Or maybe not.

Rules

There are five main rule differences between camogie and hurling:
1 It is not a foul to drop your hurley in camogie.
2 The camogie sliotar is slightly lighter than a hurling sliotar.
3 Hand-passed goals are allowed in camogie.
4 When the sliotar crosses the end-line off a defending player, the attacking team is awarded a 45 in camogie, rather than a 65.
5 Shouldering is not allowed in camogie. (This only seems to apply in theory.)

2004 Senior Championship Results

Opening Rounds

June 19	Duggan Park, Ballinasloe	Tipperary 4–8 Galway 0–8
	Glenariffe, Cushendall	Kilkenny 5–18 Antrim 0–4
June 26	Wexford Park, Wexford	Wexford 6–17 Limerick 1–4
	Mountrath, Laois	Derry give walkover to Cork
July 3	Nowlan Park, Kilkenny	Galway 5–10 Kilkenny 3–8
	Semple Stadium, Thurles	Tipperary 4–27 Antrim 1–4
	Greenlough, Derry	Wexford 3–10 Derry 1–1
July 10	Fitzgerald Stadium, Killarney	Cork 4–16 Limerick 1–6
July 17	Páirc Tailteann, Navan	Galway 9–26 Antrim 0–9
	Callan, Kilkenny	Tipperary 3–8 Kilkenny 2–9

| July 24 | Wexford Park, Wexford | Cork **1–14** Wexford **0–8** |
| | Gaelic Grounds, Limerick | Limerick **2–13** Derry **0–5** |

All-Ireland Semi-finals

| August 21 | Nowlan Park, Kilkenny | Cork **3–9** Galway **1–4** |
| | Nowlan Park, Kilkenny | Tipperary **1–10** Wexford |

All-Ireland Final

| September 19 | Croke Park, Dublin | Tipperary **2–11** Cork **0–9** |

2004 Champions

	Champions	Runners-up
Senior	Tipperary	Cork
Junior	Cork	Down
Intermediate	Galway	Tipperary
Minor A	Galway	Kildare
Minor B	Antrim	Roscommon
NL Division 1	Tipperary	Wexford
NL Division 2	Kildare	Laois

Camogie Team of the Century: 1904–2004

Eileen Duffy-O'Mahoney (Dublin) Played between the posts for Dublin from 1949 to 1957, winning eight senior All-Ireland medals.

Liz Neary (Kilkenny) Won seven senior All-Ireland titles, captaining the successful campaigns of 1981 and 1986. Also won seven All-Ireland club medals.

Marie Costine-O'Donovan (Cork) Five senior All-Ireland winners' medals, including four in a row from 1970 to 1973. Also claimed All-Ireland club title in 1980 with Killeagh.

Mary Sinnott-Dinan (Wexford) Full-back on county team that made huge breakthrough in 1968, winning the All-Ireland senior championship.

Bridie Martin-McGarry (Kilkenny) Won nine senior All-Ireland medals with her county and three with her club, St Paul's. Captained Kilkenny from centre-back in 1985 and 1987.

Sandie Fitzgibbon (Cork) Six All-Ireland senior winners' medals, one as captain (1992). Also played in four successful All-Ireland club championship campaigns with Glen Rovers.

Margaret O'Leary-Leacy (Wexford) On two-in-a-row side of 1968 and 1969, then moved to back line in successful campaign of 1975. Won four club All-Ireland titles, three with Buffers Alley, one with Eoghan Ruadh.

Mairead McAtamney-Magill (Antrim) Playing inter-county camogie for 20 years, she won two All-Ireland senior titles, in 1967 and 1979, the latter as captain.

Linda Mellerick (Cork) Six senior All-Ireland medals, captaining the successful sides of 1993 and 1997. Also claimed three club titles with Glen Rovers.

Sophie Brack (Dublin) Winnner of eight senior All-Ireland medals (the first in 1948), including six as captain.

Kathleen Mills-Hill (Dublin) The midfielder claimed 15 All-Ireland medals, captaining the side to success in 1958.

Una O'Connor (Dublin) Winner of an incredible 13 All-Ireland medals: three in a row from 1953 to 1955, then another ten on the trot from 1957.

Pat Moloney-Lenihan (Cork) Seven All-Ireland senior medals, including four in a row 1970–73. Also won an All-Ireland club medal with Killeagh.

Deirdre Hughes (Tipperary) Won the player of the match award in the breakthrough 1999 final, and has gone on to claim All-Ireland senior medals in five of the past six years.

Angela Downey-Browne (Kilkenny) Won 12 senior All Ireland medals, the ace forward captaining her side to success in 1977, 1988 and 1989.

Camogie Roll of Honour

County	No of Titles	Years won
Dublin	26	1932, 1933, 1937, 1938, 1942, 1943, 1944, 1948, 1949, 1950, 1951, 1952, 1953, 1954, 1955, 1957, 1958, 1959, 1960, 1961, 1962, 1963, 1964, 1965, 1966, 1984
Cork	20	1934, 1935, 1936, 1939, 1940, 1941, 1970, 1971, 1972, 1973, 1978, 1980, 1982, 1983, 1992, 1993, 1995, 1997, 1998, 2002

Kilkenny	12	1974, 1976, 1977, 1981, 1985, 1986, 1987, 1988, 1989, 1990, 1991, 1994
Antrim	6	1945, 1946, 1947, 1956, 1967, 1979
Tipperary	5	1999, 2000, 2001, 2003, 2004
Wexford	3	1968, 1969, 1975
Galway	1	1996

Women's Football 2005

Imagine having to play the reigning All-Ireland senior football champions four times in one championship season, en route to claiming the All-Ireland title for the first time. No one who follows women's football has to imagine it. Last season, Galway didn't just do it the hard way, they did it the unimaginable way.

Galway's improbable triumph was the perfect climax to another season of relentless progress for the code. The men's game took over a century to get where it is today; women's football hasn't been as patient. New clubs, new members, more funding and much more support – there are many men's sports in the world that can only dream of tens of thousands of supporters turning up to watch their final game of the season. Though that's not to say the aim of the women's game is to catch up with the men's code. Why set limits?

In recent years the women's senior football championship has had cyclical fortunes – teams have found it difficult to avoid a dip in form after a few seasons at the helm. Tipperary were considered the strongest county in the early years of the competition, appearing in five All-Ireland finals between 1974 and 1980, winning three. But then Kerry took over, dominating the 1980s. Waterford and Monaghan emerged and took over in the early 1990s, with very few interruptions from elsewhere until the late 1990s, when another new power emerged.

Last season was the first year Mayo haven't appeared in the senior All-Ireland final since 1998. In their fourth championship meeting with Galway – following a victory in the first round of the Connacht championship, a heavy defeat in the Connacht final, and a draw in the All-Ireland semi-final – Mayo suffered a one-point defeat in the semi-final replay. Galway then overcame Dublin, who were appearing in their second final in succession. Losing the second final was even more devastating for the Dubs than the previous season's disappointment.

Now, the dials have been reset to zero and more teams then ever are preparing for a prolonged interest in the 2005 women's football championship.

For Galway, remaining at the helm of the women's competition may not be as straightforward as it once might have been. Even retaining the Connacht title will prove a fierce struggle as Mayo will be bent on revenge – and the champions can't afford to take Roscommon for granted either.

In Munster, Cork are determined to match their Munster final performance of last year, and harbour realistic ambitions of going further than last season's All-Ireland quarter-final stage. Past masters Kerry and Waterford are regrouping, however, and it shouldn't be forgotten that Clare started last season brightly, before finding the pace a little too fast.

Another surprise last season was Donegal's impressive challenge to favourites Dublin in their All-Ireland quarter-final clash at Pearse Park. Monaghan shipped too many goals against Kerry at the same stage, but it will surely be only a short period of time before Ulster teams are back in Croke Park on women's All-Ireland football final day.

Dublin have quite recently taken over from Laois and Meath as the top side in Leinster and there is much to suggest that this season will be no different. The Dublin team has unfinished business to attend to – the small matter of two All-Ireland final defeats in as many years. The Cumann Peil Gael na mBan were confident that having the Dubs in the All-Ireland senior final would attract a record crowd to Croke Park for a women's game, with predictions ranging from 35,000 to over 40,000. However, the unfavourable weather on the day of the past two All-Ireland finals – probably more than any other reason – ensured those numbers haven't been reached, yet.

Rules

There are five main rule differences between men's and women's football.

1 The ball used is slightly smaller in women's football.
2 A player holding the ball into her body cannot be legally dispossessed.
3 Shouldering is not supposed to be permitted in women's football.
4 If the referee stops play to deal with an injured player, the team in possession retains possession on the restart (though they cannot score directly from the first kick).
5 For a kick-out in women's football, the ball may be kicked from the hand (or the ground).

2004 All-Ireland Women's Senior Football Championship Results

Leinster

Opening rounds

May 8	Hunterstown, Louth	Laois **6–10** Louth **0–6**
May 9		Longford give walkover to Dublin
May 23	Naomh Mearnog, Dublin	Dublin **0–10** Meath **0–8**
	Mountmellick, Laois	Laois **2–10** Longford **1–2**
June 6	Simonstown, Meath	Meath **2–18** Louth **0–5**
June 20	Fingallians, Dublin	Dublin **1–10** Laois **0–4**
June 27	Naul, Dublin	Dublin **5–22** Louth **2–2**
July 4	Dunsany, Meath	Laois **3–9** Meath **1–11**

Semi-finals

July 7	Naul, Dublin	Dublin **6–11** Louth **0–7**
July 11	Stradbally, Laois	Laois **4–12** Meath **4–8**

Final

July 25	Dr Cullen Park, Carlow	Dublin **2–10** Laois **0–7**

Ulster

Opening rounds

June 20	Truagh, Monaghan	Monaghan 1–11 Donegal 0–7
	Maghery, Armagh	Tyrone 1–12 Down 1–4
July 4	Crossmaglen, Armagh	Monaghan 2–15 Down 2–7
July 18	Brewster Park, Fermanagh	Donegal 2–9 Tyrone 0–12
July 25	Brewster Park, Fermanagh	Monaghan 1–14 Tyrone 1–5
	Moneyglass, Antrim	Donegal 5–26 Down 0–4

Final

August 13	Clones, Monaghan	Monaghan 3–9 Donegal 1–10

Connacht
Opening rounds

June 26	Tuam Stadium, Galway	Galway 0–9 Mayo 0–8
July 11	McHale Park, Mayo	Mayo 1–12 Roscommon 0–12
July 25	Dr Hyde Park, Roscommon	Galway 3–13 Roscommon 1–8

Final

August 8	Tuam Stadium, Galway	Galway 0–16 Mayo 0–2

Munster
Opening rounds

July 10	Emly, Tipperary	Clare 0–10 Waterford 0–10
July 11	Killorglin, Kerry	Kerry 3–11 Cork 1–11
July 24	Austin Stacks, Kerry	Waterford 2–10 Kerry 1–6
	Doonbeg, Clare	Cork 3–16 Clare 1–6
July 31	Dungarvan, Waterford	Cork 1–11 Waterford 0–10
	Abbeydorney, Kerry	Kerry 6–19 Clare 1–4

Final

August 15	Pairc Ui Rinn, Cork	Cork 4–13 Kerry 1–9

All-Ireland Quarter-finals

August 28	Pearse Park, Galway	Dublin 2–14 Donegal 2–12 AET
	Pearse Park, Galway	Galway 1–8 Laois 1–6
	O'Connor Park, Tullamore	Kerry 5–10 Monaghan 3–11
	O'Connor Park, Tullamore	Mayo 1–11 Cork 1–7

All-Ireland Semi-finals

September 11	O'Moore Park, Portlaoise	Dublin **2–14** Kerry **3–8**
	O'Moore Park, Portlaoise	Galway **1–10** Mayo **1–10**
September 18	Hyde Park, Roscommon	Galway **3–10** Mayo **3–9** (Replay)

All-Ireland Final

| October 3 | Croke Park, Dublin | Galway **3–8** Dublin **0–11** |

Roll of Honour 2004

	Champions	Runners-up
Senior	Galway	Dublin
Junior	Kildare	Sligo
Minor	Cork	Laois
NL Division One	Mayo	Cork
NL Division Two	Kildare	Louth
NL Division Three	Wexford	Limerick
NL Division Four	Offaly	Wicklow

County	No of Titles	Years won
Kerry	11	1976, 1982, 1983, 1984, 1985, 1986, 1987, 1988, 1989, 1990, 1993
Waterford	5	1991, 1992, 1994, 1995, 1998
Mayo	4	1999, 2000, 2002, 2003
Tipperary	3	1974, 1975, 1980
Offaly	2	1979, 1981
Monaghan	2	1996, 1997
Cavan	1	1977
Roscommon	1	1978
Laois	1	2001
Galway	1	2004

Decade of Champions

Senior	Winners	Runner-up
2004	Galway	Dublin
2003	Mayo	Dublin
2002	Mayo	Monaghan
2001	Laois	Mayo
2000	Mayo	Waterford
1999	Mayo	Waterford
1998	Waterford	Monaghan
1997	Monaghan	Waterford
1996	Monaghan	Laois
1995	Waterford	Monaghan

6
Results
2004

6
Results
2004

Leinster Senior Hurling Championship
Preliminary – First Round

Laois **4–19** Carlow **0–8**

Laois K Galvin | C Cuddy, Patrick Cuddy, M McEvoy | J Fitzpatrick (0–1), Paul Cuddy (0–5, four frees, one 65), R Conroy | D Rooney (0–2), J Walsh (0–1) | C Coonen, E Meagher (0–3), T Fitzgerald (1–3) | L Tynan, D Culleton (1–0), F Keenan (0–2)

Subs: E Browne (1–0) for Coonen (39 mins) | C Brophy for Walsh (51) | E Jackman (1–0) for Rooney (52) | A Delaney for Fitzpatrick (61) | D Walsh (0–2) for Tynan (65)

Carlow F Foley (0–1, penalty) | W Hickey, A Corcoran, M Kehoe | K Nolan, E Coady, A Gaul | S Kavanagh, P Coady (0–4, three frees) | P Kehoe, D Murphy, R Minchin | B Murphy, K English (0–2, one free), S Smithers

Subs: S M Murphy (0–1) for Kavanagh (9 mins) | D Shaw for Kehoe (29) | P Coady for B Murphy (50) | T O'Shea for Smithers (54) | S Sheil for Gaul (58)

Referee E Morris (Dublin)

Westmeath **6–14** Wicklow **1–13**

Westmeath M Briody | D Curley, B Murtagh, P Greville | D Gallagher (0–1), C Murtagh, D McCormack | P Williams, O Devine | R Whelan (1–2), V Bateman (1–1), A Mitchell (1–7) | D Carty, J Shaw (2–1), B Kennedy (0–1)

Subs: B Connaughton (0–1) for Williams | F Shaw (1–0) for Kennedy | S McDonnell for Devine | K Cosgrove for Carty | D Devine for Mitchell

Wicklow T Finn | J O'Neill, G Keogh, J Bermingham | S Kinsella, A O'Neill, T McGrath (0–1) | C O'Toole, G Murray | J Murphy, G Doran (0–1), C Kavanagh | A Tiernan, J O'Neill (1–11), D Moran

Subs: D Doran for Kinsella | D Moran for Tiernan | J Sinnott for Moran

Referee Fergus Smith (Meath)

Preliminary – Second Round

May 16	Cusack Park, Mullingar

Westmeath 1–18 Kildare 1–6

Westmeath M Briody | D Curley, B Murtagh, P Greville | D Gallagher, D McCormack (0–2), S McDonnell | R Whelan, B Connaughton | K Cosgrove, O Devine (0–2), A Mitchell (0–9) | D McNicholas, J Shaw, B Kennedy (0–3)

Subs: D Carty for McNicholas | J Forbes (1–2) for Cosgrove | C Murtagh for Curley | P Williams for Connaughton | N Flanagan for Shaw

Kildare C Leahy | S Crowe, D Laharte, B Maher | C Divilly (0–1), D Harney, R Hoban | C Buggy, J Brennan | J Dempsey (1–1), E Denieffe, S Joyce | A McAndrew, A Quinn (0–1), T Carew (0–3)

Subs: B White for Joyce | P Reidy for Maher | A Flaherty for Crowe | C Boran for Denieffe

Referee J Guinan (Kilkenny)

May 16	O'Moore Park, Portlaoise

Laois 1–13 Meath 0–8

Laois K Glavin | C Cuddy, Pat Cuddy, M McEvoy | J Fitzpatrick, P Cuddy (0–1), R Conway | D Rooney, J Walsh | R Jones (0–4), J Young (1–6), E Meagher (0–1) | T Fitzgerald (0–1), L Tynan, D Culleton

Subs: J Dunne for Rooney | P Mahon for Walsh | E Browne for Meagher | C Brophy for Fitzgerald

Meath M Brennan | S White, P Roche, S Moran | D Brennan, T Reilly, S Reilly (0–1) | J Canty, D Donnelly | E Lynam (0–2), S Clinch (0–1), M Burke | N Reilly, M Gannon (0–1), A Fox

Subs: M Cole (0–3) for Burke | G O'Neill for Fox | P Donoghue for Moran | J Keena for Canty

Referee J Kelly (Wexford)

Quarter-finals

Dublin **2–14** Westmeath **0–11**

Dublin G Maguire | D Spain, S Daly, A de Paor | S Hiney, R Fallon, K Ryan | C Meehan, C Keaney (1–2, one penalty, one free) | D Curtin (0–3, two frees), L Ryan (0–2), M Carton (0–1) | D O'Callaghan (1–1), K Flynn (0–1, 65), D Donnelly

Subs: P Fleury (0–2) for Donnelly (40 mins) | J McGuirk (0–1) for Curtin (53) | S O'Shea (0–1) for Meehan (60) | S McCann for Carton (68)

Westmeath M Briody | D Curley, C Murtagh, P Greville | O Devine, B Murtagh, D McCormack | R Whelan (0–1), E Loughlin (0–2) | J Forbes, V Bateman (0–1), A Mitchell (0–5, four frees) | D Carty, K Cosgrove (0–1), J Shaw (0–1)

Subs: B Kennedy for Forbes (18 mins) | N Flanagan for Carty (half–time) | S McDonnell for Cosgrove (47) | D Gallagher for Flanagan (56) | P Williams for Kennedy (64)

Referee D Kirwan (Cork)

Offaly **2–23** Laois **1–15**

Offaly B Mullins | M O'Hara, G Oakley, D Franks | K Brady, N Claffey, C Cassidy (0–3, all 65s) | M Cordial (0–1), Barry Whelahan | N Coughlan, G Hanniffy (0–1), B Murphy (1–2) | B Carroll (1–4), J Brady (0–1), D Murray (0–10, eight frees)

Subs: S Whelahan (0–1) for Brady (46 mins) | D Hayden for Whelahan (60)

Laois K Galvin | C Cuddy, D Rooney, M McEvoy | J Fitzpatrick (0–1), P Cuddy, R Conroy | D Cuddy (0–1), J Walsh | C Coonan (1–0), J Young (0–11, nine frees, one 65, one sideline cut), R Jones (0–1) | T Fitzgerald, L Tynan, D Culleton (0–1)

Subs: E Meagher for Coonan (24 mins) | C Brophy for Conroy (55) | J Dunne for Tynan (57) | F Keenan for Meagher (61)

Referee S McMahon (Clare)

Semi-finals

Wexford **2–15** Kilkenny **1–16**

Wexford D Fitzhenry | M Travers, D Ryan, D O'Connor | R McCarthy, D Ruth, J O'Connor | A Fenlon (0–1, sideline), T Mahon | P Carley (0–3, two frees), B Lambert (0–4, three frees), E Quigley (0–1) | M Jordan (0–3), M Jacob (1–2), R Jacob (1–1)

Subs: L Murphy for Lambert (50 mins) | P Codd for Mahon (62) | C Kehoe for Ryan (68)

Kilkenny J McGarry | M Kavanagh, N Hickey, J J Delaney | S Dowling (0–2, one free), P Barry, B Hogan | Lyng, P Tennyson (0–1) | J Hoyne (0–1), H Shefflin (0–5, five frees), T Walsh (0–2) | E Brennan (1–1), M Comerford (0–2), J Coogan (0–1)

Subs: DJ Carey (0–1) for Coogan (58 mins) | A Fogarty for Hoyne (65)

Referee B Kelly (Westmeath)

Offaly **2–25** Dublin **1–13**

Offaly B Mullins | B Teehan, G Oakley, D Franks | Brian Whelahan, N Claffey, C Cassidy (0–2, both frees) | M Cordial (0–3), Barry Whelahan | G Hanniffy, R Hanniffy (0–3), J Brady | B Carroll (0–4), B Murphy (2–5), D Murray (0–8, three frees)

Subs: K Brady for Franks (47 mins) | N Coughlan for Cordial (57) | S Whelahan for Brady (66)

Dublin G Maguire | D Spain, S Perkins, S Daly | A de Paor (0–2, one 65), R Fallon, K Ryan | C Meehan, J McGuirk | D Sweeney (0–1), L Ryan (0–2), K Flynn (0–2, one free) | D O'Callaghan (0–5), S Hiney, P Fleury

Subs: M Carton (1–0) for McGuirk, D Kirwan (0–1) for Meehan, P Brennan for Spain (all half–time), D O'Reilly for Perkins (65 mins), S O'Shea for Fallon (68 mins)

Referee P Ahern (Carlow)

Final

Wexford **2–12** Offaly **1–11**

Wexford D Fitzhenry | M Travers, D Ryan, D O'Connor | R McCarthy, D Ruth, J O'Connor | A Fenlon (0–1), T Mahon | P Carley (1–1, 0–1 free), E Quigley (0–3, frees), B Lambert (0–3, frees) | M Jordan, M Jacob (1–0), R Jacob (0–2)

Subs: P Codd (0–2) for Lambert (45 mins), C McGrath for Jordan (57)

Offaly B Mullins | B Teehan, G Oakley, D Franks | N Claffey, Brian Whelahan, C Cassidy (0–1) | M Cordial (0–1), Barry Whelahan (0–1) | G Hanniffy (1–0), R Hanniffy (0–1), B Murphy (0–1) | B Carroll (0–2), J Brady, D Murray (0–4, frees)

Subs: N Coughlan for Brian Whelahan (45 mins) | S Brown for Carroll (62), D Hayden for Brady (66)

Referee G Harrington (Cork)

Munster Senior Hurling Championship
First round

Waterford **3–21** Clare **1–8**

Waterford S Brenner | J Murray, T Feeney, E Murphy | T Browne, K McGrath, B Phelan | D Bennett (0–5, four frees), E Kelly (0–8, four frees) | D Shanahan (3–1), M Walsh (0–1), P Flynn (0–1) | J Mullane (0–4), S Prendergast (0–1), E McGrath

Subs: P O'Brien for Flynn (59 mins) | S Ryan for E McGrath (66) | A Moloney for Prendergast (69)

Clare D Fitzgerald | B Quinn, B Lohan, B O'Connell | G Quinn, S McMahon, C Plunkett | O Baker, D McMahon | T Griffin (1–0), C Lynch (0–1), A Markham | N Gilligan (0–4, one free), F Lohan (0–3), D Forde

Subs: T Carmody for Baker (21) | D Hoey for O'Connell (26) | J O'Connor for Markham (42) | B O'Connell for O'Connor (47) | C Forde for Quinn (60)

Referee G Harrington (Cork)

Cork **4–19** Kerry **1–7**

Cork D Óg Cusack | B Murphy, D O'Sullivan, C O'Connor | T Kenny, R Curran (0–1, free), S Óg Ó hAilpín | J Gardiner (1–1), M O'Connell (0–2, one 65) | J O'Connor (0–3), N McCarthy (0–2), T McCarthy (0–1) | B O'Connor (1–0), J Deane (1–4, two frees), J O'Callaghan (0–3, one free)

Subs: J Anderson (0–1) for N McCarthy (48 mins) | B Corcoran (1–1) for Deane (51) | P Tierney for Gardiner (55) | J Browne for Kenny (56) | B Lombard for O'Callaghan (62)

Kerry T Flynn | B Blackwell, A Healy, A Keane | K O'Sullivan, J McCarthy (0–1), C Harris | A Cronin, D Young | I McCarthy, S Brick (0–2 frees), P O'Connell (0–2, one free) | E Tuohy (1–1), JM Dooley, J Egan (0–1)

Subs: L Boyle for Young (half–time) | M Lucid for I McCarthy (54 mins)

Referee B Kelly (Westmeath)

Semi-finals

Cork **1–18** Limerick **2–12**

Cork D Cusack | W Sherlock, D O'Sullivan, B Murphy | T Kenny, R Curran, S Óg Ó hAilpín | J Gardiner, M O'Connell (0–1) | N McCarthy (0–3), J O'Connor (0–1), T McCarthy (0–1) | J O'Callaghan, B O'Connor (1–7, 1–6 frees, one 65), J Deane (0–4, three frees)

Subs: B Corcoran (0–1) for T McCarthy (54 mins) | M Byrne for O'Callaghan (65)

Limerick A Shanahan | D Reale, TJ Ryan, M Cahill | O Moran, B Geary, P Lawlor | C Smith, M Foley | N Moran (0–7, three frees), JP Sheahan (0–1), M McKenna (0–1) | A O'Shaughnessy, S O'Connor (2–0), D Sheehan (0–1)

Subs: P Tobin (0–2) for Sheahan (56 mins) | D O'Grady for Sheehan (72)

Referee S Roche (Tipperary)

Waterford **4–10** Tipperary **3–12**

Waterford S Brenner | J Murray, D Prendergast, B Wall | B Phelan, K McGrath, E Murphy | D Bennett (0–2, one 65), E Kelly (0–2, one free) | D Shanahan (2–0), M Walsh (0–1), P Flynn (0–2, one free) | J Mullane (1–0), S Prendergast (0–2), E McGrath (0–1)

Subs: P O'Brien (1–0) for E McGrath (44 mins) | S O'Sullivan for Flynn (65) | T Feeney for K McGrath (68)

Tipperary B Cummins | T Costello, P Maher, P Curran | P Kelly (0–1, one 65), D Fitzgerald, E Corcoran | E Enright, C Morrissey (1–1) | T Dunne (0–1), J Carroll, B Dunne | E Kelly (2–8, four frees), J Devane, P O'Brien

Subs: S Butler (0–1) for O'Brien, M Maher for Costello (both half–time) | C Gleeson for Carroll (46 mins) | M O'Leary for B Dunne (68)

Referee D Kirwan (Cork)

Final

Waterford **3–16** Cork **1–21**

Waterford S Brenner | J Murray, D Prendergast, E Murphy | T Browne,
K McGrath, B Phelan | D Bennett (0–1, free), E Kelly (1–1) | D Shanahan (1–3),
M Walsh, P Flynn (1–7, 1–4 from frees) | J Mullane (0–2), S Prendergast (0–1),
E McGrath

Subs: P O'Brien for Bennett (50 mins) | S O'Sullivan for E McGrath (66) |
J Kennedy for O'Brien (71)

Cork D Cusack | W Sherlock, D O'Sullivan, B Murphy | S Óg Ó hAilpin, R Curran
(0–1), J Gardiner | T Kenny (0–3), J O'Connor (0–2) | G McCarthy (1–0),
N McCarthy, T McCarthy | B O'Connor (0–4, one free, one 65), B Corcoran (0–2),
J Deane (0–9, six frees)

Subs: J O'Callaghan for N McCarthy (58 mins) | K Murphy for G McCarthy (65) |
M O'Connell for Gardiner (70)

Referee S McMahon (Clare)

Ulster Senior Hurling Championship
Quarter-final

Derry **2–14** London **0–11**

Derry K Stevenson | G Brunton, L Himphey, M Conway | B Ward, C Brunton, P O'Kane | R Convery, F Kelly (0–1) | K Himphey (1–0), G Biggs (0–3), Gary Biggs (0–2) | D McGrellis (0–3), P Hearty (0–1), G McConigle (1–4)

Sub: P Doherty for Hearty

London JJ Burke | S Dennehy, M Gordon, E Leamey | S Linnane, B Foley, E Phelan | M Hayes (0–1), K Ivors | D Bourke (0–7), N Lawlor, F McMahon (0–1) | T Ó hAilpín (0–1), C Buckley, K White

Subs: N Murphy for Buckley | C Heaney for Linnane | E Kinlon (0–1) for Lawlor | M O'Meara for Heaney

Referee J Sexton (Limerick)

Semi-finals

May 23	Casement Park, Belfast

Down **1–19** New York **1–9**

Down Graham Clarke | L Clarke, S Murray, JH Hughes | S Wilson (0–1), G Savage, G Clarke | A Savage, G Adare (0–2) | G McGrattan (0–1), P Branniff (0–8, five frees), B McGourty (0–3) | M Coulter (0–2), G Johnson (1–1), M Branniff (0–1)

Subs: J Convery for A Savage (49 mins) | E Trainor for P Branniff (60)

New York K Jordan | A Kiely, P Dalton, P Wickham | S Quirke (0–1), J Madden, T O'Callaghan | A Guinan, S Nolan | B Kennedy (1–2), V Norton (0–3) | T Fletcher, D Simms (0–2, one free), T Moylan (0–2), D McCarthy

Subs: G O'Halloran for McCarthy (half–time) | T Maher for Simms (50 mins) | D Loughnane for Fletcher (55) | C Ruth for Guinan (60)

Referee P Horan (Offaly)

May 23	Casement Park, Belfast

Antrim **2–14** Derry **0–12**

Antrim D Quinn | M McCambridge, K Kelly, B Herron | J Campbell, K McKeegan (0–1, free), C Herron | J Connolly (1–2), M Scullion | L Richmond (0–1), C McGuickian (0–1), M Herron (0–1) | L Watson (0–4, four frees), P Richmond (1–0), B McFall (0–4, three frees).

Subs: D Quinn for Watson (47 mins) | J McIntosh for Scullion (53)

Derry K Stevenson | G Brunton, L Hinphey, M Conway | B Ward, C Brunton, P O'Kane | Gary Biggs (0–1) | P Kelly | K Hinphey (0–2), Greg Biggs (0–5, three frees), P Doherty (0–1) | D McGrellis, P Hearty, G McGonagle (0–3, three frees)

Subs: B McGoldrick for McGrellis (44 mins) | A Rafferty for C Brunton (62)

Referee B Galvin (Offaly)

Final

Antrim **1–15** Down **1–15**

Antrim Damien Quinn | G Cunningham, K Kelly, B Herron | M McCambridge, K McKeegan (0–1, one free), J Campbell | C Herron, J Connolly | M Herron (1–1), C McGuckian (0–1), L Richmond | Darren Quinn (0–4), P Richmond (0–3), B McFall (0–5, two frees)

Subs: L Watson for L Richmond (45 mins) | M Kettle for Cunningham (54) | J McIntosh for Connolly (65)

Down Graham Clarke | L Clarke, S Murray, J H Hughes | S Wilson (0–1), G Savage (0–1), Gabriel Clarke | G Adair (0–1) | A Savage (0–1) | G McGrattan (0–1), J Convery (0–1), B McGourty (0–2), M Coulter (1–1, goal from penalty) | G Johnson (0–4, two frees), M Braniff

Subs: S Clarke (0–2, two frees) for Braniff (21 mins) | E Dorrian for Hughes (26) | E Trainor for McGrattan (60) | E Clarke for Johnson (64)

Referee M Haverty (Galway)

Antrim **3–14** Down **0–18**

Antrim Damien Quinn | M Kettle, K Kelly, B Herron (0–1) | M McCambridge, K McKeegan, J Campbell | C Herron (0–1), J Connolly (0–1) | M Herron (0–2), C McGuckian, L Watson (0–2) | Darren Quinn, P Richmond (2–3), B McFall (1–3)

Subs: L Richmond (0–1) for McCambridge (53) | G J McIntosh for Watson (55) | Ward for Darren Quinn (58) | M Magill for Connolly (69)

Down G Clarke | L Clarke, S Murray, E Dorrian | S Wilson (0–1), G Savage, G Clarke | G Adair (0–1), A Savage (0–1) | G McGrattan, J Convery (0–2), B McGourty (0–4) | M Coulter (0–1), G Johnson (0–2), S Clarke (0–6)

Subs: JH Hughes for Wilson (12 mins) | P Hughes for Murray (23) | A Bell for Hughes (48)

Referee Eamonn Morris (Dublin)

All-Ireland Hurling Championship Qualifiers
Preliminary – First Round

June 19 O'Moore Park, Portlaoise

Laois **3–13** Westmeath **4–5**

Laois K Galvin | L Mahon, P Cuddy, A Delaney | J Fitzpatrick, L Tynan, M McEvoy (0–1) | J Young (0–3), J Walsh | E Browne (0–1), P Mahon, C Cuddy | T Fitzgerald, D Cuddy (1–1), D Culleton (2–1)

Subs: D Walsh (0–6) for P Mahon | R Conroy for Delaney | E Jackman for Fitzgerald | R Jones for Walsh | C Coonan for Browne

Westmeath M Briody | D Curley, B Murtagh, P Greville | O Devine, C Murtagh, D McCormack (0–1) | S McDonnell, E Loughlin | K Cosgrove (1–0), V Bateman, A Mitchell (1–4) | B Kennedy, J Shaw, R Whelan (1–0)

Subs: D Gallagher for Greville | B Connaughton for Loughlin | J Forbes for Kennedy | D McNicholas (1–0) for Whelan

Referee Eamon Morris (Dublin)

Round One

Galway **5–19** Down **1–14**

Galway L Donoghue | D Joyce, D Cloonan, O Canning | D Hardiman, D Collins, F Moore | F Healy, David Hayes | A Kerins (1–2), D Forde (0–3), D Tierney (0–2, one free) | Damien Hayes (0–2), E Cloonan (4–7, 1–4 from frees), K Broderick (0–1)

Subs: M Kerins (0–1) for Broderick (42 mins) | T O'Regan for Collins (52) | R Gantley for David Hayes (65) | S Kavanagh for Hardiman (68) | J Conway for Healy (70)

Down Graham Clarke | M Braniff, E Dorrian | A Bell, L Clarke, G Savage, Gabriel Clarke | G Adair, A Savage (0–2) | G McGrattan (0–1), J Convery, B McGourty (0–2) | M Coulter (1–2, 0–1 from a free), G Johnson (0–2, one free), S Clarke (0–5, four frees)

Subs: R Conlon for Braniff (68 mins)

Referee P Horan (Offaly)

Tipperary **3–10** Limerick **2–12**

Tipperary B Cummins | M Maher, P Maher, P Curran | E Corcoran, D Fanning, D Fitzgerald | P Kelly, C Morrissey (0–2) | T Dunne (1–1, 0–1 from free), E Enright, B Dunne (0–1) | S Butler (1–2), J Carroll (1–1), E Kelly (0–3, two frees)

Subs: B O'Meara for Enright (33 mins) | L Corbett for Kelly (half–time) | T Scroope for O'Meara (60) | M O'Leary for Butler (69)

Limerick J Cahill | M Cahill, TJ Ryan, D Reale | O Moran, B Geary, P Lawlor | C Smith, M Foley (0–1) | M McKenna, JP Sheahan, N Moran (0–7, four frees two 65s) | A O'Shaughnessy (2–1), S O'Connor, D Sheehan

Subs: J O'Brien (0–1) for Sheehan (29 mins) | D Ryan for O'Connor (40) | D O'Grady (0–1) for Smith (49) | P O'Grady for McKenna (57) | P Tobin (0–1) for Sheehan (64)

Referee A MacSuibhne (Dublin)

Dr Cullen Park, Carlow

Kilkenny **4–22** Dublin **0–8**

Kilkenny J McGarry | M Phelan, N Hickey, T Walsh | R Mullally, P Barry, J J Delaney | D Lyng (0–1), K Coogan | M Comerford (0–2), J Coogan (1–2), E Brennan (1–3) | A Fogarty, D J Carey (0–4, one free, one 65), H Shefflin (2–8, 0–7 from frees)

Subs: J Fitzpatrick (0–1) for Fogarty | J Maher (0–1) for Carey | J Ryall for Barry | S Dowling for Lyng | C Phelan for Brennan

Dublin G Maguire | P Brennan, S Perkins, S Daly | S Hiney, R Fallon (0–1), K Ryan | A de Paor (0–3, two frees, one 65), C Meehan | S O'Shea (0–1), G Keogh, S McCann | D O'Callaghan (0–2, frees), M Carton, P Fleury

Subs: D Kirwan for McCann | C O'Brien for Brennan | R Brennan for Meehan | G O'Meara (0–1) for Ryan | M Breathnach for Keogh

Referee Seamus Roche (Tipperary)

Gaelic Grounds, Limerick

Clare **7–19** Laois **2–15**

Clare D Fitzgerald | T Holland, B Lohan, G O'Grady | D Hoey, S McMahon (0–1, 65), A Markham | C Lynch, D McMahon | F Lohan (0–1), G Quinn (0–1), J O'Connor | N Gilligan (2–10, 0–6 from frees), T Griffin (4–1), D O'Connell

Subs: D Forde (0–3) for O'Connell | T Carmody (1–0) for Lohan | C Forde for Holland | B Murphy (0–2) for O'Connor | B O'Connell for McMahon

Laois K Galvin | C Cuddy (0–1), P Cuddy, D Rooney | J Fitzpatrick, L Tynan, M McEvoy | J Young (0–6, frees), J Walsh | C Coonan, D Walsh, E Browne | T Fitzgerald (2–1), D Cuddy (0–4), D Culleton

Subs: J Dunne (0–1) for Browne | R Jones (0–1) for J Walsh | C Brophy for Coonan | L Mahon for Rooney | P Mahon (0–1) for D Walsh

Referee M Haverty (Galway)

Round Two

Not applicable as Galway won their Round One game

Round Three

Cork **2–19** Tipperary **1–16**

Cork D Óg Cusack | W Sherlock, D O'Sullivan, B Murphy | J Gardiner (0–1), R Curran, S Óg Ó hAilpín | T Kenny, J O'Connor (0–1) | B O'Connor (0–4, two frees), N McCarthy (1–2), G McCarthy | K Murphy (0–2), B Corcoran, J Deane (0–7, six frees)

Subs: T McCarthy (1–1) for G McCarthy (31 mins) | M O'Connell (0–1) for Kenny (64)

Tipperary B Cummins | M Maher, P Maher, P Curran | E Corcoran, D Fanning, D Fitzgerald | C Morrissey (0–1) | T Dunne | P Kelly (1–0), C Gleeson (0–1), B Dunne (0–3) | E Kelly (0–9, five frees), J Carroll (0–1), S Butler

Subs: L Corbett for Butler (50 mins) | M O'Leary (0–1) for P Kelly (58) | N Morris for Carroll (70)

Referee B Kelly (Westmeath)

Kilkenny **4–20** Galway **1–20**

Kilkenny J McGarry | J Ryall, N Hickey, T Walsh | R Mullally (0–1), P Barry, J J Delaney | D Lyng (0–1), K Coogan | M Comerford (0–2), H Shefflin (2–11, eight frees), C Phelan (0–1) | E Brennan (1–3), DJ Carey (0–1, 65), J Coogan

Subs: J Hoyne (1–0) for Comerford (60 mins)

Galway L Donoghue | D Joyce, D Cloonan, O Canning | D Hardiman, David Hayes, F Moore | F Healy, T Regan | A Kerins, D Forde, D Tierney | Damien Hayes (1–2), E Cloonan (0–7, five frees, one 65), K Broderick (0–1)

Subs: A Cullinane for Healy (26 mins) | M Kerins for Tierney (49)

Referee D Kirwan (Cork)

Gaelic Grounds, Limerick

Clare **3–16** Offaly **2–10**

Clare D Fitzgerald | B Quinn, B Lohan, G O'Grady | D Hoey, S McMahon, A Markham | D McMahon, C Lynch (0–1) | D Forde (0–2), A Quinn (0–2), F Lohan | N Gilligan (2–7, four frees), T Griffin (1–2), T Carmody (0–1)

Subs: D O'Connell (0–1) for Lohan (32 mins) | O Baker for D McMahon (61) | J O'Connor for Carmody, B O'Connell for Griffin, C Harrison for Markham (all 70 mins)

Offaly B Mullins | B Teehan, G Oakley, D Franks | K Brady, N Claffey, C Cassidy | M Cordial (0–1), Barry Whelahan (0–1) | R Hanniffy (1–2), G Hanniffy (0–1), J Brady | B Murphy (0–1), N Coughlan, D Murray (1–3, all frees)

Subs: D Hayden (0–1) for Brady (43 mins), S Brown for Brady (64) | N Mannion for Coughlan, R McRedmond for Murray (both 65 mins)

Referee P O'Connor (Limerick)

All-Ireland Hurling Championship Finals
Quarter-finals

| July 25 | Croke Park, Dublin |

Cork **2–26** Antrim **0–10**

Cork D Óg Cusack | W Sherlock, D O'Sullivan, B Murphy | J Gardiner (0–1, 65), R Curran, S Óg Ó hAilpín | T Kenny, J O'Connor (0–4) | B O'Connor (0–3, 2f), N McCarthy (0–2), T McCarthy | K Murphy (0–1), B Corcoran (2–1), J Deane (0–4, three frees)

Subs: M O'Connell (0–2) for J O'Connor (half–time) | J O'Callaghan (0–2) for B O'Connor (43 mins) | C O'Connor for Óg Ó hAilpín (58) | J Anderson (0–4) for N McCarthy (62) | J Browne for O'Sullivan (65)

Antrim D Quinn | M Kettle, K Kelly, B Herron | M McCambridge (0–1), K McKeegan, J Campbell | J Connolly, M Maill | M Herron, C McGuckian (0–1), L Richmond | L Watson, P Richmond (0–3), B McCall (0–4, one free, two side-lines)

Subs: D Quinn (0–1) for L Richmond (40 mins) | J McIntosh for Campbell (42) | G Cunningham for McCambridge, M Scullion for Connolly (both 60 mins)

Referee A MacSuibhne (Dublin)

| July 25 | Croke Park, Dublin |

Clare **1–13** Kilkenny **1–13**

Clare D Fitzgerald | B Quinn, F Lohan, G O'Grady | D Hoey, S McMahon (0–3, one free, two 65s), A Markham | D McMahon (0–1), C Lynch | G Quinn, A Quinn (0–1), D Forde | N Gilligan (1–7, five frees, penalty), T Griffin, T Carmody

Subs: J O'Connor (0–1) for A Forde (21 mins), O Baker for A Quinn (52 mins), D O'Connell for D McMahon (64)

Kilkenny J McGarry | J Ryall, N Hickey, T Walsh | R Mullally, P Barry, JJ Delaney | D Lyng, K Coogan | M Comerford, H Shefflin (0–8, six frees), P Tennyson (0–1) | E Brennan, DJ Carey (0–2, one free), J Coogan (0–1)

Subs: J Hoyne (1–0) for Brennan (half–time), S Dowling (0–1) for Tennyson (59 mins), P Mullally for Mullally (64 mins)

Referee G Harrington (Cork)

All-Ireland Hurling
Championship Finals
(Replays)

July 31 Replay · Semple Stadium, Thurles

Kilkenny **1–11** Clare **0–9**

Kilkenny J McGarry | T Walsh, N Hickey, J Ryall | M Kavanagh, P Barry, J J Delaney | D Lyng, K Coogan | E Brennan (1–2), J Hoyne (0–1), DJ Carey (0–3, one free, one 65) | M Comerford (0–2), H Shefflin (0–3 frees), J Fitzpatrick

Subs: J Maher for Shefflin (57 mins) | S Dowling for Coogan (66)

Clare D Fitzgerald | B Quinn, B Lohan, G O'Grady | D Hoey, S McMahon (0–2 frees), A Markham | D McMahon, C Lynch | J Reddan, G Quinn, F Lohan | N Gilligan (0–3, all frees), T Griffin (0–1), A Quinn.

Subs: C Plunkett for B Lohan (8 mins) | J O'Connor (0–2) for A Quinn (21) | D Forde (0–1) for Hoey (28) | B Murphy for Reddan (half–time) | O Baker for Markham (67)

Referee P Horan (Offaly)

Semi-finals

August 8	Croke Park, Dublin

Kilkenny **3–12** Waterford **0–18**

Kilkenny J McGarry | M Kavanagh, N Hickey, J Ryall | T Walsh, P Barry, JJ Delaney | D Lyng, K Coogan (0–1) | E Brennan (1–1), J Hoyne, DJ Carey (0–2, one free) | J Fitzpatrick (0–1), M Comerford (0–3), H Shefflin (2–4, 0–4 from frees)

Waterford I O'Regan | E Murphy, D Prendergast, J Murray | T Browne, K McGrath, B Phelan | D Bennett, E Kelly (0–1) | D Shanahan, M Walsh (0–1), P Flynn (0–13, eight frees, one 45) | S O'Sullivan, S Prendergast, E McGrath

Subs: J Kennedy (0–3) for O'Sullivan (half–time) | P O'Brien for E McGrath (59)

Referee A MacSuibhne (Dublin)

August 15	Croke Park, Dublin

Cork **1–27** Wexford **0–12**

Cork D Óg Cusack | W Sherlock, D O'Sullivan, B Murphy | S Óg Ó hAilpín, R Curran, C O'Connor | T Kenny (1–1), J O'Connor (0–6) | B O'Connor (0–8, five frees, one 65), N McCarthy (0–2), T McCarthy (0–2) | K Murphy (0–1), B Corcoran, J Deane (0–4, one free)

Subs: J O'Callaghan (0–2) for Deane, JP King for T McCarthy (both 61 mins) | M O'Connell (0–1) for J O'Connor (64) | J Browne for Sherlock (67) | P Mulcahy for O'Sullivan (69)

Wexford D Fitzhenry | M Travers (0–1), D Ryan, D O'Connor | J O'Connor, D Ruth (0–2, free, 65), R McCarthy | A Fenlon, T Mahon (0–2) | P Carley (0–2, frees), E Quigley (0–1), P Codd (0–2) | R Jacob, M Jacob, M Jordan (0–2)

Subs: D Lyng for J O'Connor, K Rossiter for J O'Connor (both half–time) | L Murphy for M Jacob (46) | C McGrath for Carley (59) | B Lambert for Quigley (66)

Referee B Kelly (Westmeath)

Final

September 12   Croke Park, Dublin

Cork **0–17** Kilkenny **0–9**

Cork D Óg Cusack | W Sherlock, D O'Sullivan, B Murphy | J Gardiner, R Curran, S Óg Ó hAilpín | T Kenny (0–1), J O'Connor (0–1) | B O'Connor (0–3, three frees), N McCarthy (0–3, three frees), T McCarthy | K Murphy (0–2), B Corcoran (0–2), J Deane (0–5, all frees)

Subs: J Browne for B Murphy (25 mins)

Kilkenny J McGarry | M Kavanagh, N Hickey, J Ryall | T Walsh, P Barry, JJ Delaney | D Lyng (0–1), K Coogan | H Shefflin (0–5, three frees, one 65), J Hoyne, DJ Carey | J Fitzpatrick (0–1), M Comerford (0–2), E Brennan

Subs: C Phelan for Fitzpatrick (62 mins) | S Dowling for Coogan (69)

Referee A MacSuibhne (Dublin)

Leinster Senior Football Championship
First Round

Carlow **4–15** Longford **1–16**

Carlow J Clarke | B Farrell, S O'Brien, C McCarthy | K Walker, J Hayden (0–1), J Byrne (0–1) | M Brennan, T Walsh (0–1) | P Hickey (1–1, point from free), J Nevin (0–2), M Carpenter (1–1, point from free)| S Rea (2–3, three frees, one penalty), S Kavanagh (0–3), B Carberry (0–1)

Subs: B English for Walker (33 mins) | B Kelly (0–1) for Carberry (53) | W Power for Brennan (54)

Longford G Tonra | D Ledwith, C Conefrey, S Carroll | E Ledwith, D Hannify, A O'Connor | L Kennan (0–1), T Smullen (0–1) | P O'Hara, J Kenny, P Barden (0–3), J Martin (0–1, free), N Sheridan (0–3), P Davis (1–7, four frees)

Subs: S Lynch for Kenny (45 mins) | M Lennon for Martin (51) | M Kelly for Lynch (61)

Referee T Quigley (Wexford)

Wexford **2–10** Louth **0–8**

Wexford J Cooper | C Morris, P Wallace, N Murphy | D Breen, D Murphy, G Sunderland (0–1) | P Colfer (0–1), W Carley | D Fogarty, J Hudson, R Barry | J Hearty (1–0), D Foran (1–0), M Forde (0–8, three frees)

Subs: L O'Brien for Murphy (45–47 mins) | N Lambert for Carley (48) | P Forde for Kelly (61) | J Lawlor for Hearty (63), O'Brien for Breen (65)

Louth S McCoy | S Gerard, J Clerkin, J Carr | A Page, P Mallon, R Rooney | D Devaney, P Keenan (0–2) | R Kelly, D Clarke (0–1, one free), O McDonnell (0–3, one free) | P Matthews (0–1) | D Reid, R Finnegan

Subs: D Shevlin for Mallon (16 mins) | A Hoey for Finnegan (24–27 mins) | S O'Neill for Matthews (43) | M Stanfield (0–1) for Clarke | A Hoey for Reid (both 46), C Malone for D Devaney (63)

Referee M Hughes (Tyrone)

May 23	Croke Park, Dublin

Westmeath 0–11 Offaly 0–10

Westmeath G Connaughton | J Davitt, D O'Donoghue, J Keane | M Ennis (0–1), D Healy, D Heavin | R O'Connell, D O'Shaughnessy | B Morley (0–2), G Dolan, A Mangan | F Wilson (0–1), D Glennon (0–1), D Dolan (0–5, four frees)

Subs: JP Casey (0–1) for Wilson (35 mins) | P Conway for G Dolan (66) | S Colleary for Mangan, J Fallon for Casey (both 73)

Offaly P Kelly | S Sullivan, C Evans, S Brady | B Mooney, C Daly, K Slattery (0–1) | C McManus (0–1), J Grennan (0–1) | P Kellaghan (0–2), R Malone, A McNamee | C Quinn, N Coughlan (0–1), N McNamee

Subs: J Coughlan (0–3) for Quinn (26 mins) | M Daly for Malone (44) | T Deehan (0–1) for A McNamee (56) | B Malone for Sullivan (61) | C Farrell for N McNamee (66)

Referee G Harrington (Cork)

Quarter-finals

Meath **2–13** Wicklow **1–8**

Meath D Gallagher | N McKeigue, D Fay, M O'Reilly | P Reynolds, T O'Connor, S McGabhann (0–1) | N Crawford, A Moyles | N Kelly, C McCarthy (0–2), T Giles (0–1, 45) | E Kelly (0–2), S McKeigue (0–1), D Regan (1–6, four frees)

Subs: R Kealy for N McKeigue (35 mins) | D Curtis (1–0) for N Kelly (half–time) | J Cullinane for A Moyles (50) | D Crimmins for E Kelly, Farrell for D Regan (both 65)

Wicklow R Hollingsworth | C Hyland, S Cushe, T Burke | C Davis, S Byrne, A Foley | B Sheehan, B Ó Hannaidh (0–1) | T Harney, R Coffey, A Ellis (0–1) | T Gill (0–4, two frees), T Hannon (0–1), W O'Gorman (0–1)

Subs: C Clancy for B Sheehan (27 mins) | D McGillacuddy (1–0) for Ellis (half–time) | L Glynn for Hannon (47) | D Ó Hannaidh for Harney (61)

Referee J McKee (Armagh)

Laois **0–15** Carlow **1–7**

Laois F Byron | A Fennelly, C Byrne, J Higgins | D Rooney (0–1), T Kelly, P McDonald | K Fitzpatrick (0–1), N Garvan | R Munnelly (0–4, three frees), I Fitzgerald, C Parkinson (0–1) | B McDonald (0–3, two frees), M Lawlor (0–2), C Conway (0–2, one free)

Subs: S Cooke for McDonald (35 mins) | P Clancy (0–1) for Fitzgerald (half–time) | P McMahon for Parkinson (59)

Carlow J Clarke | P Cashin, B Farrell, C McCarthy | B English, J Hayden, J Byrne | T Walsh, W Power | S Kavanagh (0–1), M Carpenter (0–1), J Nevin | S Rea (0–2, two frees), B Kelly (1–3, two frees), P Hickey

Subs: J Kavanagh for English, B Carberry for Hickey (both half time) | D Byrne for McCarthy (55 mins) | R Walker for Rea (63) | M Brennan for Walsh (67)

Referee M Ryan (Limerick)

June 6
Croke Park, Dublin

Wexford **0–12** Kildare **0–10**

Wexford J Cooper | C Morris, P Wallace, N Murphy | D Breen (0–1), D Murphy, G Sunderland | P Colfer, Willie Carley | R Barry, N Lambert, J Hudson | J Hegarty, D Foran, M Forde (0–8, five frees, one 45)

Subs: P Forde (0–2) for Lambert (31 mins) | J Lawlor (0–1) for Hegarty (half–time), L O'Brien for Sunderland (43) | R Hassey for Foran (48) | K Kennedy for Hudson (66)

Kildare E Murphy | B Lacey, R McCabe, A McLoughlin | E Callaghan, M Foley, K Ennis (0–1) | K Brennan, D Earley | D McCormack (0–1), J Doyle (0–2, both frees), A Barry | P Brennan (0–2, one free), M O'Sullivan (0–2), T Fennin (0–1)

Subs: P Hurley (0–1) for Barry (30 mins) | A Rainbow for Callaghan (31) | P Donnelly for Hurley (50) | G Ryan for Lacey (55) | T Rossiter for Fennin (68)

Referee M Curley (Galway)

June 6
Croke Park, Dublin

Westmeath **0–14** Dublin **0–12**

Westmeath G Connaughton | J Davitt, D O'Donoghue, J Keane | M Ennis, D Healy, D Heavin | G Dolan (0–1), D O'Shaughnessy | B Morley (0–1), P Conway (0–2), A Mangan (0–2) | F Wilson (0–1, free), D Glennon (0–2), D Dolan (0–3)

Subs: D Kilmartin for Davitt (22 mins) | D Mitchell (0–1) for Wilson (31) | J Fallon (0–1) for Kilmartin (69)

Dublin B Murphy | B Cahill, P Christie, P Griffin | S Ryan, C Moran (0–1), P Andrews | C Whelan, D Homan | C Keaney, D Magee, B Cullen (0–1) | A Brogan (0–4), J Sherlock (0–4), S Connell (0–2, two frees)

Subs: R Cosgrove for Keaney (49 mins) | C Goggins for Homan (54) | D Lally for Cullen (51) | T Quinn for Moran (76)

Referee M Collins (Cork)

Semi-finals

Laois **1–13** Meath **0–9**

Laois F Byron | A Fennelly, C Byrne, J Higgins | D Rooney, T Kelly, P McDonald | K Fitzpatrick, N Garvan | R Munnelly (0–6, four frees), B McDonald (0–2), P Clancy (0–1) | I Fitzgerald, C Parkinson (1–2), C Conway (0–1)

Subs: M Lawler (0–1) for Fitzpatrick (half–time)

Meath D Gallagher | N McKeigue, D Fay, M O'Reilly | P Reynolds, T O'Connor, H Traynor | N Crawford, A Moyles | S Kenny, C McCarthy, T Giles (0–1) | E Kelly, J Sheridan (0–6, four frees one 45), D Regan (0–2, one free)

Subs: D Curtis for E Kelly, O Murphy for Kenny (both 53 mins) | J Cullinane for Regan (57) | R Kealy for Traynor (63) | G Geraghty for O'Connor (69)

Referee P McEnaney (Monaghan)

Westmeath **2–15** Wexford **1–14**

Westmeath C Connaughton | J Keane, D O'Donoghue, J Davitt | M Ennis (0–1), D Healy | D Heavin (0–1) | G Dolan, D O'Shaughnessy | P Conway, B Morley (0–2), D Mitchell | A Mangan (0–2), D Glennon (0–2), D Dolan (1–7, five frees)

Subs: S Collery (1–0) for G Dolan (45 mins), C Galligan for Mitchell (48) | J Fallon for Morley (54) | J P Casey for Glennon (69)

Wexford J Cooper | D Breen (0–1), P Wallace, N Murphy | L O'Brien, D Murphy, R Barry | P Colfer, W Carley | D Fogarty (0–1), J Hudson, P Forde (0–1) | J Lawlor (1–1), D Foran | M Forde (0–8, four frees)

Subs: J Hegarty (0–2, one free) for Foran (30 mins) | D Browne for Hudson (53) | R Hassey for P Forde (60)

Referee J White (Donegal)

Final

Laois **0–13** Westmeath **0–13**

Laois F Byron | A Fennelly, C Byrne, J Higgins | D Rooney (0–1), T Kelly, P McDonald | P Clancy, N Garvan | R Munnelly (0–2), K Fitzpatrick (0–1), C Conway (0–2) | I Fitzgerald, C Parkinson, B McDonald (0–4, two frees)

Subs: M Lawlor (0–1) for Fitzgerald (23 mins) | S Cook (0–2, both frees) for Byrne (32) | G Kavanagh for Munnelly (53) | P Lawlor for M Lawlor (69)

Westmeath G Connaughton | D Healy, J Keane, J Davitt | D Heavin, D O'Donoghue, M Ennis | G Dolan, D O'Shaughnessy | B Morley, P Conway, F Wilson (0–2, frees) | A Mangan, D Glennon (0–5), D Dolan (0–4, three frees)

Subs: R O'Connell for G Dolan (20 mins) | J Fallon (0–2) for Mangan (46) | S Colleary for Wilson (57) | D Mitchell for Morley (66) | D Kilmartin for Davitt (73)

Referee P McEnaney (Monaghan)

Westmeath **0–12** Laois **0–10**

Westmeath G Connaughton | D O'Donoghue, J Keane, D Healy | D Heavin, J Davitt, M Ennis (0–1) | R O'Connell, D O'Shaughnessy | B Morley (0–1), P Conway, F Wilson (0–1, free) | A Mangan (0–4), D Glennon (0–2), D Dolan (0–3, one free)

Subs: J Fallon for Wilson (57 mins) | G Dolan for Conway (74) | S Colleary for Glennon (75)

Laois F Byron | A Fennelly, J Higgins, P McDonald | D Rooney, T Kelly (0–1), K Fitzpatrick (0–2) | P Clancy (0–1), N Garvan | R Munnelly (0–3, frees), M Lawlor, G Kavanagh | B McDonald (0–1), D Brennan (0–1), C Parkinson (0–1)

Subs: I Fitzgerald for Lawlor (31 mins, injured) | D Miller for Kavanagh (42) | M Delaney for Brennan (55) | P Conway for Higgins (64 mins, injured)

Referee M Monahan (Kildare)

Munster Senior Football Championship
First Round

May 16	Páirc Uí Chaoimh, Cork

Limerick **0–16** Tipperary **3–5**

Limerick M Jones | M O'Riordan, J McCarthy, T Stack | C Mullane (0–1), S Lucey, D Reidy | J Galvin, J Quane | S Kelly (0–1), M Gavin (0–7, five frees), M O'Brien | C Fitzgerald (0–2), E Keating (0–4, one free, one 45), J Murphy (0–1)

Subs: T Carroll for Quane (55 mins) | M Horan for Murphy (63) | M Reidy for Kelly (68)

Tipperary B Enright | B Hahessy, S Collum, N Curran | R Costigan, D Byrne, G Burke (0–1) | F O'Gallaghan, K Mulryan | L England, A Fitzgerald (1–0), M Webster | P Cahill (1–0) | D Browne (1–4, all frees), D O'Brien

Subs: J P Looby for Webster (30 mins) | P Halley for England (44) | L Cronin for Curran (54) | J Williams for Fitzgerald (63) | D Byrne for Cahill (65)

Referee M Deegan (Laois)

May 23	Cusack Park, Ennis

Kerry **2–10** Clare **0–9**

Kerry D Murphy | T O'Sullivan, M McCarthy, A O'Mahony | T Ó Sé, E Fitzmaurice, S Moynihan | D Ó Sé, W Kirby | P Galvin, D O'Sullivan, E Brosnan (1–4) | C Cooper (0–1), J Crowley (1–0), MF Russell (0–5, two frees)

Subs: M Quirke for Crowley (22 mins) | L Hassett for Galvin (45), M Ó Sé for T Ó Sé (57) | R O'Connor (Foilmore) for Quirke (64 mins)

Clare D O'Brien | P Gallagher, C Whelan, K Dilleen | N Griffin, B Considine, R Slattery | David Russell (Kilkee), D O'Sullivan | G Quinlan, Denis Russell (0–3, two frees), O O'Dwyer (0–1) | C Mullen (0–3, two frees), E Coughlan, S O'Meara

Subs: S Hickey for O'Meara, E Talty (0–1) for Griffin, M O'Shea for O'Dwyer (all half–time) | M O'Dwyer (0–1) for Coughlan (53 mins) | David Russell (Clarecastle) for O'Sullivan (58)

Referee G Kinneavy (Roscommon)

Semi-finals

June 13	Gaelic Grounds, Limerick

Limerick **1–18** Waterford **0–7**

Limerick S O'Donnell | M O'Riordan, J McCarthy, T Stack | P Browne, S Lucey, D Reidy (0–1) | J Quane, J Galvin | C Mullane (1–0), M Galvin (0–8, six frees), M O'Brien | C Fitzgerald (0–4), M Reidy (0–3), E Keating (0–1)

Subs: S Lavin for D Reidy (35 mins) | J Murphy for Keating (47) | S Kelly for Fitzgerald (49) | M Horan for O'Brien (53) | M Jones for O'Donnell (60)

Waterford P Houlihan | J Moore, E Rockett, T Costelloe | C Watt, T Dunphy, N Hennessy | K O'Keeffe, A Hubbard | J Hearne, M Aherne (0–1), J Coffey, L O Loináin, S Walsh (0–4, frees), G Power (0–2)

Subs: K Connery for Dunphy (37) | B Harty for O'Keefe (44) | T Whelan for L Ó Loinain (51) | P Ogle for Costello (53–56) | P Nagle for Coffey (57) | L Hayes for Watt (60)

Referee T Quigley (Wexford)

June 13	Fitzgerald Stadium, Killarney

Kerry **0–15** Cork **0–7**

Kerry D Murphy | T O'Sullivan, M McCarthy, A O'Mahony | T Ó Sé (0–1), E Fitzmaurice, S Moynihan | D Ó Sé, W Kirby (0–2) | L Hassett, D O'Sullivan, E Brosnan (0–1) | C Cooper (0–3), J Crowley, MF Russell (0–7, five frees)

Subs: D Ó Cinnéide (0–1) for Crowley (half–time) | P Galvin for Brosnan (63 mins) | M Ó Sé for O'Mahony (66)

Cork K O'Dwyer | S O'Brien, D Kavanagh, N O'Leary | E Sexton, M Cronin, G Murphy | G Canty, D Hurley | A Cronin (0–1), C McCarthy (0–1), C O'Sullivan | C Crowley, M Ó Croinin (0–3, two frees), K O'Sullivan

Subs: N Murphy for C O'Sullivan, K McMahon (0–1) for A Cronin (both 46) | M O'Sullivan (0–1) for Hurley (53) | F Murray for K O'Sullivan (55)

Referee B White (Wexford)

Final

Kerry **1–10** Limerick **1–10**

Kerry D Murphy | M McCarthy, T O'Sullivan, A O'Mahony | T Ó Sé, E Fitzmaurice, M Ó Sé | D Ó Sé, W Kirby | L Hassett, E Brosnan (0–1), P Galvin | C Cooper (0–2), D Ó Cinneide (0–3, all frees), MF Russell (1–4, four frees)

Subs: J Crowley for Ó Cinneide (58 mins) | T Griffin for Kirby (48) | J Sheehan for Fitzmaurice (71)

Limerick S O'Donnell | T Stack, J McCarthy, M O'Riordan | C Mullane (0–1), S Lucey, S Lavin (1–0) | J Quane, J Galvin | E Keating (0–2, two frees), M Gavin (0–4, all frees), J Stokes (0–1) | C Fitzgerald (0–2), S Kelly, M O'Brien

Subs: J Murphy for Gavin (55 mins, injured) | D Reidy for Lavin (55)

Referee G Kinneavy (Roscommon)

Kerry **3–10** Limerick **2–9**

Kerry D Murphy | M McCarthy, T O'Sullivan, M Ó Sé | T Ó Sé (1–0), E Fitzmaurice, A O'Mahony | D Ó Sé, E Brosnan (1–1) | L Hassett, D Ó Cinnéide (1–7, points from frees, goal from penalty), P Galvin (0–1) | C Cooper, J Crowley, M F Russell (0–1)

Subs: T Griffin for Crowley (26 mins) | W Kirby for Hassett (61) | S O'Sullivan for Galvin (66)

Limerick S O'Donnell | M O'Riordan, J McCarthy, T Stack | C Mullane, S Lucey, S Lavin | J Quane (0–1), J Stokes | M O'Brien, M Gavin (0–5, three frees), E Keating (1–1, penalty, free) | S Kelly (1–0), J Galvin (0–1), C Fitzgerald (0–1)

Subs: D Reidy for O'Brien (48 mins) | J Murphy for Quane (54)

Referee M Curley (Galway)

Ulster Senior Football Championship
First Round

May 9	St Tiernach's Park, Clones

Tyrone **1–17** Derry **1–6**

Tyrone J Devine | R McMenamin, C Gormley, C Gourley | B Donnelly, G Devlin, P Jordan (0–1) | C Holmes, S Cavanagh (0–4) | B Dooher (0–2), B McGuigan, E McGinley (0–1) | M Harte (0–4, one free), K Hughes (1–2), C McCullagh (0–2)

Subs: J McMahon for Donnelly (half–time) | S O'Neill (0–1) for Dooher (66)

Derry B Gillis | S M Lockhart, N McCusker, P Kelly (1–0) | P O'Kane, K McGuckin, F McEldowney (0–1) | F Doherty, Patsy Bradley | C Gilligan, E Muldoon (0–1, one free), J McBride | J Kelly, Paddy Bradley (0–4, three frees), P McFlynn

Subs: R Lynch for McFlynn (31 mins) | J Donaghy for J Kelly (50) | J Bradley for Patsy Bradley (67)

Referee B White (Wexford)

Quarter-finals

May 23	St Tiernach's Park, Clones

Armagh **2–19** Monaghan **0–10**

Armagh P Hearty | E McNulty, F Bellew, A Mallon | A O'Rourke, K Hughes, A McCann | P Loughran, P McGrane | P McKeever (0–5, one free), T McEntee (0–1), O McConville (0–5, two frees) | S McDonnell (1–4, one free), R Clarke (1–2), M O'Rourke (0–1)

Subs: B Mallon (0–1) for Clarke (58 mins) | K McElvanna for McCann (65) | S Kernan for M O'Rourke (67)

Monaghan G Murphy | G McQuaid, J Coyle, Edmund Lennon | D Duffy, D Clerkin (0–2), V Corey | J Hughes, Eoin Lennon | P Finlay (0–4, one free), T Freeman (0–1), D Mone (0–1) | K Tavey, R Ronaghan, D Freeman

Subs: R Woods (0–2, one free) for Tavey (25 mins) | J P Mone for Corey (31) | D McDermott for Edmund Lennon (32) | J Conlon for Hughes (half-time) | N Corrigan for Ronaghan (56)

Referee J Bannon (Longford)

May 16	Casement Park, Belfast

Cavan **1–13** Down **1–13**

Cavan E Elliott | E Reilly, D Rabbitte, P Brady | A Forde, T Crowe, A Gaynor | P McKenna, C Collins | L Reilly (0–1, free), M Lyng (0–6, three frees), M McKeever | G Pearson (0–3), J O'Reilly (1–2), S Johnston (0–1)

Subs: K Crotty for Collins (50 mins) | P Reilly for Johnston (63)

Down M McVeigh | M Higgins, A Molloy, A Scullion | J Clarke (0–1), M Cole, S Farrell | B Coulter (1–2), G McCartan | L Doyle (0–4, three frees, one 45), S Ward, R Sexton (0–1) | E McCartan (0–1), D Gordon, D Hughes (0–3)

Subs: J Lavery for Farrell (59 mins) | C McCrickard for G McCartan (61) | A O'Prey (0–1) for E McCartan (72)

Referee D Coldrick (Meath)

May 30 Replay   Breffni Park, Cavan

Cavan **3–13** Down **2–12**

Cavan E Elliott | E Reilly, D Rabbit, P Brady | A Forde, T Crowe (0–1), A Gaynor | P McKenna (0–1), K Crotty | L Reilly, M Lyng (0–4, frees), M McKeever (0–3, 2 frees) | G Pearson (0–1), J O'Reilly (1–2), S Johnston

Subs: C Collins for Crotty, D McCabe (1–0) for Pearson, P Reilly (1–1) for Johnston (all half–time) | R Donohoe for Brady (59 mins) | S Brady for McKeever (70)

Down M McVeigh | B Grant, A Molloy, A Scullion | J Clarke, M Cole, S Farrell | B Coulter (2–2), G McCartan (0–3, frees) | A O'Prey (0–3), S Ward, R Sexton | E McCartan, D Gordon (0–1), D Hughes (0–2, 1 free)

Subs: R Murtagh (0–1) for Ward (22 mins) | A Rodgers for Sexton (52) | J Lavery for E McCartan (60)

Referee S McCormack (Meath)

May 30   Mac Cumhaill Park, Ballybofey

Donegal **1–15** Antrim **1–9**

Donegal P Durcan | N McCready, R Sweeney, D Diver | E McGee, B Monaghan, K Cassidy | B Boyle (1–0), B McLoughlin | C Toye, M Hegarty (0–3), S McDermott | C McFadden (0–3), A Sweeney (0–5, three frees), B Devenney (0–3, one free)

Subs: P McGonigle for McLaughlin (59 mins) | K Lacy for McCready (66) | S Carr for McGee (70) | B Roper for Toye (71 mins)

Antrim S McGreevy | N Ward, C Brady, T Convery | G Adams, S Kelly, A Finnegan | J Quinn, M McCrory | M McCarry, K Brady, K McGourty (0–1) | P Doherty, D O'Hare (1–1), K Madden (0–6, four frees)

Subs: M Dougan for McCrory (3 mins) | J Marron (0–1) for Doherty, J McKeever for Ward (both 57) | K Murray for Adams (61)

Referee P Fox (Westmeath)

June 6	St Tiernach's Park, Clones

Tyrone **1–13** Fermanagh **0–12**

Tyrone J Devine | R McMenamin, C Gormley, C Gourley (0–1) | J McMahon, G Devlin, P Jordan | C Holmes, S Cavanagh (0–1) | E Mulligan (0–5, three frees), B McGuigan (0–1), S O'Neill (0–1) | M Harte (1–2, penalty and one free), K Hughes (0–2), C McCullagh

Subs: G Cavlan for McCullough (half–time) | M Coleman for Holmes (62 mins)

Fermanagh N Tinney | N Bogue, B Owens, H Brady | R Johnston, S McDermott, D Kelly (0–1) | M McGrath 0–2, L McBarran | E Maguire (0–1, free), J Sherry (0–2), M Little (0–1) | C O'Reilly, S Maguire, (0–5, four frees), C Bradley

Subs: P Sherry for Owens (34 mins) | M Murphy for O'Reilly (46) | D McGrath for Bradley (70 mins)

Referee S McCormack (Meath)

Semi-finals

Armagh **0–13** Cavan **0–11**

Armagh P Hearty | E McNulty, F Bellew, A Mallon | K Hughes, A O'Rourke, A McCann | J Toal, P McGrane | P McKeever (0–1), T McEntee, O McConville (0–5) | S McDonnell (0–2), R Clarke (0–1), M O'Rourke

Subs: K McElvanna (0–1) for Mallon (43) | D Marsden (0–1) for McEntee (48) | K McGeeney for McCann (57) | B Mallon (0–2) for Clarke (60)

Cavan E Elliott | C Collins, D Rabbit, R Donohoe | A Forde, A Gaynor, K Crotty | P McKenna, T Crowe | L Reilly (0–3, one free), M Lyng (0–4, four frees), M McKeever | J Reilly, P Reilly, G Pearson (0–3)

Subs: D McCabe (0–1) for P Reilly (29 mins) | M Bride for Donohoe (35) | S Cole for Crowe (62) | S Johnston for J Reilly (70)

Sent off: McKenna (1)

Referee M Monahan (Kildare)

Donegal **1–11** Tyrone **0–9**

Donegal P Durcan | N McCready, R Sweeney, D Diver | E McGee, B Monaghan (0–1), S Carr | B Boyle, B McLaughlin | C Toye, M Hegarty (0–1), B Roper (0–1) | C McFadden (1–7, five frees, 50), A Sweeney (0–1, free), B Devenney

Subs: S McDermott for B McLaughlin (30 mins) | S Cassidy for B Devenney (61) | J Gildea for C Toye (72)

Tyrone J Devine: R McMenamin, C Gormley, C Gourley | J McMahon (0–1), S Sweeney, P Jordan | G Cavlan, S Cavanagh (0–1) | B Dooher, B McGuigan (0–1), S O'Neill (0–1, one free) | M Harte (0–1), K Hughes, E Mulligan (0–4)

Subs: E McGinley for M Harte (52 mins) | McMcGee for C Gourley (54) | C Holmes for J Hughes (61)

Referee G Kinneavy (Roscommon)

Final

Armagh **3–15** Donegal **0–11**

Armagh P Hearty | E McNulty, F Bellew, A Mallon | K Hughes, K McGeeney, A O'Rourke | P Loughran (0–1), P McGrane | P McKeever (1–3), T McEntee (0–2), O McConville (1–3, 0–1, one free) | S McDonnell (0–2), R Clarke (0–1), D Marsden (1–2)

Subs: B Mallon (0–1) for R Clarke (63 mins) | J Toal for Loughran (64) | J McNulty for McGeeney, A McCann for Bellew, J McEntee for Marsden (all 67 mins)

Donegal P Durcan | N McCready, R Sweeney, D Diver | E McGee, B Monaghan, S Carr | B Boyle, S McDermott | C Toye, M Hegarty (0–1), B Roper (0–1) | C McFadden (0–4, all frees), A Sweeney (0–1), B Devenney (0–2, frees)

Subs: J Gildea (0–1) for McDermott, R Kavanagh (0–1) for Toye (both half–time) | P McGonagle for Roper (53 mins) | J Haran for A Sweeney (63) | K Lacy for McGee (65)

Referee M Collins (Cork)

Connacht Senior Football Championship
First Round

Mayo **3–28** New York **1–8**

Mayo P Burke | D Geraghty, P Kelly, G Ruane | F Costello (0–1), D Sweeney, J Nallan | D Heaney, D Brady | J Gill (0–2), A Dillon (0–1), A Moran (0–5) | C Mortimer (1–12, six frees), B Maloney (0–1), M McNicholas (0–2)

Subs: A O'Malley (1–3) for Maloney (35) | R McGarrity for Heaney (49) | M Moyles (1–1) for Dillon (53) | P Gardiner for Nallan (55) | G Mullins for Costello (61)

New York E Doherty | D Costello, P O'Connor, P Murphy | M Sloey, K Newell, D Callaghan | K O'Connor (1–1), J Killeen (0–3) | S McInerney, E Bradley (0–2), B O'Driscoll | K Lilly, S Russell, B Newman

Subs: G Dowd for McInerney, J Shaw for Callaghan (both 28) | P Higgins for Russell (35) | M Dobbin (0–2, frees) for O'Driscoll (40)

Referee M Collins (Cork)

Galway **8–14** London **0–8**

Galway B O'Donoghue | B Dooney, K Fitzgerald, C Monaghan | D Meehan, P Clancy, S de Paor (0–1) | J Bergin (1–1), S Ó Domhnaill (1–1) | T Joyce (1–1), M Donnellan (2–1), J Devane (0–2) | M Meehan (1–0), P Joyce (2–3), N Joyce (0–3)

Subs: M Clancy (0–1) for T Joyce | D Savage for Devane | M Comer for Monaghan | N Meehan for Donnellan | D Burke for de Paor

London G McEvoy | C Harrison, D McKenna, S Murphy | A McLarnon, J Niblock, K Scanlon | G Kane (0–1), P Quinn | S Doran (0–3), F McMahon (0–2), B Egan | P Lynott, D Kineavey (0–1), B McDonagh

Subs: S Byrne for McDonagh | G Weldon (0–1) for Lynott | M Drea for Murphy | T Ó hAilpín for Byrne | M Lillis for McEvoy

Referee J White (Donegal)

Roscommon **1–10** Sligo **0–13**

Roscommon S Curran | J Whyte, M Ryan, J Nolan | D Casey, F Grehan, J Rogers | S O'Neill (0–1), S Lohan | G Cox, N Dineen (0–1), D Connellan | G Heneghan, K Mannion (1–1), F Dolan (0–7, three frees, two 45s)

Subs: P Noone for Casey (24) | J Tiernan for Connellan (49) | J Egan for Heneghan (60) | B Higgins for O'Neill (63)

Sligo P Greene | N McGuire, P Naughton, B Philips | J Martyn, M Langan, P Gallagher | G Maye, S Davey (0–2) | K Quinn, M Brehony (0–2), E O'Hara | D Sloyan (0–5, all frees), M McNamara (0–1), G McGowan (0–3, one free)

Subs: P Doohan for Gallagher (30) | B Curran for Quinn (46) | P Neary for Maye (63) | J Davey for McGowan (70)

Referee J McQuillan (Cavan)

Roscommon **2–16** Sligo **1–15**

Roscommon S Curran (1–1, penalty, one free) | J Whyte, M Ryan, J Nolan | P Noone (0–1), F Grehan (0–2), J Rogers | S O'Neill (0–2), S Lohan | G Cox (0–1), N Dineen, B Higgins | G Heneghan (1–1, goal from penalty), K Mannion (0–2), F Dolan (0–3, two frees)

Subs: D Connellan for Higgins (25) | J Dunning (0–1) for Heneghan, A McPadden (0–1) for Rogers (both half–time) | D Casey for Dineen (63) | E Towey for Noone (67) | J Tiernan (0–1) for Connellan (80)

Sligo P Greene | J Martyn, N McGuire, B Phillips | D Durkin, M Langan, P Doohan | E O'Hara, S Davey (0–3) | B Curran, M Breheny (0–2), M McNamara (0–1) | D Sloyan (0–4, three frees, one 45), P Taylor (1–4, penalty, two frees), G McGowan

Subs: D McGarty for Curran (64) | J Davey (0–1) for Durkin (69) | K Quinn for McGowan (74) | P Durcan for McNamara (80)

Referee A Mannion (Kerry)

Semi-finals

| June 20 | Seán McDermott Park, Leitrim |

Leitrim **1–10** Roscommon **0–13**

Roscommon S Curran | J Whyte, M Ryan, J Nolan | D Casey, F Grehan (0–2), A McPadden | S O'Neill (0–3), S Lohan (0–1) | B Higgins, F Dolan (0–6, four frees, one sideline), G Cox (0–1 free) | N Dineen, K Mannion, G Heneghan

Subs: J Rogers for McPadden (half–time) | J Hanley for Dineen (47) | J Tiernan for Higgins (63) | E Towey for Heneghan (64)

Leitrim G Phelan | D Reynolds, J McKeon (0–1), M McGuinness | N Gilbane, S Quinn, B Prior (0–1) | D Maxwell (0–1), C Carroll | J Goldrick (0–1), J Guckian, C Regan (0–2) | D Brennan, F McBrien (0–1), M Foley (1–1, penalty, one free)

Subs: S Canning (0–1) for Guckian (42) | P Farrell (0–1) for Goldrick (55) | N Doonan for McBrien (63)

Referee M Hughes (Tyrone)

| June 26 Replay | Dr Hyde Park, Roscommon |

Roscommon **1–9** Leitrim **0–5**

Roscommon S Curran | J Whyte, M Ryan, J Nolan | E Towey, F Grehan, D Casey | S O'Neill, S Lohan | D Connellan, J Hanly (1–1), G Cox (0–2) | G Heneghan, K Mannion, F Dolan (0–3, 2 frees)

Subs: J Dunning (0–1) for Heneghan (25) | J Tiernan (0–2) for Connellan (half–time) | J Rogers for Casey (49) | B Higgins for Cox (68) | D O'Connor for Hanly (71)

Leitrim G Phelan | D Reynolds, S Quinn, M McGuinness | N Gilbane, J McKeon, B Prior | D Maxwell, C Carroll | J Goldrick (0–1), J Guckian, C Regan | D Brennan, F McBrien (0–1), M Foley (0–3, two frees)

Subs: S Canning for Maxwell (half–time) | P Farrell for Brennan, D Kennedy for Goldrick (both 58) | B Brennan for McBrien (64)

Referee J Geaney (Cork)

Mayo **0–18** Galway **1–9**

Mayo F Ruddy | C Moran, D Heaney (0–1), G Ruane | G Mullins, J Nallen, F Costello | J Gill (0–2), R McGarritty (0–1) | M McNicholas, K McDonald (0–3, 1 45), A Dillon | C Mortimer (0–8, 5 frees), T Mortimer (0–1), B Maloney (0–2)

Subs: D Brady for McNicholas, P Gardiner for Costello (both half–time) | A Moran for Mortimer (64) | P Kelly for Mullins (66)

Galway B O'Donoghue | M Comer, K Fitzgerald, B Doney | D Meehan, P Clancy, T Meehan | J Bergin, S Ó Domhnaill | M Meehan (1–1), M Donnellan (0–3, one free), M Clancy | D Savage, P Joyce (0–5, two frees), T Joyce

Subs: D Burke for Comer (25) | K Walsh for T Joyce (50) | J Devane for Ó Domhnaill (59)

Referee D Coldrick (Meath)

Final

Mayo **2–13** Roscommon **0–9**

Mayo F Ruddy | C Moran (0–1), D Heaney, G Ruane | G Mullins, J Nallen, F Costello | D Brady, R McGarrity | J Gill, K McDonald (0–1), A Dillon (0–1, free) | C Mortimer (0–9, six frees), T Mortimer (1–1), B Maloney

Subs: P Gardiner for Mullins (21) | P Kelly for Costello (55) | A Moran for Dillon (61) | A O'Malley (1–0) for Maloney (65) | D Sweeney for Moran (68)

Roscommon S Curran | J Whyte, M Ryan, J Nolan | D Casey, F Grehan, A McPadden | S O'Neill, S Lohan (0–1) | G Cox, J Hanly (0–1), J Tiernan | J Dunning, K Mannion, F Dolan (0–1, free)

Subs: G Heneghan (0–5, all frees) for Dolan, N Dineen (0–1) for Hanly, J Rogers for Nolan (all half–time) | D Connellan for Dunning (56) | R Cox for Tiernan (60)

Referee B White (Wexford)

All-Ireland Football Championship Qualifiers
Round One

June 12	O'Rahilly's, Drogheda

Louth **2–13** Antrim **0–14**

Louth S McCoy | J Clerkin, P Mallon, J Carr | D Shevlin (0–1), S Gerrard, R Rooney | D Devaney (0–1), P Keenan (0–2) | R Kelly, D Reid, N McDonnell (0–1) | A Hoey (0–3, one free), M Stanfield (1–2, one penalty), O McDonnell (0–1)

Subs: D Clarke (0–1, free) for Kelly, A Page for Reid (both 35) | J P Rooney (1–1) for N McDonnell (59) | N McDonnell (extra–time), P Matthews for Hoey (89)

Antrim S McGreevy | N Ward, C Brady, T Convery | G MacAdaim (0–1), S Kelly (0–1), A Finnegan | J Quinn, M McCrory | M McCarry, K McGourty (0–3), J Marron | K Brady (0–1), D O'Hare, K Madden (0–7, three frees)

Subs: K Niblock for Quinn (45) | J McKeever for Convery (63) | A McClean (0–1) for McCarry (69) | M Dougan for O'Hare (80), K Murray for Kelly (88)

Referee P McGovern (Galway)

June 12	Cusack Park, Ennis

Clare **1–15** Sligo **1–7**

Clare D O'Brien | P Gallagher, C Whelan, K Dilleen | A Clohessy (0–1), B Considine, R Slattery | David Russell, G Quinlan (0–1) | Denis Russell (1–5, four frees), C Mullen (0–1), M O'Shea | E Coughlan (0–1), O O'Dwyer, M O'Dwyer (0–5)

Subs: E Talty for Dilleen (12) | S Hickey for O'Shea (35) | S O'Meara (0–1) for Mullen (43) | C Considine for M O'Dwyer (55) | D Blake for Talty (62)

Sligo P Green | J Martyn, N McGuire, N Carew | P Doohan, N Clancy, M Langan | K Quinn (0–1), S Davey | E O'Hara, B Curran, D McGarty | D Sloyan (0–1), P Taylor, M McNamara (1–1)

Subs: G McGowan (0–3, two frees) for Taylor (28) | M Breheny (0–1) for McGarty, J Davey for Carew (both 35) | D Durkin for Clancy (43) | P Durcan for S Davey (54)

Referee M Deegan (Laois)

| June 12 | Dr Cullen Park, Carlow |

Down **1–19** Carlow **1–13**

Down M McVeigh | B Grant, A Molloy, A Scullion | J Clarke (0–1), M Cole, S Farrell | D Gordon, G McCartan (0–2, frees) | E McCartan, S Ward (0–2), R Sexton | B Coulter (1–3, one free), A O'Prey (0–3), D Hughes (0–4)

Subs: R Murtagh (0–1) for E McCartan (half–time) | L Doyle (0–3) for G McCartan (45) | A Brannigan for Farrell (59) | C McCrickard for Grant (68) | S Kearney for Hughes (70)

Carlow J Clarke | P Cashen, B Farrell, C McCarthy | J Kavanagh, J Hayden, J Byrne | D Byrne, W Power (0–1) | S Kavanagh, J Nevin (0–1), M Carpenter (1–1) | S Rea (0–7, four frees, one 45), B Carbery (0–2), B Kelly (0–1)

Subs: M Brennan for D Byrne (half–time) | T Walsh for Nevin (45) | P Hickey for Kelly (54) | K Walker for McCarthy (60)

Referee John Geaney (Cork)

| June 12 | St Tiernach's Park, Clones |

Longford **4–15** Monaghan **1–17**

Longford D Sheridan | D Brady, C Conefrey, S Mulligan | M Mulleady (0–1), E Ledwith, D Reilly | L Keenan (1–0), D Hannify | J Kenny, P Barden (1–1), P O'Hara | T Smullen (1–1), N Sheridan, P Davis (0–11)

Subs: D Barden (1–0) for Kenny | A O'Connor for O'Hara | S Lynch (0–1) for Mulligan | D Ledwith for Hannify | S Carroll for Mulleady | Ledwith for O'Connor | B Burke for Ledwith

Monaghan G Murphy | P McKenna, J Coyle, Edmund Lennon | G McQuaid (0–2), J P Mone, V Corey | Eoin Lennon, D Duffy (0–1) | N Corrigan (0–2), R Woods (0–3), D Clerkin | T Freeman (0–2), P Finlay, D Freeman (1–3)

Subs: M Slowey for Finlay | K Tavey (0–4) for Woods | J Hughes for McKenna | R Ronaghan for Tavey | Woods for Ronaghan | D Mone for McQuaid | D Larkin for D Freeman

Referee M Duffy (Sligo)

| June 12 | Aughrim Park, Wicklow |

Derry **1–15** Wicklow **1–10**

Derry B Gillis | K Guckian, N McCusker, G O'Kane | F McEldowney, S M Lockhart, P Kelly | F Doherty, Patsy Bradley | J Donaghy (0–3), J McBride (0–4), C Moran | J Kelly, Paddy Bradley (1–8), E Burke

Subs: C Gilligan for Kelly

Wicklow R Hollingsworth | C Hyland, S Cush, T Burke | L Glynn, D Ó hAnnaidh, A Foley | B Ó hAnnaidh, G Doran | T Harney, T Doyle (1–5), A Ellis | T Gill (0–3), R Coffey (0–1), W O'Gorman

Subs: C Clancy for D Ó hAnnaidh | P Dalton (0–1) for Harney | B Mernagh for Foley | C Davis for B Ó hAnnaidh | P Cronin for O'Gorman

Referee P Russell (Tipperary)

| June 12 | Parnell Park, Dublin |

Dublin **3–24** London **0–6**

Dublin S Cluxton | B Cahill, P Christie, P Griffin | S Ryan, D Magee (0–1), P Andrews | C Whelan, D O'Mahony (0–1, one free) | C Moran (0–2), T Quinn (1–5, penalty, one free), S Connell (0–7, six frees) | A Brogan (2–4, one side-line), J Sherlock (0–1), J McNally

Subs: P Casey for Ryan (half–time) | D Henry for Griffin (43) | C Goggins for Andrews (44) | D Lally for McNally (47) | R Cosgrove (0–3) for Moran (56)

London M Lillis | C Harrison, B McGonigle, S Murphy | J Niblock, D McKenna, A McLarnon | G Kane, P Quinn | S Doran (0–1), F McMahon (0–3, one 45, one free), B Egan (0–1) | G Weldon, D Kineavey, P Lynott

Subs: T Ó hAilpín for Lynott, C Slane for Niblock (both 33) | C Scanlon for Weldon (54) | S Byrnes (0–1) for McLarnon (60)

Referee B Tyrrell (Tipperary)

June 12	St Conleth's Park, Newbridge

Offaly **2–17** Kildare **1–16**

Offaly P Kelly | S Sullivan, C Evans, S Brady | B Mooney, C Daly, K Slattery |
M Daly (0–2), J Grennan (0–1) | N McNamee (1–1), P Kellaghan (1–3),
J Coughlan (0–6) | N Coughlan (0–2), T Deehan (0–2), J Reynolds

Subs: J O'Neill for M Daly (47) | A McNamee for Grennan (66) | C Quinn for
P Kellaghan (68) | R Malone for N McNamee (71)

Kildare E Murphy | D Hendy, R McCabe, A McLoughlin | E Callaghan, M Foley
(0–1), G Ryan (0–1) | D Earley (0–1), K Brennan | K Ennis, M O'Sullivan,
D McCormack (0–1) | T Rossiter, P Donnelly (0–1), J Doyle (0–8)

Subs: E Fitzpatrick for Hendy (24) | T Fennin (1–3) for Rossiter (28) | A Rainbow
for McCabe, W Heffernan for Brennan (both 38) | A Barry for Donnelly (41)

Referee J McQuillan (Cavan)

Fermanagh **v** Tipperary

Fermanagh walkover: Tipperary withdrew.

Round Two

O'Moore Park, Portlaoise

Longford **1–14** Waterford **1–5**

Longford D Sheridan | D Brady, C Conefrey, B Burke | M Mulleady, E Ledwith, D Reilly | L Keenan, D Hannify (0–1) | A O'Connor, P Barden (0–4), T Smullen (0–2) | D Barden (0–1), N Sheridan (0–2), P Davis (1–4)

Subs: S Mulligan for Mulleady, S Carroll for O'Connor (both 64) | B Sheridan for Brady (68) | E Williams for Davis (70)

Waterford P Houlihan | L Kavanagh, E Rockett, T Costelloe | P Queally, K Connery, N Hennessy | C O'Keeffe, A Hubbard | J Hearn, B Harty (0–1), P Ogle | L Ó Lolain, N Curran, G Powell

Subs: L Hayes (1–2) for Ó Lolain (29) | C Power (0–1) for Queally (half–time) | J Moore (0–1) for Harty (53) | T Dunphy for Kavanagh (70)

Referee J McKee (Armagh)

Pairc Esler, Newry

Tyrone **1–15** Down **0–10**

Tyrone P McConnell | R McMenamin, C Gormley, C Gourley | J McMahon, S Sweeney, P Jordan | K Hughes, S Cavanagh (1–1) | B Dooher, B McGuigan (0–2), G Cavlan | M Harte (0–7, three frees), O Mulligan (0–3), S O'Neill

Subs: C McCullagh (0–2, one 45) for O'Neill (half–time)

Down M McVeigh | M Higgins, A Molloy, A Scullion | J Clarke (0–2), M Cole (0–1), S Farrell | D Gordon, G McCartan (0–1) | L Doyle (0–3, one free), S Ward, R Murtagh | B Coulter (0–1), A O'Prey (0–1), D Hughes

Subs: B Grant for Scullion (46) | S Ward for McCartan (56) | C McCrickard (0–1) for Ward (62) | A Fagan for Murtagh (64)

Referee M Monahan (Kildare)

July 3   Cusack Park, Ennis

Cork **0–15** Clare **0–11**

Cork K O'Dwyer | S O'Brien, D Kavanagh, G Murphy | E Sexton (0–1), G Canty, M Cronin | D Hurley, N Murphy | A Cronin (0–1), M Ó Cróinín (0–1), C McCarthy (0–1) | C Crowley (0–2), C Corkery (0–6, five frees), B J O'Sullivan (0–1)

Subs: C O'Sullivan (0–1) for O'Sullivan (42) | M O'Sullivan (0–1) for Hurley (45) | S Levis for Ó Cróinín (49) | K O'Sullivan for A Cronin (62)

Clare D O'Brien | P Gallagher, C Whelan, K Dilleen | A Clohessy (0–2, one free), B Considine, R Slattery | David Russell (Kilkee) (0–1), G Quinlan | Denis Russell (0–7, five frees), S Hickey O O'Dwyer | E Coughlan, M O'Shea, R Donnelly (0–1)

Subs: N Griffin for Considine (12) | S O'Meara for O'Dwyer (35) | D O'Sullivan for Hickey (54) | David Russell (Clarecastle) for O'Shea (63)

Referee S McCormack (Meath)

July 3   St Tiernach's Park, Clones

Fermanagh **0–19** Meath **2–12**

Fermanagh N Tinney | N Bogue, B Owens, H Brady | R Johnston, S McDermott, D O'Reilly | M McGrath, L McBarron | E Maguire (0–2), J Sherry (0–2), M Little (0–3) | C O'Reilly (0–2), S Maguire (0–3, one free), C Bradley (0–6, two frees)

Subs: P Sherry for Owens (18) | R McCluskey for McBarron (36) | E Sherry for C O'Reilly (53) | S Goan for D O'Reilly (66) | D McGrath (0–1) for S Maguire (72) | C Boyle for Brady (76)

Meath D Gallagher | N McKeague, D Fay, M O'Reilly | P Reynolds, T O'Connor, T Giles (0–1, free) | N Crawford, A Moyles | E Kelly (0–1), C McCarthy, S Kenny (0–1) | D Regan (2–6, 0–4 from frees), S McKeague, J Sheridan

Subs: O Murphy (0–1) for McCarthy (29) | D Crimmins (0–1) for S McKeague (50) | N Kelly (0–1) for O'Connor (56) | D Byrne for Kelly (66) | D Curtis for Regan (86) | C McCarthy for Byrne (86)

Referee M Daly (Mayo)

Galway **2–8** Louth **0–9**

Galway B O'Donoghue | T Meehan, K Fitzgerald, G Fahy | D Meehan, P Clancy, B Dooney | J Bergin, K Walsh (0–1) | T Joyce, P Joyce (1–3, three frees), M Donnellan (0–2) | M Meehan, D Savage (0–1), M Clancy (0–1)

Subs: N Meehan (1–0) for T Joyce (half–time) | D Burke for Dooney (51) | J Devane for M Clancy (65)

Louth S McCoy | P Mallon, A Hoey, J Carr | D Shevlin, S Gerard, R Rooney | D Devaney, P Keenan (0–1) | R Finnegan, O McDonnell, A Page, M Stanfield (0–5, all frees), J P Rooney (0–2), N McDonnell (0–1)

Subs: D Clarke for O McDonnell (61) | P Matthews for Devaney (68) | R Kelly for Stanfield (71)

Referee J McQuillan (Cavan)

Dublin **1–13** Leitrim **0–4**

Dublin S Cluxton | B Cahill, P Christie, C Goggins | P Casey (0–1), B Cullen (0–1), P Griffin | J McGee, D McGee | D Lally, C Whelan, S Connell (1–2) | A Brogan (0–3), J Sherlock (0–2), T Quinn (0–3, two frees)

Subs: I Robertson for Lally (15) | D Farrell (0–1) for Quinn (53) | R Cosgrove for Sherlock (63) | D O'Mahony for D McGee (68) | S Ryan for J McGee (70)

Leitrim G Phelan | D Reynolds, S Quinn, M McGuinness | N Gilbane, P Flynn, C Regan | N Doonan, C Carroll | J Glancy, J Guckian, B Prior (0–1) | J McGuiness, P Farrell, M Foley (0–2, frees)

Subs: F McBrien (0–1, free), for J McGuinness (24) | S Canning for Farrell (40) | P McGuinness for Clancy (55) | D Gilhooley for Foley (57)

Referee B Crowe (Cavan)

July 4   Celtic Park, Derry

Derry **0–25** Cavan **2–9 (AET)**

Derry B Gillis | K McGuckin, N McCusker (0–1), G O'Kane | P Kelly (0–1), P O'Kane, F McEldowney | F Doherty (0–1), Patsy Bradley (0–1) | C Moran (0–1), J McBride (0–2), J Dinghy (0–2) | E Muldoon (0–6, two frees), Paddy Bradley (0–8, four frees), J Bradle

Subs: P McFlynn (0–1) for P O'Kane (56) | C Gilligan (0–1) for Moran (61) | Fergal McEldowney for Dinghy (65)

Cavan E Elliott | C Collins, A Forde, D Rabbit | K Crotty, A Gaynor, E Reilly | S Cole, T Crowe | M Brides, M Lyng (0–4, two frees), M McKeever (0–3) | J O'Reilly (1–0), L Reilly (0–1), G Pearson (1–1)

Subs: D McCabe for Brides (42) | R Donohue for Collins (48) | M Hannon for Crotty (56) | S Johnston for Pearson, N Walsh for Cole (both 80)

Referee J Bannon (Longford)

July 10   Wexford Park

Wexford **2–14** Offaly **0–15**

Wexford J Cooper | C Morris, P Wallace, N Murphy | D Breen, D Murphy, L O'Brien | P Colfer, W Carley (0–1) | R Barry (0–1), P Forde, D Fogarty (0–1) | J Lawlor (0–1), D Browne, M Forde (2–10, 0–2 from frees)

Subs: D Foran for Browne (60) | P Curtis for O'Brien (63) | R Hassey for Carley (65)

Offaly P Kelly | S Sullivan (0–1), C Evans, S Brady | B Mooney, C Daly, K Slattery | M Daly (0–1), J Grennan (0–1) | N McNamee, P Kellaghan (0–1), C McManus | J Coughlan (0–7, two frees), N Coughlan (0–1), J Reynolds (0–1)

Subs: B Malone for C Daly (31) | R Malone for Reynolds (50) | C Quinn (0–2) for M Daly (57)

Referee A Mangan (Kerry)

Round Three

Dublin **1–17** Longford **0–11**

Dublin S Cluxton | B Cahill, P Christie, C Goggins | P Casey, B Cullen, P Griffin | D Homan, D Magee | J Sherlock (0–2), C Whelan (0–2), S Connell | A Brogan (0–4), I Robertson (1–1), T Quinn (0–6, three frees, one 45)

Subs: S Ryan (0–1) for Casey (40) | D Farrell (0–1) for Brogan (58) | J Magee for Homan (59) | R Boyle for Robertson (64) | R Cosgrove for Connell (66)

Longford D Sheridan | D Brady, C Conefrey, B Burke | M Mulleady, E Ledwith, D Reilly | L Keenan, D Hannify | A O'Connor, P Barden, T Smullen (0–2) | D Barden (0–2), N Sheridan, P Davis (0–7, five frees)

Subs: S Carroll for Mulleady (12) | S Mulligan for Carroll (47) | J Kenny for O'Connor (50)

Referee M Curley (Galway)

Fermanagh **0–18** Cork **0–12**

Fermanagh N Tinney | N Bogue, B Owens, R McCluskey | R Johnston, S McDermott, D O'Reilly (0–2) | M McGrath, L McBarron | E Maguire (0–2), J Sherry (0–4), M Little (0–2) | C O'Reilly, S Maguire (0–6, four frees), C Bradley (0–1)

Subs: T Brewster (0–1) for C O'Reilly (32) | P Sherry for McCarron (44) | D Kelly for D O'Reilly (64)

Cork K O'Dwyer | S O'Brien, D Kavanagh, G Murphy | E Sexton, S Levis, M Croinín | M O'Sullivan, G Canty (0–1) | N Murphy (0–1), C O'Sullivan, C McCarthy (0–2) | C Crowley, C Corkery (0–6, three frees), A Cronin

Subs: C Brosnan for O'Brien (29) | B O'Sullivan (0–2) for Levis (half–time) | F Murray for C O'Sullivan (57) | K O'Connor for Sexton (60) | M Ó Cróinín for Crowley (64)

Referee M Deegan (Laois)

Tyrone **1–16** Galway **0–11**

Tyrone P McConnell | R McMenamin, C Gormley, C Gourley | J McMahon, S Sweeney (0–1), P Jordan (0–1) | K Hughes, S Cavanagh (0–3) | B Dooher (0–1), B McGuigan (1–0), G Cavlan | M Coleman, O Mulligan (0–5, two frees), S O'Neill (0–4, two frees)

Subs: P Canavan (0–1) for Coleman (55) | L Meenan for Mulligan (69) | B Collins for Dooher (71)

Galway B Donoghue | K Fitzgerald, G Fahey, T Meehan (0–1) | D Burke, P Clancy, D Meehan | J Bergin, S Ó Domhnaill (0–1) | M Meehan, M Donnellan (0–2, one free), M Clancy | D Savage (0–1), P Joyce (0–4, three frees), J Devane (0–1)

Subs: T Joyce (0–1) for M Clancy (30) | N Meehan for M Meehan (59) | N Joyce for Savage, D Mullahy for Bergin (both 67)

Referee M Monahan (Kildare)

Derry **2–16** Wexford **2–5**

Derry B Gillis | K McGuckin, N McCusker, G O'Kane | F McEldowney, P McFlynn, P Kelly | F Doherty, P Bradley | J Donaghy (0–1), J McBride (0–1), C Moran | J Bradley, P Bradley (0–8, three frees), E Muldoon (1–5, three frees)

Subs: S Lockhart for Kelly (46) | C Gilligan (0–1) for Dinghy, D McIvor (1–0) for J Bradley (both 51) | E Burke for Muldoon, P O'Kane for McGuckin (both 67)

Wexford J Cooper | P Curtis, P Wallace, N Murphy | D Breen, D Murphy, L O'Brien | P Colfer (1–0), W Carley | J Hudson (0–1), P Forde, D Fogarty | J Lawlor, R Barry, M Forde (1–4, three frees)

Subs: J D'Arcy for Forde (30) | K Kennedy for Hudon, D Kinsella for Carley (both half–time) | G Sunderland for O'Brien (46) | J Hegarty for Lawler (65)

Referee J Geaney (Cork)

Round Four

Fermanagh **1–10** Donegal **0–12 (AET)**

Fermanagh N Tinney | N Bogue, B Owens, R McCluskey | T Johnston,
S McDermott (0–1), D O'Reilly | M McGrath (0–2), L McBarron | E Maguire
(1–0), S Maguire (0–4, frees), M Little | C O'Reilly, J Sherry, C Bradley (0–2)

Subs: T Brewster (0–1, one free) for McBarron (blood sub 3–35) | D Kelly for
D O'Reilly (27) | P Sherry for Bogue (45) | Brewster for O'Reilly (46) | H Brady
for McBarron (53) | S Goan for McCluskey (67) | M Murphy for Sherry (77) |
McCluskey for Brewster (83) | D McGrath for S Maguire (88)

Donegal P Durcan | N McCready, R Sweeney, N McGinley | K Lacey,
B Monaghan, S Carr | J Gildea (0–1), B Boyle | P McGonigle, M Hegarty (0–2),
B Roper (0–2) | C McFadden (0–1, one free), A Sweeney (0–3, one free),
B Devenney (0–3, two frees)

Subs: C Toye for McFadden (34) | S McDermott for McGonigle (half–time) |
B Dunnion for McGinley (42) | K Cassidy for Toye (67) | R Kavanagh for
J Gildea (extra–time) | J Haran for Roper (82) | S Cassidy for A Sweeney (88)

Referee J McQuillan (Cavan)

Derry **0–10** Limerick **0–7**

Derry B Gillis | K McGuckin, N McCusker, G O'Kane | F McEldowney,
P McFlynn, P Kelly | F Doherty, Patsy Bradley | J Donaghy, J McBride, (0–1),
C Moran (0–2) | J Bradley, Paddy Bradley (0–2, one free), E Muldoon (0–4, two
frees)

Subs: C Gilligan for Donaghy (20) | S M Lockhart for McCusker (61) |
G Donaghy (0–1) for Gilligan (66) | M Lynch for J Bradley (70)

Limerick S O'Donnell | M O'Riordan, J McCarthy, T Stack | C Mullane,
S Lucey, S Lavin | J Stokes, J Galvin | S Kelly, M Gavin (0–1), M O'Brien (0–1) |
C Fitzgerald (0–2, one free), O Keating (0–3 frees), M Reidy

Subs: J Quane for Reidy (21) | J Murphy for Gavin (29) | D Reidy for Mullane
(45) | P Browne for Stokes (69)

Referee D Coldrick (Meath)

August 1 Croke Park, Dublin

Tyrone **3–15** Laois **2–4**

Tyrone P McConnell | R McMenamin, C Gormley, M McGee | J McMahon, S Sweeney, P Jordan | K Hughes, S Cavanagh (0–3) | B Dooher (0–1), B McGuigan (0–2), G Cavlan | M Harte (2–3, three frees), E Mulligan (1–3, one free), S O'Neill (0–3)

Subs: C Gourley for McMahon (15) | B Collins for Mulligan (39) | J Devine for McConnell (57) | C Lawn for Sweeney (67)

Laois F Byron | A Fennelly, C Ryan, P McDonald | D Rooney, T Kelly, P McMahon | P Clancy, N Garvan | R Munnelly, K Fitzpatrick (1–0), C Parkinson | P Lawlor, S Cooke (0–2, one free), B McDonald (1–1, one free)

Subs: G Kavanagh for Munnelly, D Miller (0–1) for Lawlor (both half time) | C Bergin for McDonald (62, injury) | P Conway for Ryan (69)

Referee M Collins (Cork)

August 1 Croke Park, Dublin

Dublin **1–14** Roscommon **0–13**

Dublin S Cluxton | B Cahill, P Christie, C Goggins | P Casey, B Cullen (0–2, 45), P Griffin | D Homan (0–1), D Magee | C Keaney (0–1, free), C Whelan (0–2), S Connell (0–1) | A Brogan (0–3), I Robertson, J Sherlock (1–4)

Subs: J Magee for Homan (45) | S Ryan for Goggins (49) | D Farrell for Keaney (56) | T Quinn for Farrell (62)

Roscommon S Curran | R Cox, M Ryan, J Whyte | A McPadden, D Casey, M Ennis | S O'Neill (0–1), S Lohan (0–3) | J Hanly, F Grehan, G Cox (0–1) | J Dunning, N Dineen (0–2), G Heneghan (0–5, four frees)

Subs: J Tiernan (0–1) for R Cox (31) | K Mannion for Lohan (51) | F Dolan for Dunning, J Rogers for Towey (54) | B Higgins for Hanly (65)

Referee G Harrington (Cork)

All-Ireland Football Championship Finals
Quarter-finals

Mayo **0–16** Tyrone **1–9**

Mayo P Burke | D Heaney, G Ruane, C Moran | F Costello, J Nallen, P Gardiner | R McGarrity (0–1), D Brady (0–3) | J Gill, K McDonald (0–1, free), A Dillon (0–6, four frees) | C Mortimer (0–3, one free), T Mortimer (0–2), B Maloney

Subs: P Kelly for Costello (36) | A Moran for C Mortimer (61) | D Sweeney for Heaney (64) | A O'Malley for Maloney (70)

Tyrone P McConnell | R McMenamin, C Gormley, M McGee | J McMahon, S Sweeney, P Jordan | K Hughes, S Cavanagh | B Dooher, G Cavlan (0–1), C Gourley | M Harte (0–1, one free), O Mulligan (0–3, one free), S O'Neill (1–3)

Subs: D Carlin for Gormley (17) | P Canavan (0–1) for Sweeney (23) | B McGuigan for Harte (55), C McCullagh for McGee (66)

Referee P Russell (Tipperary)

Fermanagh **0–12** Armagh **0–11**

Fermanagh N Tinney | N Bogue, B Owens, R McCluskey | R Johnston, S McDermott, P Sherry | M McGrath, L McBarron | E Maguire (0–1), J Sherry (0–1), C Bradley (0–2, one 45) | C O'Reilly, S Maguire (0–5, four frees), M Little

Subs: T Brewster (0–3, one free) for O'Reilly (24) | H Brady for M McGrath (37–half-time, temporary) | H Brady for McBarron (42–44, temporary) | D McGrath for J Sherry (58)

Armagh P Hearty | E McNulty, F Bellew, A Mallon | K Hughes, K McGeeney (0–1), A O'Rourke | P Loughran, P McGrane | P McKeever (0–1, free), T McEntee, J Toal | S McDonnell (0–7, three frees), R Clarke, D Marsden (0–1)

Subs: B Mallon for Toal (31) | A McCann for B Mallon (half–time) | K McElvenna for O'Rourke (54) | O McConville for McKeever (56) | B Mallon for Clarke (61)

Referee J Bannon (Longford)

August 14	Croke Park, Dublin

Kerry **1–15** Dublin **1–8**

Kerry D Murphy | T O'Sullivan, M McCarthy, M Ó Se | A O'Mahony, E Fitzmaurice, T Ó Sé | D Ó Sé, P Kelly | E Brosnan, D O'Sullivan (0–1), P Galvin (0–1) | MF Russell, D Ó Cinnéide (1–5, three frees), C Cooper (0–5, two frees)

Subs: L Hassett (0–1) for Russell (48) | W Kirby (0–2) for Kelly (52) | J Crowley for D O'Sullivan (63) | J Sheahan for T Ó Sé (69) | S O'Sullivan for O'Mahony (73)

Dublin S Cluxton | B Cahill, P Christie, P Griffin | S Ryan, B Cullen, P Casey | D Homan (0–2), D Magee | C Keaney (0–1, free), C Whelan, S Connell (0–5, frees) | A Brogan, I Robertson, J Sherlock (1–0)

Subs: T Quinn for Keaney (54) | R Cosgrove for Robertson (58) | J Magee for Cullen (60) | D O'Mahony for Homan (63)

Referee P McEnaney (Monaghan)

August 14	Croke Park, Dublin

Derry **2–9** Westmeath **0–13**

Derry B Gillis | L McGuckin, N McCusker, S M Lockhart | F McEldowney, P McFlynn, P Kelly | F Doherty, Patsy Bradley | J Donaghy, J McBride, C Moran | J Bradley, P Bradley (1–2, 0–1 from free), E Muldoon (1–6, four frees)

Subs: G Donaghy for Moran (55) | E Burke (0–1) for J Bradley (59) | C Gilligan for McBride (63) | G O'Kane for McCusker (63)

Westmeath G Connaughton | D Healy, J Keane, D O'Donoghue | M Ennis, J Davitt, D Heavin | R O'Connell, D O'Shaughnessy | B Morley, P Conway, F Wilson (0–2, frees) | A Mangan (0–1), D Glennon (0–2), D Dolan (0–5, four frees)

Subs: J Fallon (0–2, frees) for Wilson (36) | S Colleary for Morley (46) | G Dolan (0–1) for Conway (50)

Referee M Curley (Galway)

Semi-finals

August 22	Croke Park, Dublin

Mayo **0–9** Fermanagh **0–9**

Mayo P Burke | C Moran, D Heaney (0–1), G Ruane | P Gardiner, J Nallen, P Kelly | R McGarrity, D Brady | J Gill, K McDonald (0–1), A Dillon (two frees) | C Mortimer (0–4, two frees), T Mortimer (0–1), B Maloney

Subs: A Moran for Maloney, G Mullins for Brady (both 53) | M McNicholas (0–1) for Dillon (60)

Fermanagh N Tinney | N Bogue, B Owens, R McCluskey | R Johnston, S McDermott, P Sherry | M McGrath, L McBarron (0–1) | E Maguire (0–1), J Sherry (0–1), M Little (0–1) | C O'Reilly, S Maguire, C Bradley (0–3)

Subs: T Brewster (0–1, free) for Little (42) | H Brady for P Sherry (43) | M Murphy for J Sherry (70)

Referee M Collins (Cork)

August 28 Replay	Croke Park, Dublin

Mayo **0–13** Fermanagh **1–8**

Mayo P Burke | G Ruane, D Heaney, P Kelly | P Gardiner, J Nallen, C Moran | R McGarrity (0–1), F Kelly | J Gill, K McDonald (0–2), A Dillon | C Mortimer (0–5, two frees), T Mortimer (0–3), B Maloney

Subs: D Geraghty for Moran (half–time) | A O'Malley (0–1) for B Maloney (45) | D Brady (0–1) for Kelly (52) | D Munnelly for Gill (65)

Fermanagh N Tinney | N Bogue, B Owens, R McCluskey | R Johnston, S McDermott, P Sherry | M McGrath, L McBarron | E Maguire, T Brewster (0–1, a free), M Little (0–1) | C O'Reilly, S Maguire (0–2, frees), C Bradley (0–3, two frees)

Subs: H Brady for P Sherry (22) | J Sherry (1–1) for O'Reilly (29) | D O'Reilly for Owens (half–time)

Referee J Bannon (Longford)

Kerry **1–17** Derry **1–11**

Kerry D Murphy | M McCarthy, T O'Sullivan, M Ó Sé | A O'Mahony,
E Fitzmaurice, T Ó Sé (0–2) | D Ó Sé (0–1), W Kirby (0–1) | L Hassett, E Brosnan
(0–1), P Galvin (0–1) | D O'Sullivan (1–0), D Ó Cinnéide (0–2, 45 and free),
C Cooper (0–6, three frees)

Subs: MF Russell (0–2) for D Ó Sé (22) | P Kelly (0–1) for Hassett (59) | T Griffin
for Kirby (64) | J Crowley for Cooper (67)

Derry B Gillis | K McGuckin, N McCusker, S M Lockhart | F McEldowney,
P McFlynn (0–1), P Kelly | F Doherty (0–1), Patsy Bradley | J Donaghy,
J McBride, C Moran | J Bradley, E Muldoon (1–1), Paddy Bradley (0–6, four
frees)

Subs: G O'Kane for McEldowney (37) | G Donaghy for Moran (40) | E Burke for
J Bradley (42) | C Gilligan (0–2) for J Donaghy (48) | M Lynch for McBride (53)

Referee B White (Wexford)

Final

September 26	Croke Park, Dublin

Kerry **1–20** Mayo **2–9**

Kerry D Murphy | A O'Mahony, M McCarthy, T O'Sullivan | M Ó Sé,
E Fitzmaurice, T Ó Sé (0–1 each) | E Brosnan, W Kirby (0–3) | L Hassett,
D O'Sullivan (0–1), P Galvin (0–1) | C Cooper (1–5, one free),
D Ó Cinnéide (0–8, five frees, one 45), J Crowley

Subs: S Moynihan for Hassett (55) | MF Russell (0–1) for Crowley (58) |
R O'Connor for Ó Cinnéide (63) | P Kelly for Galvin (68) | B Guiney for T Ó Sé
(72)

Mayo P Burke | G Ruane, D Heaney, D Geraghty | P Kelly, J Nallen, P Gardiner |
R McGarrity, F Kelly | T Mortimer, C McDonald (0–3, two frees), B Maloney (0–1
each) | C Mortimer (0–1), J Gill, Alan Dillon (1–2, one free)

Subs: D Brady for F Kelly (25) | C Moran for Geraghty, M Conroy (1–1) for Gill
(both half–time) | A Moran (0–1) for C Mortimer (48) | P Navin for Heaney (66)

Referee P McEnaney (Monaghan)